ENGLISH
FRENCH
UNITED STATES
BOLIVIA
CHINA
UNITED KINGDOM

SWEDEN
RUSSIAN FEDERATION
POLAND

EXIT
ENGLISH
FRENCH
RUSSIAN
KUWAIT
NETHERLANDS
PERU

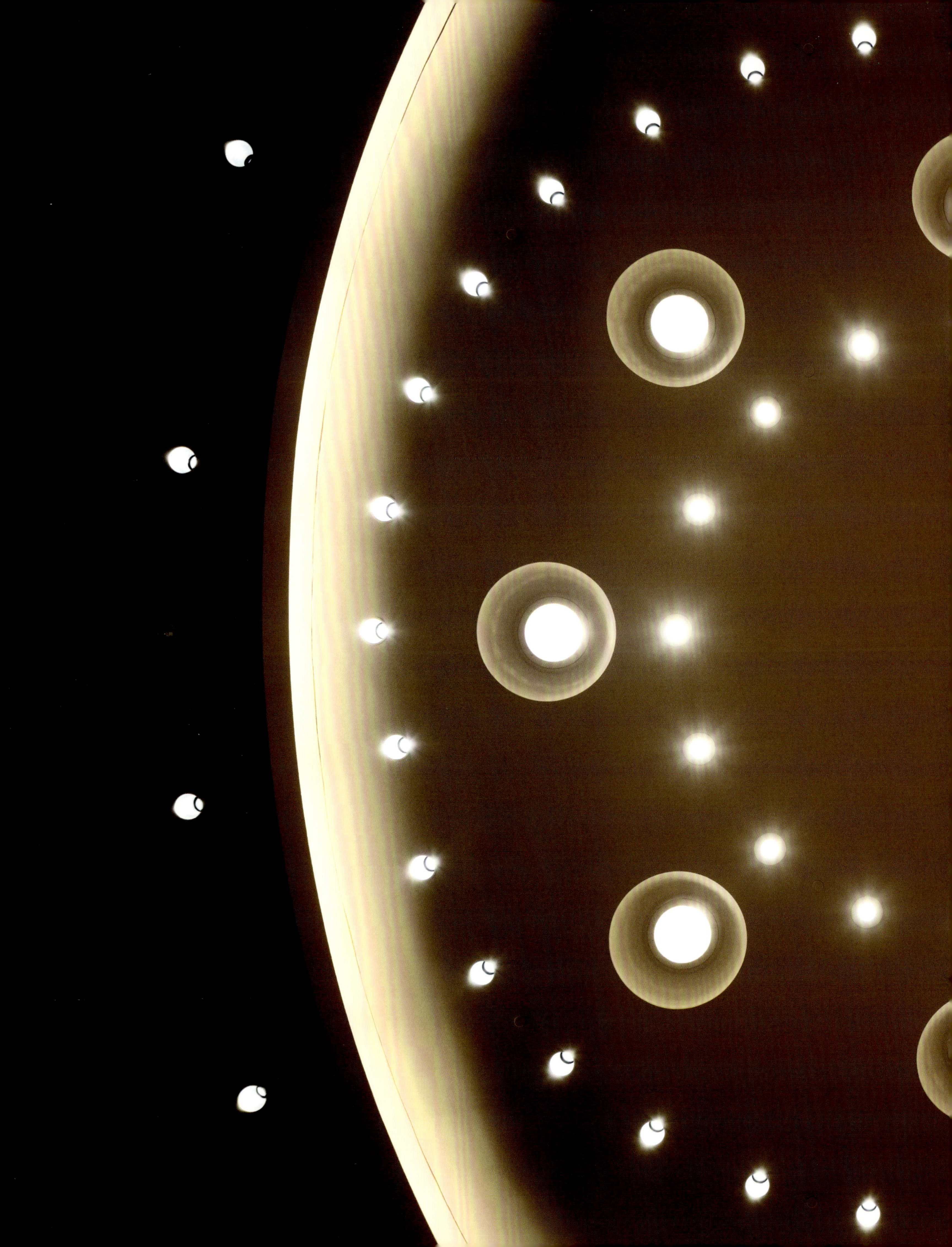

FRENCH
RUSSIAN

The room

Since the completion of the UN Security Council Chamber in New York in 1952, the world's foremost leaders and diplomats have come together here to resolve crises and preserve world peace. To design the interior of such an important space was, of course, a highly prestigious task. The UN buildings were designed by the most prominent international architects of the day. That the job of decorating the most important room in the entire UN complex went to Norway, and to the architect Arnstein Arneberg, is nothing less than incredible. Every indication is that the Norwegian Trygve Lie, the UN's first secretary-general, was a driving force behind this decision.

The interior of the Security Council Chamber was designed by Arnstein Arneberg. The configuration of the chamber had already been determined, so Arneberg's task was to decorate the walls and ceiling. In addition he designed the seats for the delegates and secretariat, the entry doors with intarsia patterns, the railings and other details. Aiding Arneberg in this effort was a group of Norwegian artists and designers. Per Krohg created the large mural. The textile artist Else Poulsson designed the curtains and the royal blue and yellow wallpaper, Klare Schee designed the Biri wallpaper that covers the back wall and Birgit Wessel designed the blue-striped furniture textile that covers Arneberg's chairs.

The Security Council Chamber

Editor

Jørn Holme

Contributors

Michael Adlerstein
Nina Berre
Ingeborg Glambek
Ulf Grønvold
Vibeke Waallann Hansen
Guri Hjeltnes
Sarah A. Lichtman
Maria Csaszni Rygh
Loraine Sievers
Linda Veiby
Siri Wolland

Photos by

Ivan Brodey

Forlaget Press 2018

I remember well my first visit to the UN complex. It was the early 1980s and I was a young student. When the tour was over, Norway was the only country that had been mentioned twice. First the guide talked about the Norwegian Trygve Lie, the UN's first secretary-general. The high point of this standard guided tour, however, was the Security Council Chamber. Here we learned that Norway had been responsible for its decoration, and heard the name of the architect Arnstein Arneberg.

The history of the UN headquarters in New York is one that can both inspire and shock today's building developers. No competition, no openness. Decisions made at record speed behind closed doors, and exclusively by men. The buildings went up rapidly. The huge Secretariat was completed less than a year after the cornerstone was laid. The General Assembly and the conference building were finished in 1952.

At the center of this project was the UN's first secretary-general, Trygve Lie. He hired the head architect, Wallace K. Harrison, and closely followed the planning and construction of the complex. Trygve Lie also played a key role in the decision to invite Norway, Denmark, and Sweden to decorate the three council chambers in the conference building. Lie's friend Arnstein Arneberg received the most high-status of the three commissions: the Security Council Chamber.

The idea for this book emerged out of the debate as to whether or not the modernist government buildings in central Oslo that had been damaged in the 22 July 2011 terrorist attack should be torn down. The Norwegian architect Erling Viksjø was strongly influenced by the UN buildings' architecture when he designed the government quarter in the years after the war. During the debate that followed the terrorist attack, however, there were many who argued that such concrete buildings from the 1950s and 60s were ugly, and that we needed government buildings with a more contemporary look.

The story of the Security Council Chamber is unfamiliar to most people. The National Museum – Architecture has a unique collection of drawings by Arneberg and letters between him and Trygve Lie. Both the Directorate of Cultural Heritage and the National Museum agreed that we needed a book about the Security Council Chamber in order to illuminate Lie's role in the building of the UN headquarters and to draw attention to Arnstein Arneberg, the painter Per Krohg, and the textile artist Else Poulsson, who worked together to create this important space.

Preface

In connection with the major modernization of the UN headquarters during the years 2008–2103, the Directorate of Cultural Heritage was brought in by the Ministry of Foreign Affairs as an advisor for the work on the Security Council Chamber. The history of such a restoration deserves, in and of itself, to be told – in large part so that it may serve to inspire all of those who always want only to build something new. To retain the best of the past is is never unwise when constructing the future. The work on the Security Council Chamber should, then, be a role model for future restoration projects. Our position was, and is, clear: modernism is modern, not unmodern. Today, of the large meeting rooms in the UN complex, the Security Council Chamber is the one that has undergone the fewest changes. It will be the setting of decisive debates about the world's security for many years to come. At the same time that Forlaget Press is publishing this book, the National Museum is holding an exhibition of important drawings, documents, and other materials that illuminate the history of the chamber.

One of the paths to this book project has already been trod by Ingeborg Glambek, a Norwegian professor of art history whose 2005 article "The Council Chambers in the UN Building in New York" in the *Scandinavian Journal of Design History* offers a solid introduction to the UN complex and a comprehensive history of the Scandinavian council. An abridged and updated version of this article also appears in this book.

We have collected writings by a number of authors with the goal of illuminating the Security Council Chamber and its history from various angles and perspectives. Our primary objective has not been to provide extensive technical data, but to bring together a range of stories about a room that very few people know much about. We are especially pleased to have contributions by three American writers. The man behind the restoration of the main UN building, Michael Adlerstein, tells about this immense project and about the challenges that arose along the way. Adlerstein, more than anyone else, is responsible for the extraordinary success of this nearly two billion dollar effort. Sarah A. Lichtman writes about Else Poulsson, the Norwegian textile artist who designed the Security Council Chamber's textile wallpaper and curtains, and Loraine Sievers outlines the chamber's history as a setting of international politics and diplomacy from 1952 to the present.

The book is richly illustrated with drawings and photographs, so that the reader can experience the chamber as it appears today while also getting a taste of its remarkable history. The new photographs of the Security Council Chamber were taken by Ivan Brodey. Picture editor Tone Svinningen has worked hard to hunt down the other illustrations, while Rune Døli has brought all of these ingredients together into a thing of beauty.

The book's editor-in-chief is Jørn Holme, head of the Directorate of Cultural Heritage. The other members of the editorial team are department director Nina Berre (National Museum), project coordinator Maria Csaszni Rygh (National Museum; Directorate of Cultural Heritage), section chief Linda Veiby (Directorate of Cultural Heritage), communications director Siri Wolland (Directorate of Cultural Heritage), picture editor Tone Svinningen, and graphic designer Rune Døli.

For practical support and contributions to this project, the editors are grateful to the Ministry of Foreign Affairs, the Norwegian Consulate-General and UN delegation in New York, the archival and photo offices of the UN Secretariat, ArkDes in Stockholm and the Directorate for Cultural Heritage. The collaboration with Forlaget Press and house editor Trygve Riiser Gundersen has been both inspiring and impeccable.

Jørn Holme
Oslo, May 2018

The Security Council Chamber

Published in cooperation with the Norwegian Directorate for
Cultural Heritage and the National Museum of Norway

Design: Rune Døli, Modest Design
Photos: Ivan Brodey, with the exception of historical
photos, see list of images on page 216.
Photo editor: Tone Svinningen
Captions and introductory texts: Maria Csaszni Rygh
Translation: Bruce Bawer

Type: GT America
Paper: 170 gsm Gardamatt Smooth/120 gsm Tauro Offset
Printing and binding: Printer Trento, Italy

ISBN 978-82-328-0203-6

Forlaget Press, Kongens gate 2, 0153 Oslo, Norway
www.forlagetpress.no

Contents

SIMONIZ
LASTING BEAUTY FOR FLOORS

The site

In his first speech as the UN's secretary-general, Trygve Lie asked the question: "Where is the centre of the world?" Which country should host the UN's new headquarters? The answer came pretty quickly: the United States. With that decision began an intense struggle among several major American cities for the honour of becoming the UN's home. For a long time, Philadelphia and San Fransisco were ahead. The majority, however, wanted New York, although there was an extreme lack of suitable sites in the city centre.

The search for a location lasted a year; in the meantime, the UN made do with temporary headquarters. Eventually, some of New York's most powerful citizens took action. Over the course of a single week in December 1946, everything was settled. The solution was Turtle Bay, a run-down neighbourhood along the East River in Manhattan, where the city's slaughterhouses had previously been located. The site was owned by property magnate William Zeckendorf, who had big plans for residential development there. But after securing financing from the Rockefeller famiily and support from New York Mayor William O'Dwyer and city planner Robert Moses, the architect Wallace K. Harrison worked out a deal with Zeckendorf to sell the stretch of land along the river to the Rockefellers, who were then able to present it to the UN as a gift. The new world organization had finally found a home.

Page 16–17: In 1949, the work on the UN Secretariat was underway. The site along the East River had previously been a neighbourhood of slaughterhouses. Now the UN's permanent headquarters was being built here. With its central location in Manhattan, the three-part building complex rose gradually over the course of the next three years.

Page 18–19: With its greenish glass windows that extend over 39 floors, the Secretariat building is a landmark. The building was the first in New York to have a façade that was fully covered by windows; this is known as a curtain wall.

Page 20: The low, rectangular conference building houses the Security Council Chamber, the windows of which face the East River. The Secretariat and the General Assembly building are located on either side of the conference building and closer to the street.

S
KWOOD

Jørn Holme

Introduction – The World's Most Important Room

The history of the founding of the United Nations on 24 October 1945, in the wake of the Second World War, is nothing less than fascinating. How was it possible, while large parts of the globe lay in smouldering ruins, to establish, in the space of a few short months, something that was, in many ways, a new world order? Almost as exciting as the founding narrative of this new organization is the story of its buildings: how did the secretary-general and a group of selected architects manage, in the course of a few years, to create a magnificent modernistic headquarters in the middle of New York City. The UN buildings are at once an important civic landmark and an international symbol of world peace. The grounds are dominated by the Secretariat, one of the city's great office towers, while the General Assembly's low-lying building, with its striking dome, houses the world's most important gathering place for national leaders. The building is still used for the purpose for which it was originally intended, even though the number of member states has risen from 51 to 193 and the UN bureaucracy has grown correspondingly.

The United Nations is based on the principle of the equality of sovereign states – but also on the recognition that certain nations play a more crucial role than others do in ensuring world peace. In the General Assembly, which approves budgets and chooses members of the Security Council and other key UN bodies, every country has one vote, independent of size. At the same time, five of the victors in the Second World War – the United States, Britain, France, the Soviet Union (now Russia) and China – hold special positions of power, with permanent seats and the right to veto in the most powerful of international bodies, the United Nations Security Council.

The Security Council, which consists of five permanent members and ten elected non-permanent members, can literally make the difference between war and peace in the world. It can decide to intervene in a military conflict or impose sanctions on countries that threaten other states or that refuse to respect human rights. Nevertheless, it is a complicated game. Even though the Security Council adopts its binding resolutions by majority vote, any of the five permanent members can block any measure through the use of its veto power.

Several books have been published about the UN buildings, not least in connection with the extensive renovations that were completed in 2013. However, most readers are unaware of Norway's role in the original building project, especially with regard to the Security Council Chamber. This story deserves to be told. The tale begins with the man

Page 22–23: The UN's garden is located in the northern part of the grounds. The General Assembly is the most organically formed building. It has a fan-like shape, with windows facing the garden and a cupola that forms the ceiling of the General Assembly chamber. The skyscraper's side walls are clad in light marble.

Page 24: The Secretariat's glass façade seen from 43rd Street in midtown Manhattan.

who ran the whole project – Trygve Lie, a Norwegian and the United Nations' first secretary-general.

Where would the UN be located?

On 1 February 1946, at the first meeting of the UN General Assembly, Norwegian Foreign Minister Trygve Lie was chosen to be the organization's first secretary-general. The vote was 46 for and 3 against. Thus, he enjoyed almost unanimous support. He became the organization's most powerful man and would remain so as long as both the United States and the Soviet Union trusted him.

The first meeting of the UN General Assembly took place at Central Hall in London, a Methodist church near Westminster Abbey. As Guri Hjeltnes recounts in her article in this book, one of the first matters the UN had to address was the question of where its main headquarters would be located. Trygve Lie began his inaugural address by asking, "Where is the centre of the world?" He answered his own question without hesitation: "The world's new centre of gravity should be on the northwest shore of the Atlantic."[1] It was, after all, the United States, under the leadership of the late President Roosevelt, that had been the major force behind the establishment of the new organization.

The USSR supported Lie's proposal, mostly because it did not want too many American diplomats in Europe. So the UN would be based in America. But where? Several cities were suggested – Boston, Chicago, Philadelphia, San Francisco, and New York.

Trygve Lie must have recognized early on that he was not equipped to negotiate the complex legal and political issues raised by this huge, important construction project alone. He quickly established a building site committee, with delegation leaders from several different countries. As to the question of who would lead the construction project, the issue resolved itself when the site was finally chosen and key partners were brought on board.

The UN's building site committee brought in architects and engineers to evaluate several possible sites on the west coast of the United States. When it became clear that New York was a real candidate, the city established its own committee, led by the wealthy businessman Nelson Rockefeller. New York's mayor, William O'Dwyer, offered a large green area: Flushing Meadows in Queens, east of Manhattan, where the 1939 World's Fair had been held. As Guri Hjeltnes explains, Flushing Meadows was not a particularly popular choice in the UN system: the UN employees wanted to be closer to the heart of the city.[2]

It was John D. Rockefeller Jr., the financier and philanthropist, who solved the problem. His son Nelson negotiated John D.'s purchase, for $8.5 million, of a site that was then presented to the United Nations as a gift. Both the site committee and, later, the General Assembly supported Lie's approval of the site.

How exactly did the Rockefellers acquire the site? The family had quietly purchased a rundown industrial parcel along the East River in Manhattan, between 42nd and 46th streets. The land was bought from property magnate William Zeckendorf, who had planned to fill the site with office buildings. This commercial development, which was to be called "X City", had been designed by the celebrated American architect Wallace K. Harrison, famous for the two spectacular pavilions, the Trylon and Perisphere, that he had designed for the 1939 World's Fair. In addition, Harrison was the Rockefeller family's house architect, a consultant to the city's own building site committee, and a close ally of Mayor O'Dwyer and the city's powerful construction coordinator, Robert Moses. Harrison wanted to be in charge of the work on the new UN headquarters. It was on New Year's Day 1947 that he presented his ideas to Trygve Lie. Only five days later, Lie offered him the job as head of the Headquarters Planning Office.

Harrison had great respect for the bear-like and effective secretary-general. In her biography of Harrison, Victoria Newhouse writes about Lie: "In Harrison's eyes, he possessed the one indispensable quality for a client: like Nelson Rockefeller, Robert Moses and William Zeckendorf, he was a man who could get things done."[3] From the first day, there was a strong chemistry between Lie and Harrison. Lie would later praise Harrison's forthrightness, good sense, and diplomatic skills, as well as his proficiency as an architect. They became close friends.[4]

On 28 January 1949, Secretary-General Trygve Lie signed the building contract. To Lie's right sits Wallace K. Harrison, who was head of the planning office. To his left sits Lou R. Crandall, who represented the four firms Fuller, Turner, Walsh and Slattery Inc., which merged in order to carry out the prestigious construction project.

Trygve Lie was against holding an architectural competition – there was no time for that. As Nina Berre shows in her article, Lie's disinclination to hold a competition was influenced partly by memories of the scandal surrounding the interwar architectural competition for the League of Nations headquarters in Geneva, the *Palais des Nations*. One of the winners of that competition had been the Swiss-French architect Le Corbusier, but his extremely modernistic design encountered massive resistance. Other architects in the competition were awarded the commission instead, and the result was a pompous classical complex.

The site committee turned into a building committee under the leadership of U.S. Ambassador Warren Austin. Among the other committee members was Norwegian UN Ambassador Finn Moe. There was close contact between Lie and some of the more important ambassadors.[5] Years later, in 1956, Trygve Lie would develop ties with the Zeckendorf family, which had sold the UN site to the Rockefellers, when his daughter Guri married William Zeckendorf, Jr., the son of William Zeckendorf.

The architects

Early in the process, Harrison decided to involve several of the world's best architects in the work on the UN buildings. They would work together on the headquarters in a "workshop for peace". But who should be chosen? It was important to bring in people from most of the continents, and invite candidates from countries that had not been among the enemies in the Second World War. A list of 33 names was ultimately reduced to 10, all of them well-known architects, who were appointed to the so-called Board of Design.

Sven Markelius became Sweden's, and thus also the Nordic countries', representative on the Board of Design. His appointment was a typical example of how Lie and Harrison went about ensuring that the names of their desired candidates were submitted by their respective homelands. The countries were formally asked to submit suggestions, but at the same time, Lie and Harrison made it clear with whom they wanted to work. On 13 January 1947, Lie asked the Swedish UN delegation for a candidate for the group of architects. A few days later, Harrison's office suggested to Swedish diplomats that Markelius would be a good choice.[6] The Swedish architect and Harrison had both made names for themselves at the World's Fair, where Markelius had designed the Swedish pavilion. Alvar Aalto was Harrison's first choice from the Nordic countries. Aalto had designed the Finnish pavilion, for which Harrison himself had been the contractor. Nevertheless, politics made the difference: Finland was not yet a member of the UN and was viewed by many as having been on the wrong side in the war.[7]

Other than Harrison himself, the architects who set the tone for the headquarters were Le Corbusier and Oscar Niemeyer, a Brazilian. Harrison was a skilled administrator, whose impressive diplomatic gifts proved useful at meetings of the architects' group. The disagreements among several of them were often intense. Harrison managed to hold it all together and keep things on track. In the spring of 1947, the group held no fewer than 45 meetings.

Le Corbusier turned out to be the greatest challenge. He considered himself the obvious choice for chief architect, having been kicked to the curb in the League of Nations fiasco, and the tension between him and Niemeyer was palpable. However, the great Swiss modernist received considerable support. Le Corbusier is credited with the design of the Secretariat. He had proposed a low-lying conference building to be used by the General Assembly as well as by the three UN councils. Niemeyer altered this concept – supposedly on a day when Le Corbusier was sick and absent from a meeting – so that there would be a separate building for the General Assembly and, for the other councils, a long, low conference building behind the Secretariat, facing the East River. For this idea, Nieyemer received the full approval of his fellow architects.

On 21 May 1947, Harrison presented the architect group's proposal to the 16 members of the building committee. The proposal was approved, and each of the architects went home with a check for $5,000 – apart from Le Corbusier, who wanted to stay on as *chef d'atelier*. Not until Trygve Lie threatened him with reprisals did Le Corbusier return to Switzerland.[8]

There is no indication that Trygve Lie intervened in any of the decisions made by the architects during the spring 1947 working process. In all things, Harrison was his rock. For Lie, the most important thing was to maintain momentum and keep expenses down. When Harrison's cost estimate turned out to be $84 million, a shocked Lie had to cut the budget by about $20 million.[9] This meant that Harrison had to make immediate changes in the plans for the building complex. The office building for the UN's subsidiary bodies on the short northern side of the complex was removed and the Secretariat was reduced from 45 to 39 storeys. One of the two conference rooms in the General Assembly building was also dropped. Funding, however, remained a problem, and the situation was not resolved until President Truman persuaded Congress to grant the UN an interest-free loan in the amount of $65 million.

The Board of Design for the UN headquarters was appointed and led by Wallace K. Harrison. The ten hand-picked architects were distinguished representatives of the architectural profession from around the world. Here is the entire group, gathered together in April 1947 in front of an early model of the UN headquarters. Among the most prominent members of the team were Le Corbusier (second from the left in the top picture) and Oscar Niemeyer (in the middle, wearing a dark tie and smiling at the camera). Scandinavia's representative, Sven Markelius (on the far left) also decorated the chamber of the Economic and Social Council (ECO-SOC).

All indications are that Trygve Lie decided early on to involve the architect Arnstein Arneberg, a personal friend, in the work on the Security Council Chamber. This was the most prestigious space in the entire UN complex, even more so than the General Assembly. On 26 December 1946, before Harrison was hired, Lie sent a letter to Arneberg asking him to suggest a Norwegian architect for the headquarters.[10] At the time, Arneberg was deeply involved in another project. He was one of the two principal architects responsible for the construction and furnishing of the new Oslo City Hall, which was to be completed in 1950. In September 1948, Arneberg and Harrison met in Paris to discuss the job before the cornerstone was laid. Why Paris? Probably because the Security Council was meeting there instead of in New York. Arneberg was thereby given an opportunity to follow the negotiations and come up with a design. The framework for the new chamber in New York had been established and the dimensions were determined in detail, as was the case with the other large spaces in the conference building. Each of the chambers had an amphitheatre-like design, and all of them had similar areas in the rear of the auditorium for members of the public and press. It is not unthinkable that the Security Council Chamber at the UN's temporary headquarters at Lake Success was in Harrison's thoughts, and that it may have contributed to the guidelines he gave Arneberg. Other features of this space were a horseshoe-shaped table, built-in press boxes in the walls, and a sloping press and audience gallery.

What was left for the nordic whitecoat to do was to design the ceiling, the floor, and the walls – and, not least, the furniture for the delegates. The press and audience seats had already been chosen – they would keep the ones that were already being used at the temporary headquarters at Flushing Meadows. In her article, Ingeborg Glambek recounts Arneberg's work on the design of the chamber, while Ulf Grønvold and Nina Berre provide a portrait of Arnstein Arneberg as an architect, revealing more background about the selection of Arneberg for work on the Security Council Chamber.

Through Arneberg, Lie persuaded Norway to become the first country to pay for artwork for the headquarters – specifically, for the Security Council Chamber. In fact, Arneberg himself chose the painter Per Krohg and brought in the textile artist Else Poulsson. Both were major artists with whom the architect had worked closely on the decoration of Oslo City Hall. Per Krohg and the painting in the Security Council Chamber are discussed more fully in Vibeke Waallann Hansen's article in this book, while Else Poulsson's art and her collaboration with Arneberg are examined in more detail in Sarah A. Lichtman's article.

More than a year later, Trygve Lie invited Sweden and Denmark for the first time to decorate the two other large chambers, those intended for use by the Trusteeship Council and the Economic and Social Council. The distinctively Scandinavian modernism was possibly an argument for this choice.[11] However, by extending such invitations, Lie also avoided criticism for having accorded his own country special treatment.[12]

The Security Council's first meeting in the Palais de Chaillot in Paris was held on 16 September 1948. Arneberg was himself in Paris at this point, and probably attended one of the Security Council meetings. The semicircular table with a Secretariat table in the middle brings to mind Arneberg's final arrangement of the council's permanent chamber in New York.

Sven Markelius (on the left) presents the model of the ECO-SOC Chamber at his Stockholm office in September 1950. Beside him stand Wallace K. Harrison and representatives of the Board of Art Advisors, Jaques Carlu from France and Howard Robertson from England. The model shows the large glass window at the end of the room that faces the river. A horse-shoe-shaped meeting table is also central to the design of this chamber.

The Security Council, the Trusteeship Council, and the Economic and Social Council (ECO-SOC) are three of the UN's six principal organs. The three others are the General Assembly, the Secretariat (the secretary-general and administration), and the International Court of Justice, the latter located in The Hague. The now defunct Trusteeship Council's mandate was to oversee countries with the status of trust territories and to help guide them toward independence. The Economic and Social Council consists of a selection of member countries (now 54 in number) and is tasked with coordinating all economic and social questions facing the UN and to serve as a liaison to all of the UN's subsidiary bodies.

In the design of the chambers for the Trusteeship Council and Economic and Social Council, Harrison played a more central role from day one, without Lie himself getting involved. Harrison's suggestion that the ECO-SOC chamber be decorated by Sven Markelius, who three years earlier had been a member of the central architects' group, was approved. Harrison's office had already sounded out Markelius about the job in the spring of 1950, before the Swedish government officially appointed Markelius to the position. Sweden was offered the ECO-SOC chamber after Denmark had been approached about the Trusteeship Council chamber. The reason was reportedly that Sweden, in the view of Harrison and Lie, was a "socially pioneering nation".[13]

As Ingeborg Glambek has pointed out, the three Scandinavian architects approached the tasks they had been assigned in different ways: Markelius came up with the most modernistic – even brutalist – solution. It was the ceiling over the area for the public and press that was most surprising. All of the technical installations, ventilation shafts, pipes, and wires are open to view instead of being hidden behind a ceiling. By making this choice, Markelius created an illusion of greater headroom in the rear of the auditorium. This part of the ceiling occasioned widespread debate; President Eisenhower is said to have commented, "You surely do not need to be so foolish just to be modern."[14] The ceiling above the delegate area, however, was entirely different – a hanging white cladding that formed a dramatic contrast to the ceiling in the back of the chamber. The walls of the delegates' area were covered with vertical laths that resembled narrow organ pipes. The surface of the large window facing the East River was covered with two sets of curtains.[15]

The relatively unknown Danish interior architect Finn Juhl was given responsibility for the Trusteeship Council chamber. Officially, it was the council of the Royal Danish Academy that appointed Juhl. That the choice fell on him can probably be credited to the Danish-American Abel Sørensen, who had been working on the UN's site project since 1946. By the summer of 1947, Sørensen had been named chief architect for the interiors and had travelled to several countries, including Sweden and Denmark, in search of inspiration. He met Juhl in Copenhagen in 1948 and was fascinated by the young furniture designer.[16]

At first, Denmark wanted only to donate a work of art, but Juhl managed to persuade his country's Foreign Ministry that it would be better to sponsor the interior decoration of a chamber – with himself as architect. The art could come later.[17]

Like Markelius, Juhl was exasperated by the lack of leeway given him as an architect, and like his Swedish colleague, he made the ceiling the room's most important interior surface. While Markelius located his modern open ceiling over the public and press section, Juhl placed his open ceiling over the delegate and press areas, where the headroom was greatest. The ceiling is dominated by a series of transverse trellises with rectangular wooden boxes of different heights, painted in strong colours. The lighting fixtures were placed in the boxes. The concrete ceiling above the boxes and trellises is painted sky blue. Juhl got the idea from an exhibition in Switzerland, where thousands of colourful flags hung vertically in long rows. Juhl also used wooden panels on the walls, in Danish ash, except at the back of the audience area. As a furniture designer by profession, Juhl designed all of the furniture – brass reflector lamps, wall clocks, tables and chairs for the delegates and their secretaries. It was important to Juhl that the room serve as a practical working space, while also standing as an expression of modern elegance.[18]

The furnishings in the ECO-SOC chamber and the Trusteeship Council's chamber have been altered several times in accordance with the major changes that have taken place at the UN since 1952. The great increase in the number of member nations and the need to use the chambers for meetings other than council meetings led to the complete transformation of the furnishings in the delegate areas of both chambers in 1964 and again in 1977. In addition, the Trusteeship Council was abolished as a permanent organ in 1994. Both chambers had originally been dominated by horseshoe-shaped meeting tables for the delegates, as in the Security Council Chamber. Now these chambers are more traditional auditoriums – smaller versions, more or less, of the General Assembly. The press and public areas of the Trusteeship Council have also been reduced in size to make room for more delegates. The extensive use of these chambers has led to considerable wear and tear, which has necessitated, for example, the replacement of the curtains on several occasions.

The Security Council Chamber has also been altered since 1952. All of the textiles and threadbare materials have been removed, but aesthetically the space has undergone minimal changes in comparison with the two other chambers. As Loraine Sievers points out in her article on the use of the Security Council, it has been important to maintain the Security Council Chamber's distinctive and conservative look. The most visible difference is that the meeting table for the secretaries in the middle of the horseshoe has disappeared. In 1965, the large horseshoe table was discreetly lengthened at both ends to increase the number of chairs to 21. The marble fence that separated the delegate area from the press and public was also removed.

A headquarters for the future

Between 2009 and 2013, the UN building underwent an extensive renovation, with a budget of $1.9 billion. Most of the member countries contributed. Norway provided a grant in the amount of NOK 47 million and covered the cost of new wallpaper for the Security Council Chamber that was based on the original pattern. In their articles, Michael

Adlerstein and Linda Veiby describe the restoration of the UN headquarters generally and the Security Council Chamber in particular, and explain Norway's role in this work.

The headquarters complex still consists almost entirely of the exact same buildings as in 1952. In 1961, the Dag Hammarskjöld Library replaced the structure that originally contained the library. This low, four-storey building on the right flank forms an elegant frame for the headquarters. Harrison himself was the architect. The building was commissioned by Lie's successor as secretary-general, Dag Hammarskjöld. The secretary-general died tragically in an aeroplane accident a few months before the library was completed. The General Assembly honoured Hammarskjöld by naming the building for him. At the beginning of the 1980s, a large new cafeteria was built at the foot of the Secretariat facing northeast and overlooking the East River.

New York did not pay tribute to Trygve Lie as the UN's first secretary-general until September 2016. The occasion was the dedication by Norwegian Prime Minister Erna Solberg of Trygve Lie Plaza and the Peace Clock at the corner of First Avenue and 42nd Street. Also present were two of Trygve Lie's three grandchildren, Arthur and William Zeckendorf. The event took place, of course, on the piece of land that their grandfather had sold 70 years earlier so that it could become the site of the UN headquarters.

The Security Council Chamber is located in the anonymous conference building facing the river. Here, in the smallest of the three large meeting rooms, the Security Council gathers for meetings, usually several times a week, for briefings, debates, and, not least, to formulate and vote on resolutions that will be binding for all of the member nations. Nowadays, the chamber is closed to the public during meetings; for reasons of security, the public no longer has access to the Security Council. Thanks to television cameras from around the world, however, the room is one of the world's most famous, and for this reason, when the Security Council is not in session, its chamber is the most popular destination for the tens of thousands of tourists who take the UN's guided tours every year. The Security Council Chamber has been the focus of critics and the press ever since 1952, and Siri Wolland recapitulates some of the media coverage in her article in this book.

Of all the important rooms at the UN headquarters, this room has undergone the least transformation. Over the years, the Security Council's permanent members have made their position clear to the UN administration: this room must be preserved in its original form. Even during the renovation of the UN, when the Security Council had to meet temporarily in the large meeting room outside the General Assembly chamber, a half-sized reproduction of Per Krohg's painting was mounted on the wall as a sign of historical continuity.

Despite its secluded location, the Security Council Chamber is perhaps the world's most important room, and it has a Norwegian background. It is this distinctive history that we want to tell in this book.[19]

The building process

The UN headquarters went up fast. The cornerstone was laid in the autumn of 1949, and in April 1952 the first meeting was held in the Security Council Chamber. The construction costs were dizzying, the time pressure intense.

To ensure that the work got done as quickly as possible, Lie eschewed a time-consuming architectural competition and instead named Wallace K. Harrison – the architect who had played the central role in acquiring the East River site – as head of construction. Harrison then put together a "Board of Design" made up of ten international architects. The project would be an international collaboration – a "workshop for peace". The many strong personalities in the group of architects, however, also made the work very challenging.

The construction of the Security Council Chamber was also a demanding process. Tight deadlines, strict budgets, and long geographical distances made the work difficult for Arneberg and the other Norwegian participants. But on 4 April 1952 the chamber was ready for its very first official meeting. In the summer of 1952 Per Krohg's painting was also finally installed, and the completed chamber was dedicated in a solemn ceremony on 22 August 1952.

In the summer of 1951, the work on the Security Council Chamber was well underway. In Arneberg's original design, the press and audience gallery were separated by a marble balustrade on which there were plans to place a decorative relief by the Norwegian sculptor Emil Lie. This work was never created, and the balustrade was later removed.

CHILE
CHINA
ASSISTANT SECRETARY GENERAL
FRANCE CHAIR.
SECRETARY
GREECE

Ingeborg Glambek

The Security Council Chamber – from Idea to Reality

Page 36–37: The delegates' meeting table being put together in the summer of 1951. The table was made of ash wood and produced in the USA. In 1952 the table consisted of 19 modules. Later the number grew to 21. In the sunken part of the floor was the meeting board for members of the Secretariat. This table was later moved, and the sunken part of the floor raised to the same level as the rest of the floor.

Page 38–39: The Security Council's chamber, photographed in February 1952, a mere two months before the first meeting was held in the chamber. Owing to delays, Per Krohg's painting was not placed in the chamber until September of the same year. The curtains are always drawn for reasons of security, so the picture provides a rare glimpse of how the chamber looks in daylight.

Page 40: The original secretariat's table was used by translators and employees of the press office of the Security Council. The table, like the horseshoe-shaped table, was made of ash wood. The chairs were designed by Arnstein Arneberg.

The three UN council chambers are located in the conference building.[1] The building is tucked away, facing eastward, and when viewed from First Avenue, it is partly hidden by the more predominant Secretariat and General Assembly buildings. From the river to the east, however, the conference building is fully visible, rising above the heavily trafficked FDR Drive (short for Franklin D. Roosevelt Drive, and still often referred to by its former name, the East River Drive).

The conference building had already been designed when the job of furnishing the three chambers was assigned to the three Scandinavian countries. The general architectural concept had thus already been established. The architects who were brought in for this work therefore had quite limited options, and they were unable to do anything that might conflict with the overall plan.

The tasks assigned to the Scandinavian architects were to make decisions about what would be done with the walls and ceilings, to select carpets and curtains, and to suggest lighting and fixtures, as well as to design doors, parapets, and railings between the separate areas for delegates, journalists, and members of the general public. They also needed to design chairs for the delegates and secretaries. The chairs for members of the press and public, which are immovable and identical in all of the chambers, were designed by the Danish-American architect in the Planning Office, Abel Sørensen. They had previously been used at the UN's temporary headquarters at Flushing Meadows (see p. 105). The three chambers – those intended for the Security Council, the Trusteeship Council, and the Economic and Social Council – are nearly identical. Nevertheless, since the eastern façade of the building is a bit curved because it follows the riverbank, one of the chambers – that of the Security Council – is slightly smaller than the others. The difference, however, is insignificant and almost unnoticeable. The floor area of each chamber measures approximately 48 metres by 25 metres. These are rather long and narrow rooms, difficult to furnish. The rooms are oriented in such a way that one of the short sides faces the river to the east. The wall here is eight metres high and consists of wall-to-wall, floor-to-ceiling windows that look out on a terrace. The daylight that pours through these large windows has caused major problems.

Each chamber is now divided into two approximately equal parts, one for delegates and their colleagues, the other for press and the general public. The latter part is built stepwise, as in a theatre, with the public seated in back and the press in front. Each chamber contains about 120 seats for journalists and about 400 for visitors. It was a guiding principle that UN meetings and negotiations should be open to the public. Large portions of the General Assembly, council chambers, and conference rooms were therefore set aside for visitors. The delegates sit at the front of each chamber, on a sort of stage.

The different levels have their own entrances, with the areas for the delegates and those for the press and public clearly divided from each other by balustrades and railings – except for the Trusteeship Council, where the architect chose another, more open solution. Because of the raised floor in the rear part of the room, the wall above the audience gallery is only three metres high – five metres lower in height, that is, than the window on the facing wall. On the delegate side of the chamber, the side walls are fitted with two rows of low windows that open onto smaller rooms that include seats for simultaneous translators, sound and TV recording, and so on.

The delegates and their advisors were placed around large horseshoe-shaped tables. The secretaries and advisors were seated immediately behind the delegates. The orientation of the rooms made it natural for those chairing the meetings to sit at the head of the delegate table, facing the chamber, with their backs to the window. This placement was problematic, however, because the strong light coming in from the window illuminated those sitting at the head of the table from behind, making them appear in silhouette from the audience's perspective. Hence, the three architects all faced the same task. In an extremely thorough assessment of the furnishings in the American periodical *Interiors* in August 1952, the anonymous author compared the difficulty facing these architects with the tasks presented to students in examinations for classical architecture and design courses: students are given identical challenges and are expected to solve them in their own individual ways. Viewed from this perspective, the three council chambers offer model responses to the challenge. All three architects addressed the same problem in extremely different ways. The result was three rooms, each of which had its own unique character. Two of them are strongly influenced by modernism, while the third, the Security Council Chamber, is more traditional and conservative – the *Interiors* author claims (see also pp. 81 og 109).

In principle, the three main UN councils are equal. The Security Council is special, however, partly because it has five major world powers as permanent members and partly because these members also possess veto power. This imbalance of power stands in sharp contrast to the organization's otherwise strictly egalitarian structure, and gives the Security Council a special status. That this council meets frequently, while the other two originally met only once or twice a year, also causes it to be regarded as more important than the other two. The distinctive nature of the Security Council was obvious from the UN's earliest days.

Arneberg's work

I have not found any sources that provide an unambiguous explanation of the origin of the idea to invite the three Scandinavian countries to furnish the three chambers or of the process by which it was decided

The Trusteeship Council's chamber in 1952. The chamber was designed by the Danish architect and furniture designer Finn Juhl. The ceiling is the most distinctive design element: clear, contrasting colours decorate the modules that hide the air-conditioning system. A wooden grid binds the ceiling elements together. Almost all of the items of furniture in the chamber were designed by Juhl and produced in Denmark.

The Economic and Social Council's chamber in 1952. The chamber was designed by the Swedish architect Sven Markelius. The sunken roof above the delegate area features round spotlights. The roof over the audience and press gallery represents a more radical move on Markelius's part: to increase the height, he left the construction and pipe systems uncovered, a choice that was widely commented on after the chamber's completion.

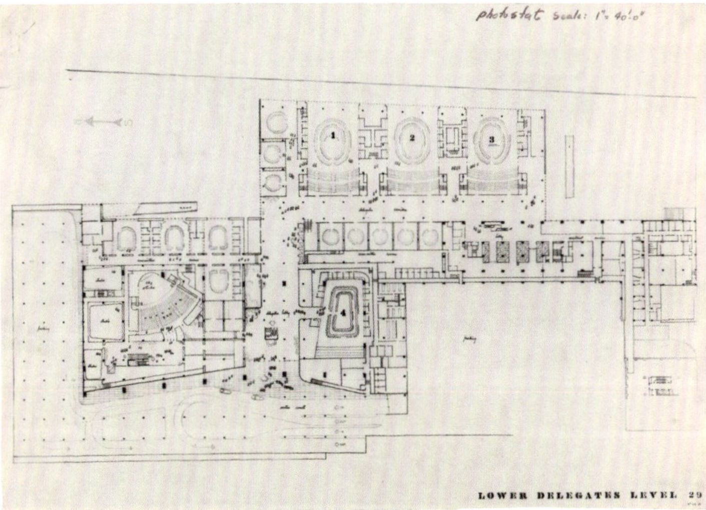

The three Scandinavian meeting chambers are laid out in a row in the conference building seen on the upper part of the drawing. The blueprint shows how similar they are in size and shape. Of the three spaces, the Security Council's chamber is the furthest to the right. The blueprint is from Arneberg's archive and was most likely sent to him from the building office in New York while the complex was under construction.

which country would get which chamber. In the minutes of meetings, letters, and other documents, the decisions are hidden behind the neutral formulation "It was determined that..." Why, for example, was Norway assigned the Security Council Chamber? It seems likely, however, that the UN's Norwegian secretary-general, Trygve Lie, saw to it that Norway was given responsibility for the furnishing of the most important of the three spaces. Since the organization's very earliest days, it was clear to Lie that the Security Council already enjoyed great prestige; being a master strategist, he undoubtedly foresaw that it would receive much more worldwide attention in the future than the others, with photographs of its chambers appearing in the media to a far greater extent than photographs of the other two chambers. Thanks to his close ties to the Labour Party government back home, moreover, Lie was in a position to see to it that the Norwegian state covered at least part of the cost of the furnishings. There is reason to believe that Lie played an important role here, and that he made it possible for Norway to come into the picture at an early point, before the subject had been taken up formally either at the UN or back in Oslo.

Trygve Lie wrote an official letter, dated 20 April 1950, to all of the member nations, asking for contributions to help pay for the furnishing of the chambers. The decision about Norway's contribution and the selection of a Norwegian architect seem to have been undertaken almost a year earlier than the corresponding actions in regard to Sweden and Denmark. Nor is it entirely clear who chose Arnstein Arneberg to be responsible for the prestigious assignment, even though there are indications that in this matter, too, it was Lie who took the initiative (see also pp. 84–88). The decision was hardly an unreasonable one: at the time, Arneberg was one of Norway's most notable architects, and a great many examples of his work could be found all over the country. In his autobiography, Lie wrote, "The Security Council Chamber had been assigned to Norway, and my good friend the architect Arnstein Arneberg was charged with its planning and design."[2]

There was no architectural competition. As mentioned, the two men were friends, and Arneberg had designed Lie's mountain cottage, Lieset, in Røros. Lie also had a cottage in Nesodden, near Oslo, that Arneberg had extensively rebuilt. The head of the Planning Office, Wallace K. Harrison, had been in contact with Arneberg as early as 1947. They had planned to meet in Stockholm, but Harrison was unable to make it, so the two did not meet until September 1948 in Paris. That December, Harrison sent Arneberg a Christmas greeting and at the same time requested materials for the Security Council Chamber.[3] Arneberg's reply must have been sent to Harrison in the same month or early in January 1949.[4] Arneberg's first written descriptions of the chamber's design appear in a letter in which he suggested that it should have a limestone or marble floor and a parapet made of coloured stucco. To attain a decorative effect, he wanted to use stainless steel in simple inlaid patterns. The doors could also be made of stainless steel, preferably with a small artistic sculpture made of gold in each centre span. The alternative was doors made of inlaid wood.

Arneberg envisaged illuminating the space with strips of lights that would run along the ceiling between the shorter walls to emphasize the room's length. At the centre, over the round table, he wanted the ceiling to be slightly raised. To mark the delegates' area and lend a touch of variety to the expansive ceiling surface, he thought that a portion of the ceiling might be decorated by an artist. In an area between the windows, he wanted to place a mosaic or fresco. Next to the windows, he wanted decorative silk curtains.

Harrison replied to Arneberg in a friendly letter dated 5 January 1949, but did not comment in detail on Arneberg's ideas.[5] Instead, he asked Arneberg to come to New York to examine the site in person.

On 30 March 1949, Arneberg sent Harrison his first sketches.[6] That April, Arneberg was in New York to study the site and the plans, and of course to present his own proposals for the decoration of the chamber. The visit thus took place six months before construction began.

While the work was underway, there were many other things that had to be settled – for example, the financing. Who would pay for what? What would be covered by the UN's own budget, and what would be paid for by the expected cash gift from the Norwegian government? It is clear that from the very beginning, there was a good deal of uncertainty and confusion surrounding this question, and it soon became clear that Arneberg's earlier visions of what could be accomplished had been too optimistic. Budget cuts were in order. The UN had appropriated $120,000 for the decoration of the Security Council Chamber.[7] That sum would cover the work on the walls and ceiling, the furniture, the railings, and the marble. Arneberg's first estimate exceeded this sum by a considerable amount, although the cost of artwork was not included. He was therefore asked to lower the estimated price. He did so, regretfully, for example by reducing the amount of marble and by painting the railings instead of using stainless steel.[8]

When the idea of allowing individual countries to take responsibility for parts of the decoration was introduced, the objective was not merely to make a symbolic statement but to reduce the burden on the UN's own budget. Norway's total contribution came to NOK 109,000. Of this, NOK 60,000 was paid to Per Krohg, plus NOK 15,000 cover his travel expenses. A sum of NOK 10,000 set aside for the design of the tapestries. The amount was granted by a royal resolution dated 7 January 1950. The appropriation was not discussed in the Norwegian Parliament, a fact that irked members of the parliamentary Committee on Foreign Affairs and the Constitution and led to the demand that the audit Committee investigate the matter.[9] Because of the misunderstanding and uncertainty as to what the gift from Norway actually entailed, the Norwegian Ministry of Foreign Affairs issued a press release stating that the gift would only cover artistic ornamentation – in other words, painting and sculpture.[10] The other costs of decoration would have to be paid by the UN itself. The Norwegian government's allocation did not include a fee for the architect – a fact that led to a good many problems.

The correspondence between Arneberg and the headquarters' Planning Office during the period 1950 to 1952 reveals many other problems, both large and small, along the way. Among the larger non-financial problems were New York's extremely strict restrictions in regard to the flammability of materials used in decoration. The idea of using Norwegian pine for the delegates' table, for example, had to be discarded because of fire safety rules. The toughest challenge of all, however,

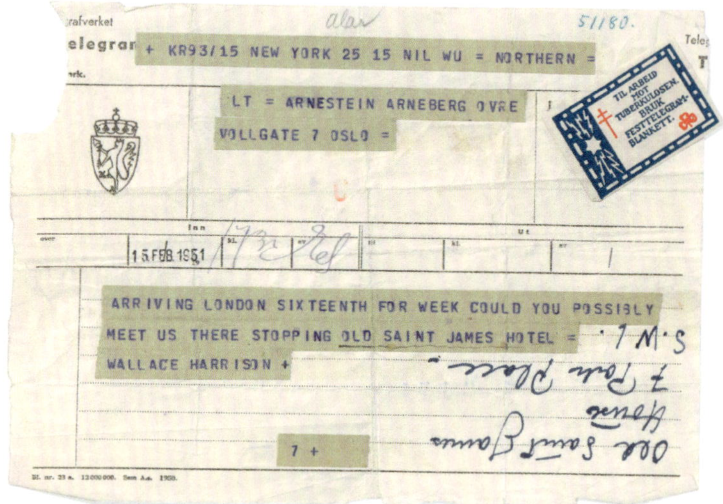
+ KR93/15 NEW YORK 25 15 NIL WU = NORTHERN =
LT = ARNESTEIN ARNEBERG OVRE VOLLGATE 7 OSLO =
ARRIVING LONDON SIXTEENTH FOR WEEK COULD YOU POSSIBLY MEET US THERE STOPPING OLD SAINT JAMES HOTEL =
WALLACE HARRISON +
7 +

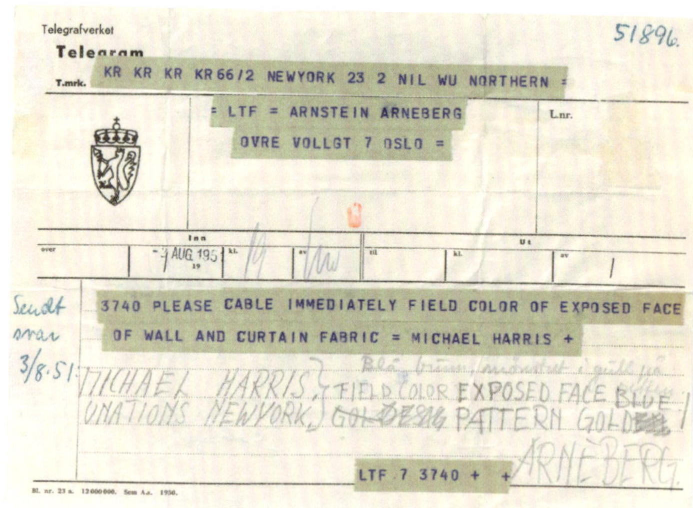
Telegrafverket
Telegram
KR KR KR KR66/2 NEWYORK 23 2 NIL WU NORTHERN =
= LTF = ARNSTEIN ARNEBERG
OVRE VOLLGT 7 OSLO =
3740 PLEASE CABLE IMMEDIATELY FIELD COLOR OF EXPOSED FACE OF WALL AND CURTAIN FABRIC = MICHAEL HARRIS +
LTF 7 3740 + +

Arneberg's archives provide a glimpse into the extensive exchange of letters with the building office in New York. Harrison and Arneberg also met several times. Telegrams were sent to confirm appointments for meetings. Aside from the occasions on which Arneberg was in New York, the architects met in Paris and London. The tone and content of the letters show how the communication varied from friendly chitchat and exchanges of gifts to frustration and disagreement.

involved the textiles for the wall coverings. Before they were hung, the textiles had to undergo treatments to render them less flammable. To the despair of the architects and the producers of the material, it turned out that the Norwegian-woven textiles, created by the Oslo firm of Joh. Petersen, shrank and became twisted as a result of the treatment. For a long time, it looked as though these difficulties were insurmountable, but the tapestries finally went up, even though Arneberg bemoaned the fact that they were not installed in an entirely attractive way (see also p. 144). Arneberg insisted on the importance of the chamber's being something more than a meeting space or "political workshop." At the time, the word "workshop" was widely used in connection with the work of the UN; indeed, it was pretty much a catchphrase there. Harrison himself liked to call his own Planning Group a "workshop for peace." Markelius (the Swedish architect) was comfortable enough with this kind of language, and even Juhl (the Danish architect) accepted it to a certain degree. Arneberg did not. He maintained that it was important for the Security Council Chamber to be more than a mere "workshop". It should be representative of contemporary Norwegian culture – which meant that it should contain works by Norwegian artists.

Problems with Per Krohg's painting

It was clear early on that the UN could not cover the cost of artwork for the Security Council, and that they would have to be funded by another source – namely, the Norwegian government. Arneberg wanted to decorate the space in a monumental fashion and suggested, probably after consulting with Trygve Lie, the artist Per Krohg (see also pp. 119–122). No competition was announced. Another long-lived intention was to decorate the chamber with sculptural works in the form of bas-reliefs. The sculptor Emil Lie was contacted, and he drafted some sketches. The budget included NOK 25,000 to pay for the reliefs, but they never saw the light of day, principally for economic reasons.[11]

When Arneberg suggested, at the very earliest phase of the project, that the chamber should contain a large painting, neither the Planning Office nor Harrison opposed the idea. Eventually, however, objections were raised. In 1950, the Board of Art Advisors was formed. Its task was to evaluate the various proposals for artwork to be displayed at the UN headquarters. To win approval, a work of art would have to be suited to the function of the specific space for which it was intended as well as to the overall design of the building.

The Board of Art Advisors did not immediately accept the idea of having a mural in the Security Council Chamber. The panel's members thought that the council chambers should have the feel of working spaces, and that putting artwork on the walls was therefore inappropriate. They said that art would disturb the delegates' concentration and suggested placing the mural from Norway somewhere else in the building. Arneberg strongly rejected this idea. He maintained that the painting was very important for the impression that the room would make as a window on Norwegian art and culture. He also argued that the appropriation for the artist's fee would be withdrawn if the artwork were not placed in the Security Council Chamber.[12] Trygve Lie very

Ahmed Shah Bokhari of Pakistan, president of the Security Council for that month, led the very first meeting in the Security Council Chamber on 4 April 1952. Norway's ambassador, Arne Sunde (at the far left of the table), was invited to sit with the Security Council and received a ceremonial expression of gratitude for Norway's contribution to the interior of the chamber. Per Krohgs mural was not yet in place.

likely shared Arneberg's idea. To persuade Harrison and the Board of Art Advisors, it was arranged that Harrison and two of the members of the Board, Jacques Carlu from France and Howard Robertson from Britain, would visit Scandinavia in August 1950.

In Oslo, Trygve Lie himself was present, and the representatives were shown monumental Norwegian paintings, especially Per Krohg's. They were, or at least appeared to be, convinced that the painting could be suitable for the chamber. One factor that may have contributed to this decision was that there was not much time left. In correspondence about the decoration, the importance of a quick decision was constantly emphasized: the chamber had to be ready for use in the autumn of 1952 at the latest. If this matter dragged out, the artist would have too little time to complete the work. It was extremely important for the headquarters to be completed by the projected date.

The UN's Board of Art Advisors must also have known that that Trygve Lie preferred conservative art. Lie was not fond of abstract art – a matter of taste that was demonstrated by his rejection in 1948 of an offer from none other than Pablo Picasso to provide a mural for the UN.[13]

The Security Council held its first meeting in the new chamber on 4 April 1952. Krohg's painting was still not in place. It was hung that summer and was there for the chamber's official dedication on 22 September 1952.

The result

In the end, Arneberg chose to give the space a unified feel by giving the two parts of the room – the part for delegates and the part for observers ("stage and auditorium") – a visual coherence. The ceiling is plastered and painted white with recessed lighting, as well as indirect lighting to mark the transition between the ceiling's two levels. The points of light look almost like a star-splashed sky. Above the delegates' table, the lights are arranged in a circle, mirroring the shape of the table.

The long walls are covered with blue damask rayon wallpaper with yellow motifs – anchors, ears of wheat, and hearts – symbolizing faith, hope, and charity. The artist responsible for these textiles was Else Poulsson, one of Arneberg's collaborators on the interior of Oslo City Hall. The delegates' portion of the room is framed with a marble parapet that turns into a railing separating the space from the press seats. Marble, quarried in Gjellebekkbruddet in Norway, also frames the large Per Krohg painting behind the delegate table.

The back wall high above the audience gallery is covered in wallpaper of Biri straw. The carpet, produced by Firth & Sons in York, England, is grey.

The pale ash doors have intarsia patterns made of tin. There are recessed torches and swords – ancient symbols of war – to emphasize the council's responsibility to preserve the peace, investigate conflicts, and take action, if necessary with military force. The doors, which have large, rectangular wooden handles, were produced by the Norwegian firm Rasmusson and Hansen.

The press and audience seats were designed and manufactured in the United States. They lacked armrests and had tubular legs that contained wires and cables connected to the translation headphones. Arneberg influenced the design by selecting the fabric for these chairs. The delegates' and secretaries' chairs, 44 in all, were designed by Arneberg's young assistant, Finn Nilsson, and manufactured in Norway by furniture maker Johan Fr. Monrad. It was important for the delegates' chairs to be comfortable, with cloth-covered armrests. The secretariat chairs were to be simpler, lack armrests, and resemble office chairs. The chairs are made of ash and mahogany and are covered with striped blue and yellow wool. The meeting table was designed by Arneberg's office but was produced in the USA.[14] The table is in the shape of a half-circle and consists of different sections. Its surface is a massive piece of ashwood, while the side slabs and the surfaces facing the inside of the circle are veneered. The table's shape and weight emphasize community and the seriousness of the decisions to be made around it. The large painting by Per Krohg hangs on the eastern short wall. The window columns between the painting and the side wall are covered by thick curtains made of the same material as the wallpaper. When Arneberg was in New York to inspect the site in April 1949, he was presented with preliminary sketches of the chamber that helped him realize where Per Krohg's painting should go. At the time, the plan was for the short wall to contain a fixed central panel and two glass side panels. The large screen cried out for decoration, as Arneberg himself wrote in *Byggekunst* in 1952 when he described the project to the Norwegian public. This idea changed over the course of the project's development, and in each of the three chambers, the short wall ended up consisting entirely of glass. This, however, did not involve alteration of Arneberg's concept of a decorative central field. The large painting by Per Krohg dominates the room completely. It is easy to agree with the *Interiors* writer who characterized the picture as "the most unique feature of the room". The painting measures about five meters by nine meters. In its lower portion, it is dark and grim, depicting dungeons and caves, dragons and other fantasy creatures, soldiers and machines of war. Human beings climb and contort and struggle to free themselves from chains and fetters. Many of them form silhouettes against the upper, lighter portion of the canvas. This part is divided into seven separate fields set against a light background. The fields are organized symmetrically, with three on each side of an almond-shaped central portion.

Beneath this, at the very centre of the picture, a phoenix rises out of a world of ashes. In the almond-shaped central part are a man and woman kneeling and facing each other with flowers in their hands. They are surrounded by children with flowers and wreaths. Depicted in the upper fields are human beings opening windows and doors onto light and sun. They are singing and dancing, or active in the work of building and creating. In brief, the picture shows in an extremely simple and unambiguous manner the new, harmonic, and brightly lit world that has overcome the forces of evil.

12
1
2
3
4
5
6
7
8
9
10
11

Per Krohg

D'IVOIRE
EQUATORIAL GUINEA
ETHIOPIA
FRANCE
SECRETARY-GENERAL
PRESIDE

ZAKHSTAN
DIRECTOR
KUWAIT
NETHERLANDS
PERU
POL

STAIR I
ESCALIER I

Ulf Grønvold

Anstein Arneberg between Past and Present

> Up from the ruins of the old world rises (...) the new, orderly society, for which the goal is Peace and Happiness and the colours of which are bright and clear, while the underworld is depicted in verdigris, iron red, and steel blue.
>
> *Per Krohg on his painting in the Security Council Chamber*[1]

In 1945, the great bloodbath was over. A new epoch began. What was needed now were joint institutions dedicated to cooperation and progress.

One way in which the new world order was manifested was in magnificent modern structures. The UN's elegant headquarters in New York and the large, Y-shaped UNESCO building in Paris were both completed during the 1950s.

At the start of the decade, the Oslo City Hall, the structure on which Arnstein Arneberg (and Magnus Poulsson) had laboured for three and a half decades, was opened with great fanfare. Two years later, on 4 April 1952, the first meeting was held in the Security Council Chamber. In this immense room in New York, the capital of the world, important and difficult political decisions would be made. The Oslo City Hall would be a landmark in the Norwegian capital for the unforeseeable future. Arneberg would remain professionally active right up until his death in 1961, but it would be hard for him to surpass these two major triumphs.

Both buildings are located at water's edge and are visible from a considerable distance. Otherwise, they are very different. This is owing to the size of the UN headquarters and its articulation of specific functions. The flat park site is like the surface of a table on which distinctive figures are placed alongside one another: the Secretariat's 39-storey slice stands in front of a narrow, elongated four-storey-high conference building. The General Assembly building, with its two long concave sides and curved roof, is sculptural in shape. Oslo City Hall is also composed of distinctive parts: two office towers face the city; between them stands the Central Building, containing the City Council chamber; and facing the fjord is the Main Hall, in which all the public rooms are located. As in New York, each of the principal parts can be read separately. The difference is that those in the City Hall are combined into a single compact brick building, a single condensed display of power.

The first modernistic public structure in the Nordic countries was the Skansen restaurant in Oslo. Completed in 1927, it came on the heels

Page 56–57: Per Krohg's painting is the most eye-catching part of the chamber. It is divided into symmetrical fields. Krohg did this consciously in order to make his message clear: the UN was responsible for establishing order in a chaotic world. In the picture, freedom, equality, and brotherhood are symbolized in various scenes. At the top left is a group of people who share grain equally among themselves. The rearing horse has won back his freedom. In the two rectangular fields closest to the centre, several smiling women and men carry a ribbon in UN blue. In the central, almond-shaped field, a family is harmoniously reunited. Below them sits the phoenix bird, which has conquered the dark underworld. The dragon has been impaled on a sword, and on each side prisoners are set free and helped into the bright part of the painting.

of the earliest European buildings in the new style. The restaurant, erected only a few hundred metres from the site on which Oslo City Hall would soon be built, was designed by Lars Backer (1892–1930), who had worked as an assistant to Arneberg and Poulsson from 1914 to 1919. Now, in 1927, their former apprentice introduced modern functional architecture to the Nordic region. The start date for Oslo City Hall was approaching, and Arneberg and Poulsson came to the realization that it would become old-fashioned even before it was finished. They had to adjust their plans, and it was then, in 1930, that they gave Oslo City Hall its final design. Thus, credit must be given to a 35-year-old architect, Lars Backer, for introducing "the new era" to Oslo in 1927. Modernism's three foremost pioneers were more experienced: the Swiss Le Corbusier (1887–1965) and the two Germans, Walter Gropius (1883–1969) and Mies van der Rohe (1886–1969) were about the same age as Arnstein Arneberg. The latter was never an avant-garde architect, but he was not hostile to the new trends. He had one foot in each camp, a fact that would later turn out to be his strength.

Verticality and modernity

The origins of Oslo City Hall go back in time. In 1918, Arnstein Arneberg and Magnus Poulsson won the second round of the competition to design the city hall for Kristiania, as Oslo was called at the time, with a design proposal laden with a certain medieval heaviness. Thirteen years would pass before construction started in 1931. In the course of these years, architecture underwent changes in form, from national romanticism to neo-classicism, and then finally to functionalism. The City Hall architects were not uninfluenced by these developments and drew up a total of eight different City Hall projects.

After many revisions, they submitted their final plan. Though thoroughly influenced by functionalism's formal simplification, the proposal also bore many traces of earlier versions, and was rich in historical references. The façades are made of bricks that form art deco patterns and reliefs that are unusual and medieval in style. The City Hall chamber and the large public rooms, indeed, were clearly inspired by northern Italian palaces of the Middle Ages.

In 1918, the jury was not entirely satisfied with the winning project, and asked Arneberg and Poulsson to rework their proposal. They did more than that, and returned to the jury with a radically different solution: a 55-metre-high skyscraper. Six storeys of offices were stacked up on top of the public rooms so as to turn the building into a looming tower. Arneberg and Poulsson, along with the other participants in the architectural competition, had submitted proposals that, in various ways, drew upon European architectural traditions. The "skyscraper project", however, was something new. The important art historian Carl W. Schnitler (1879–1926) described it as an "emphatically modern building". The City Hall plans, he said, had gone through "a marked development from the romantic – with an echo of old notes – to a full-fledged modern formal feeling".[2] The jury did not want the project, however, and Arneberg and Poulsson had to revert to their preceding romantic entry. Not until the final version was completed in

Arneberg worked on the Oslo City Hall for over 30 years, from 1918, when he submitted his first competitive draft, to 1950, when the building was finally completed. Toward the end of the construction, he also began work on the Security Council Chamber. The two projects share a number of common features: For example, Else Poulssons provided textiles and Per Krohg provided art for both places.

1930 did they return to the modern and vertical. The two 66-metre-high office towers that flank the main entrance introduced modern standards into the Norwegian capital.[3] Yet Arneberg wanted to go further. In 1932, he submitted plans for an office building for the Federation of Norwegian Industries. It was to have a prominent location on Karl Johans gate and be a full 26 storeys high. It was not very tall compared to the 102-storey Empire State Building in New York, which had been completed only one year earlier, but in Europe the tower in Oslo would have been an attention-getter.

Not until some twenty years later would Arneberg actually create a new tower. The Whaling House in Sandefjord, which opened in 1959, contains spaces with various functions that are placed on top of one another: club rooms for the city's shipping magnates and industrialists, offices for the man who had commissioned the building (Anders Jahre, Norway's leading shipowner), and a hotel. Located next to a park, the 10 storey brick building stands out in the urban landscape. A sturdy tower, it is a close relative of the 1918 skyscraper version of the Oslo City Hall. Arneberg dreamed of modern verticality through most of his professional career.

One of Arneberg's sketches for one of the major works of his later career, The Whaling House in Sandefjord. The sketch is dated 6 December 1956, the year before the construction began.

In the 1930s, by which time modernism had become completely accepted in Norway, Arneberg had no problem making use of the new formal language. The result was no masterpiece, however. Stortingsgata 12 in Oslo (1934) is a simple office building that competently addresses the challenges posed by a corner lot. Hafrsfjordgata 2 (1933) is a standard block of flats with brick façades. The villas he built for rich men during this era were sometimes given contemporary-looking white brick façades that were polished or washed, but their relationship to 1930s functionalism was rather half-hearted. One might make the same comment about the large residence at Skaugum that Arneberg designed for Norway's Crown Prince and Princess. All in all, then, modernism remained a sidetrack for Arnstein Arneberg, an architect whose professional style had been forged in an earlier time and under other influences.

The natural gift

On 7 May 1947, Norway's Ministry of Supplies released a letter stating that "a number of leading men have joined together to secure a hunting cabin for Secretary-General Trygve Lie".[4] Naturally enough, Labour Party politicians in Norway were proud of their colleague Lie, who, the year before, had won the top job at the UN (see pp. 98–101), and now they wished to honour him with the most 'Norwegian' gift one could imagine: a mountain cabin.

In her definitive five-hundred-page work about Swedish cabins, the Swedish art historian Ann Katrin Pihl Atmer maintains that Norway is unique in the world when it comes to leisure residences: : "According to figures from around 1993, Norway has the largest number of cabins per capita in the world", she writes.[5] She is probably right: today, according to Statistics Norway, Norwegians, who number five million in all, own about 460,000 leisure residences. Norwegians enjoy spending their free time out in the countryside, and they are drawn to varied and dramatic landscapes to a greater extent than most other nationalities.

Trygve Lie's cabin is a log house with a slate roof. It consists of a ground floor and a smaller, transverse second storey. Including the two upstairs rooms, there are six bedrooms in all. The living room measures about forty square metres. A protruding side wing contains a hallway with a main entrance and side rooms, including a bathroom, shower, drying room, dogs' room, and a wood storeroom.

There were several reasons why this cabin was an appropriate gift for Trygve Lie. It was stately enough to suit Lie's historical significance as the first secretary-general of the United Nations, but not too lavish for a leading member of the party representing the working class or for a representative of the down-to-earth Norwegian people. As it happened, the beautiful site on Rugelsjøen, near the town of Røros, was carved out from the property of Johan Falkberget (1879–1967), a Labour Party politician and leading author who had written popular novels about the local copper miners. Despite its spaciousness and luxurious appointment at the time, the cabin was not so grand as to appear to be a violation of Lie's Social Democratic convictions. For Arneberg, the cabin project must have brought back memories of the early days of his career. Back then, some forty years earlier, he had not been designing a chamber for the secretary-general of an international organization, but, rather, restoring a residence as a gift to the Norwegian royal couple.

A feeling of national pride

Arnstein Arneberg grew up in Lysaker, west of Oslo. It was a special place. The fairy tale illustrator Erik Werenskiold lived there, as did Gerhard Munthe, the artist who had illustrated *Snorre*, a famous collection of medieval Norwegian legends. In 1890, the polar hero and national icon Fridtjof Nansen moved into his newly constructed home, Godthåb, down by the fjord. Later, Nansen built the fortress-like residence Polhøgda on a ridge that afforded a fine view. A foreign minister, a philanthropist, and several rich people settled there, too. In Lysaker, then, there was money and art, both of which were bound up with a belief in the future, resulting in a unique environment. Indeed, contemporary life took on something of a mythical quality, and the era of the Norwegian sagas was seen as being yoked to a new era of national heroes. The young Arnstein must have grown up, then, in a stimulating environment, one in which there was no sense of any conflict between past and future.

Like his good friend Magnus Poulsson, Arneberg studied first at the Drawing School in Kristiania (now Oslo); in 1903, he took part in the regular survey tour given by his teacher Herman Major Schirmer. This tour provided him with an intimate knowledge of the old farm buildings in the valleys of East Norway – their construction styles, details, and proportions. He later completed his architectural education at the Royal Institute of Technology in Stockholm. It was supposedly during his time in Sweden that he formulated his professional mission: to develop an independent Norwegian architecture that made use of traditional Norwegian means of construction.[6]

When Trygve Lie turned 53, he was presented with the gift of a cottage by a group of major Labour Party politicians. The cottage was designed by Arneberg. It is located on Rugel Lake, near Røros, and was given the name *Lieset*.

In 1906, he returned to Kristiania, where he took part the next year, along with the experienced Ole Sverre, in the competition to design the Royal Villa, a holiday residence near Voksenkollen that was to be the Norwegian people's gift to Haakon and Maud, the new royal couple. He won second prize, and received a great deal of attention. The major art historian Andreas Aubert (1851–1913) wrote, "Arnstein Arneberg – he is the new force; he is the one we have been looking for all these years. (...) Finally we have found, in a young architect, the artistic nerve and sensitive mind that turn what he touches into art, and that gives us hope for our architecture."[7]

Quite appropriately, Ole Sverre's 25-year-old collaborator was praised for having exhibited a deeper feeling for traditional Norwegian farm buildings than did his competitors. Later, Arneberg persevered in his search for a 'Norwegian' architecture, studying such works as the Eidsvold Country College (1908), the railroad stations over the mountain from Otta to Dombås (1912), and, together with Magnus Poulsson, the stave church-inspired Seamen's Church in Rotterdam (1914). Four years later, when the competition for the Kristiania City Hall was over, Arneberg and Poulsson found themselves challenged with a task that would leave an indelible mark on their professional lives. The fact that each of them, individually, had the talent to develop a significant architectural practice of his own and to produce work of consistently high quality was definitely not a drawback.

An important and renowned Arneberg project was the set of three museum buildings he constructed to house the Viking ships in Oslo. Two of the halls were completed in 1932, and the third in 1957. The form of the buildings enclosing the ships is simple and sacral.

The official architect

The Norwegian society appreciated Arneberg's work. He was the first architect to receive an official artist's salary grant from the government and was accorded more official honours than any other Norwegian architect. The royal family, in particular, valued him highly and awarded him several commissions: the royal apartments at the Royal Palace, the decoration of the royal yacht *Norge*, and, as mentioned above, the reconstruction of Skaugum, the residence of the Crown Prince and Princess. Arneberg also provided the Viking ships, a national treasure, with a worthy and sober setting. The vaulted roofs in the Viking ship museum form an ideal mirror image of the ships' elegant curved hulls. His restoration jobs were many; the most important of them include Akershus Fortress and Oslo Cathedral. He was the closest thing Norway had to an 'official' architect, and it was therefore natural that he was asked to serve as the artistic consultant for the new series of banknotes issued by Norges Bank in 1948. The images on the banknotes were based on the frescoes on the Oslo City Hall.[8] Arneberg had many good friends among the artists and was himself an eager draughtsman – which was one of the reasons why he enjoyed decoration so much.

He was also the upper class's architect of choice, designing residences for factory owners, shipping magnates, and landowners. The expansion of the shipping business around the time of the First World War, in particular, provided Arneberg with the opportunity to design a number of opulent residences. The Ivar An Christensen house (1918), a mansion that stands at the head of Bygdøy allé, one of Oslo's most elegant thoroughfares, is a solid cube with a large, almost pyramidal roof and two side wings. The palatial residence Midtåsen in Sandefjord (1933), which he designed for the shipowner Anders Jahre, occupies a majestic spot at the end of a plateau and has a central axis that ends in an impressive stairway that runs down the side slope.

For the nature-loving upper class, Arneberg designed not only principal residences but also large holiday homes and hunting lodges. He received a large number of commissions, too, from the nation's most prominent lawyers, engineers, and doctors. When Oslo's leading citizens met at the legendary Norske Selskabs club in the centre of that city, they were surrounded by an interior created by Arneberg. Nor should it be forgotten that the products of his firm also included a number of farmsteads, hotels, offices, and churches. On top of everything else, he is considered the pioneer of Norwegian naval architecture.

The advantage of hybrids

When Oslo City Hall opened in 1950, there was great excitement among the public and the press. Many professionals were more reserved. Younger architects, especially, felt alienated by the building's heavy brick architecture. The newly educated Christian Norberg-Schulz, premier spokesman for the new generation of Norwegian architects, wrote about the City Hall in several articles and books and was always highly critical of it. A few years later, his close friends at the Office of the City Architect, Sverre Fehn and Geir Grung, would lead Norwegian architecture in an entirely different direction than the trail blazed by the City Hall. Nothing was more natural than that. When a work of architecture takes so long to complete, it must mark the end and not the beginning of a period. It is therefore understandable that another of the younger architects, Kjell Lund, said, "We saw the City Hall as the way forward."[9]

Arneberg and Poulsson apparently took the criticism calmly. "A building like the City Hall has to stand there for a while, develop a patina. In ten years you can hold a more valuable discussion of the building", said Magnus Poulsson at the opening in 1950. Arneberg suggested that it would take even more time for reasonable judgements to be made: "A half century needs to pass before you can know how it's going to hold up."

They were both right. In April 1966, the American architect Louis Kahn visited Oslo. He was a modernist who, at the same time, had re-introduced something timeless into architecture. In an interview with *Aftenposten*, the only building he praised highly was the City Hall. His enthusiasm for it made a strong impression on the members of the board of the Oslo Architects' Association who drove him around the city. When *VG* held a competition in 1999 to identify the Norwegian building of the century, a professional jury chose the Oslo City Hall. Its position as the major work of twentieth-century Norwegian architecture would seem, then, to be secure.

After the dominance of functionalism in the 1930s, the early postwar years in Norway were marked by the matter-of-fact stolidity of the rebuilding effort. Gabled roofs were preferred, both for residential structures and for public buildings; there was no room for the visionary and experimental. In the late 1950s, however, modernism returned,

Another feature shared by the interior of the Oslo Court House and the Security Council Chamber is the combination of the rich materials – especially marble – and artistic decoration. Here we see Axel Revold's fresco "Fish and agriculture" in the City Hall's Main Hall. Revold and Krohg were two of the so-called "fresco brothers", a group of artists who became famous in Norway for their large decorative works.

thanks to a new generation of talented young architects. They were very familiar with the refined glass and steel works of minimalistic classicism that Mies van der Rohe had produced in the 1940s. The UN headquarters bears a relation to Mies van der Rohe's buildings, but it also possesses a certain sensuousness, thanks to Oscar Niemeyer's long-lined design.

Oslo City Hall was thoroughly out of step with these new tendencies. What could be discerned more clearly afterwards was the building's concentrated power and the love of rich decoration that had gone into its creation. The City Hall was out of step because it was a hybrid. When the criticism of modernism's anaemic poverty began, the City Hall's impurity became one of its great advantages.

When he went to New York, Arneberg took with him his experience working on Oslo City Hall; as a result, he produced an auditorium in New York that set itself apart from the rest of the UN complex. Norwegian materials and professionals were employed in both places. The back wall of the Security Council Chamber is covered with a light-coloured straw tapestry from Biri, a village in Norway, that can also be found in the City Council Chamber at Oslo City Hall. Norwegian marble is used in both locations. Else Poulsson designed curtains and furniture materials for the City Hall, and for the UN building she devised the pattern for the blue rayon material that covers the walls of the Security Council Chamber.

Per Krohg decorated the walls of Oslo City Hall's Eastern Gallery, and in the Security Council Chamber, his large painting establishes an almost sacral atmosphere, lending an air of seriousness, even solemnity, to the events taking place in the room. Here, in contrast to the two other chambers, the view of the East River is blocked – presumably enhancing the ability of diplomats to concentrate on the serious decisions they are being paid to make.

The delegates sit around a table that forms three-quarters of a circle, a clear geometric form that underscores the chamber's simple contemporary layout. But Arneberg impregnated this simplicity with sensuality drawn from the past, thereby producing a memorable hybrid.

The architect

The decoration of the Security Council Chamber marked a high point in Arnstein Arneberg's (1882–1961) long career. During the years after the Second World War, he was Norway's leading architect and the head of the country's largest architectural firm. He was also in the process of completing Oslo's large City Hall, a project that had been underway for several decades. He was a hard-working and highly experienced professional, with a unique position in the Norwegian architectural community.

At the same time, Arneberg was in many ways a man of the past, most of whose life's work already lay behind him. During his entire career, Arneberg's architecture had bridged tradition and modernity. This was the background of the man who in 1948 stepped onto the international stage by agreeing to design the Security Council Chamber.

In Arneberg's 1949 sketches for the chamber, we can see that he was at work deciding on the look of the space from an early date. He experimented with colours, patterns, and decor. In all the drawings, the painting is placed behind a horseshoe-shaped table that was the room's focal point. The sketches also show that even at this stage, the architect and the artist were already in dialogue about the theme and content of Per Krohg's painting.

Since the room's proportions were fixed, Arneberg considered it important to work with materials, effects, and colours. In letters exchanged with Harrison in late 1948, Arneberg wrote that he pictured a room that was decorated by frescos, fabric-covered walls, decorative curtains, and a stone floor. In the spring of 1949 he worked on developing his ideas and made sketches for the chamber. In April, he went to New York to inspect the site and present his ideas. In a series of five drawings he experiments with colours and decor. The first is undated and possibly one of the early sketches. Three of the sketches are dated March 1949. The last sketch – which most resembles the chamber as it finally turned out – was possibly done somewhat later.

The first sketch, at the top on the facing page, shows a mural that is a central element in the chamber. For a long time, the idea was to have red curtains to contrast with the blue wall, as seen in Else Poulsson's drawings. In his article about the completed chamber in *Byggekunst*, Arneberg found it regrettable that there had not been time to bring this idea to fruition. Above the door are high wall panels in a darker colour. The second sketch below is dated and depicts a more worked-through draft. The curtains here are also red, while the walls are now white without the high panels. Here, too, the focus is on the mural, and the ceiling above the delegate table has been embellished.

This and the next spread: Two of the dated drawings show the chamber as seen from each of the two short walls. The ceiling ornamentation is at the centre of the sketch that shows the chamber from the delegates' perspective. In the sketch showing the room from the top of the audience area, the mural is the focal point. The sketches are entirely in line with Arneberg's descriptions in a 30 March 1949 letter to Harrison: to set the delegates' area apart, Arneberg wanted a ceiling decoration to be designed by an "outstanding artist". As a unifying element in the chamber, he wanted a mosaic or fresco to be installed on the wall behind the delegate area, provided that the commission was awarded to a "truly gifted artist". Arneberg originally wanted the sculptor Emil Lie to contribute to the artistic embellishment in the form of reliefs. In a letter to Emil Lie, he wrote that he personally put great emphasis on these reliefs as a small break with the chamber's monotony. Emil Lie replied that he imagined a relief that would decorate the balustrade between the auditorium and the negotiating space. The other two reliefs would decorate the window spaces on the long sides of the chamber. Arneberg persuaded the Norwegian government to cover Lie's fee on the condition that the UN paid the costs of the materials – an expense that, in the end, could not fit into the UN budget.

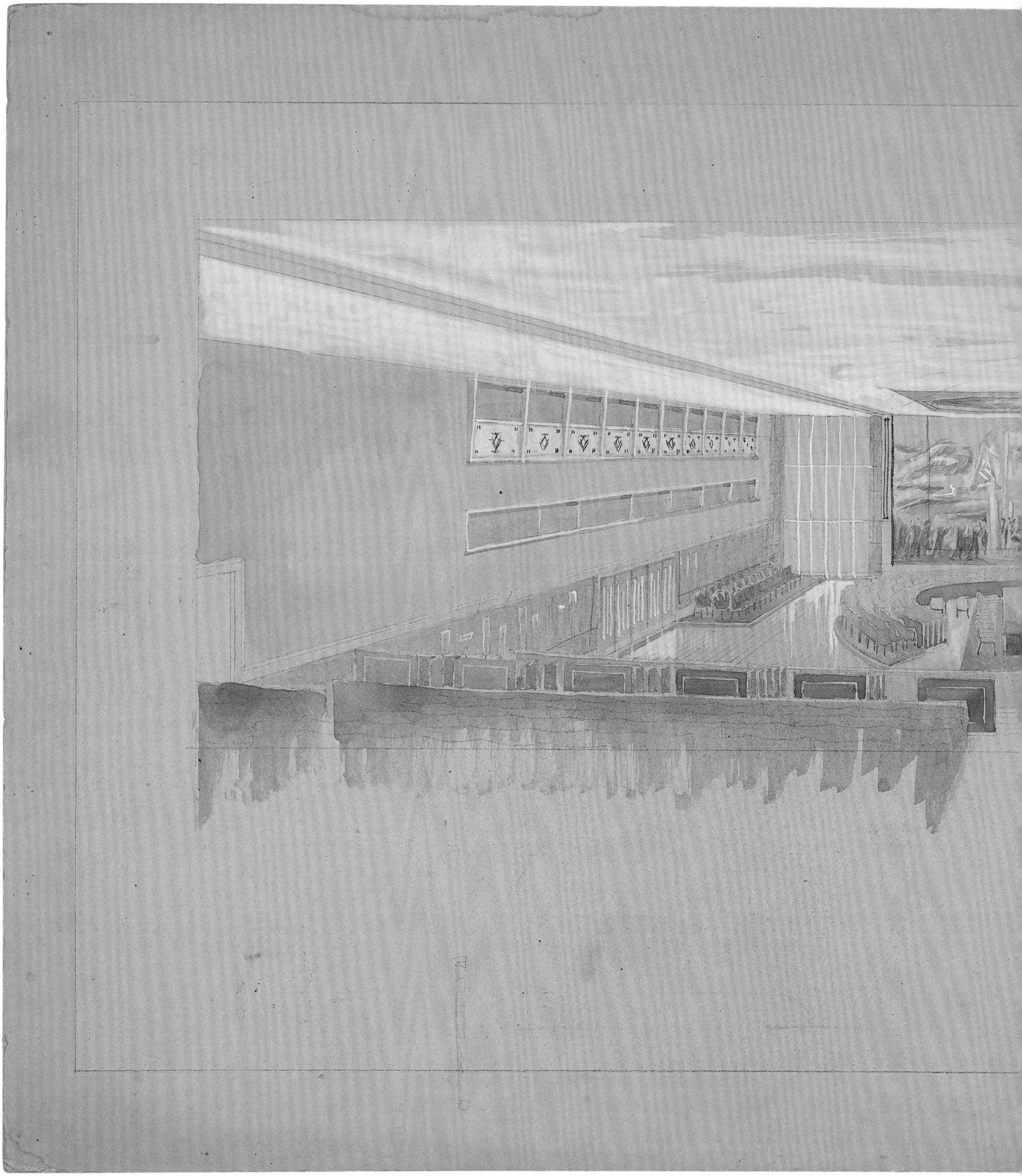

Arnstein Arneberg mars 41.

The last sketch is undated and bears the greatest resemblance to the chamber as it ultimately turned out. It was possibly created at a later date. The sketch shows the blue covering on the Secretariat chairs. The panel now looks more like marble. The blue wall textile and the blue curtains bring to mind Poulsson's wallpaper, but here they feature a white pattern. The correspondence reveals that Arneberg wanted at one point to use the UN blue and white emblem as a pattern for the fabric-covered walls, but it turned out to be absolutely impossible to make it look even and precise. Another interesting feature of the sketch is that the rendering of the painting is largely consistent with the painting itself as Per Krohg described it in a 22 February 1950 letter: "The columns will hold up the new world. Human beings escape from misery, and emerging from the dark ruined cities they meet one another and are united as they head upward toward the sun. We will look ahead; the young people will form a harmonic whole; and in this way the UN's and the Security Council's work will form the germ of a new and prosperous life."

Nina Berre

Arneberg on the International Stage

The UN complex in New York, a modernistic icon on the East River, is the product of what may have been the most prestigious building commission of the immediate postwar era. The two powerful star architects Le Corbusier and Oscar Niemeyer played central roles in the project, along with a team of top colleagues from several UN member nations. The New York architect Wallace K. Harrison, who had recently completed Rockefeller Center, led the collective design process.

From this crowd of internationally famous architects, Norwegian Arnstein Arneberg was chosen to serve as architect of the Security Council Chamber, which was perhaps the UN complex's most important room. Arneberg had been one of Norway's leading architects since the 1910s, ran a large office that was responsible for several major construction jobs, and enjoyed great recognition in his homeland (see also pp. 68–70). But the first reaction to Arneberg's design was cool (see also pp. 199–201). According to American critics, the room was uninteresting, "expensively ugly", and fell short compared to the chambers that had been designed by Finn Juhl of Denmark and Sven Markelius of Sweden. One critic, to be sure, described Arneberg's room as rich and consistent, but at the same time "curiously antique". If not quite old-fashioned, the interior alluded to the late Middle Ages: it was as if the room had been restored by the nineteenth-century French architect Viollet-le-Duc.[1]

What I want to examine here is the apparently paradoxical encounter between Arneberg and the international modernists in Manhattan. While Le Corbusier was a radical and avant-garde architect, Arneberg is best known for his efforts to breathe new life into the Norwegian tradition. Even though he had strong ties to Secretary-General Trygve Lie, it is a bit of a mystery that the Norwegian architect, who was never an adherent of modernism, could play such a central role in the creation of the authoritative example of the International Style. What common denominators can be found between Le Corbusier and Arneberg? And how does the chamber look today when measured against the still hypermodern UN complex that surrounds it?

Incommensurable! The competition in 1927

Le Corbusier and Arneberg had actually crossed paths in 1927 when they both took part in the competition to design the League of Nations Palace in Geneva. This competition, which is a significant event in the

Arnstein Arneberg at the drafting table in his own home on Madserud allé in Oslo in December 1950.

UN's prehistory, figures in the chronicles of modern architecture as both a scandal and a kind of harbinger.

A neutral people's palace, where representatives from all of the world's countries would meet, was an entirely new concept, involving complexities beyond those posed by the great majority of public construction projects of earlier times.[2] The competition attracted the interest of architects from around the world. By the January 1927 deadline, 377 proposals had been submitted. In Norway, there was keen interest in the competition. Some forty architects ordered the competition programme, and there was actually bickering over the copies that the Norwegian Architects Association (NAL) had ordered from Geneva.[3] When the NAL had only three copies left of the programme, published in French, it told architectural offices requesting additional copies that they should contact Arneberg, who had eagerly ordered the text translated into Norwegian.

A highly professional jury with members from a number of European countries spent six weeks in the spring of 1927 evaluating the submitted drafts. The proposed projects seemed to represent all imaginable styles, some of them dating as far back as the late nineteenth century. But there were also experimental and radical drafts.[4] The jury chose no winner, but awarded first prize to nine drafts, second prize to nine more drafts, and third prize to yet another nine drafts. Le Corbusier's proposal was one of the first-prize recipients, and has since come to be viewed as emblematic of the development of modernistic architecture. Four jury members recommended that he be declared the winner, but the majority felt that his plans violated the competition rules, since Le Corbusier had submitted them in the form of dyeline prints instead of pen drawings.[5]

The competition ended with a group of diplomats awarding the job to a handful of the participating architects as a sort of team project. The result of their long and costly effort was a neoclassical palace. Le Corbusier's rejection was viewed as a scandalous snub, and helped lead to the establishment of the *Congrès Internationaux d'Architecture Moderne* (CIAM) in 1928.[6] Both the competition and the building that resulted from it were strongly criticized; the various countries' architectural organizations sent in petitions, and the media published indignant commentaries. One of them appeared in the Norwegian publication *Byggekunst*, in which one critic wrote, "Thus are representatives of traditional architecture given the job of creating the symbol of the new spirit that will radiate from Geneva." There was much speculation as to the cause of "this comic game": "The real reason is likely that the old and new architecture in Europe, as they currently stand in opposition to each other, are in reality incommensurable."[7]

What was it that was so incommensurable? What was so essentially different about the drafts, and how does Arneberg's project fit into this picture? It has not been possible to find published records of all the proposals, despite the appeal by architectural organizations in several nations that the League of Nations make the entire competition public.[8] There was one person, at any rate, who studied many of the submitted drafts. His name was John Ritter, and he wrote about them in the magazine *Architectural Review* in 1964. In his article, he categorized a third of them as representing an "accepted historical style" – they were drafts that emphasized composition, dignity, and the use of symbolism. At the other extreme, there were radicals, such as Le Corbusier and Hannes Meyer, whose designs were rooted in function and not symbolism. Between these two poles there were several projects that could be grouped according to their geographic origin: the so-called academic proposals came from Central Europe, while more elegant, neo-classical ones emphasizing function were the work of Scandinavians.[9] Arneberg's project fits best into this latter group, but not merely because of its geographical origins. His draft takes the form of an elongated rectangle that runs alongside the lake and surrounds an enormous inner courtyard. A rotunda that was intended to house the 'parliament' itself is located at one end of the rectangle. The rotunda is located above a square base, probably inspired by Gunnar Asplund's municipal library in Stockholm (1920–28). With its arcade motifs and closely placed windows, Arneberg's draft is less abstract than Asplund's library. However, just as in Asplund's design, the rotunda lacks a cupola, a symbol of the non-modern.

In the Norwegian art lexicon, Arneberg is described as an architect who never became a proponent of "international classisism".[10] Similarly, Ulf Grønvold maintains that the City Hall collaborators Arneberg and Poulsson never became "full-blooded neoclassicists", although they tried out several different artistic schools: "To be sure, they attempted as early as 1918 to simplify their City Hall draft and rid themselves of the most painterly motifs".[11] Like some of the City Hall drafts, Arneberg's project for a people's palace in Geneva seems highly distinguished and suggestive of an elegant Nordic neoclassicism.

The classicism of the 1920s was not just a precursor to certain elements of modernist architecture, but was an integral part of the new modernity, which was particularly concerned with understanding the city.[12] In the Stockholm library, Asplund makes use of historical elements, but ties the structure directly to the new and modern city. It is here that the greatest difference between Asplund's library and Arneberg's attempt to design a people's palace in Geneva emerges: while the library is directly connected to the cityscape of Stockholm, Arneberg's is a historicizing monument located in an open landscape on a lake. And measured against the radical modernists in the competition, whose projects were imagined as free, and free-standing, forms on the landscape, Arneberg's draft seems outdated.

It is unlikely that anyone studying Arneberg's Geneva draft would have thought of him as a prime candidate for the UN project in Manhattan. Besides, Arneberg had hardly been the only Norwegian to enter the Geneva competition. But although it is unknown exactly how many Norwegian architectural firms actually submitted proposals,[13] the fact remains that Arneberg drafted a specific plan that, however indirectly, ended up as a part of the UN's architectural prehistory. It is possible, indeed, that some people involved with the UN project were familiar with his League of Nations effort. Secretary-General Lie, for example, may have appreciated the insight into the League of Nations' thinking and organization that Arneberg had acquired while putting together his proposal. If nothing else, Arneberg had had to seriously assess the challenge at hand and determine which type of aesthetic expression

Arneberg's 1927 competitive draft for the League of Nations Palace in Geneva shows an immense building complex in a style influenced by nordic new classisism. Arneberg did not go any further in the competition.

was best suited to a people's palace intended to represent all the countries of the world.

But the jury in Geneva ignored Arneberg's project, which was soon forgotten. The neglect of Le Corbusier's draft, however, had consequences with regard to his later role in the design of the UN"s new complex in New York. He received a good deal of support from many quarters, including the Museum of Modern Art. In a modest 1946 exhibition called "illustrated statement", the museum summed up the competition in Geneva as follows: "A Competition Failed. A Building Failed. The League Failed". Le Corbusier, insisted MoMA, had been the true winner in Geneva.[14]

The test of time: the UN in New York

When the UN set out to create a new headquarters in New York after the war, the challenge was the same as in Geneva. But this time it had to work. The idea was to create a neutral architectural framework for all nations, one that did not make use of familiar and distressing symbols. The process involved an extensive period of preliminary work entailing prolonged discussions as to the selection of a site, the choice of an architect, and the adoption of a strategy that would avoid commissioning a work of architecture that would end up as a traditional example of monumentality.

Nothing in this preliminary process points to the fact that someone like Arneberg would play an important role in the creation of the UN complex. In line with the UN's spirit of international collaboration, it was decided that a group of architects from member countries would work together on the design. The idea of a "Board of Design" fit into Wallace K. Harrison's strategy of creating a "workshop for peace" the goal of which was to produce a work of architecture that bore no resemblance to the pompous people's palace. Memories of the 1927 fiasco made it seem advisable not to hold a hasty competition. Besides, Le Corbusier had, in many ways, already secured for himself the principal commission.

A special issue of *The New York Times* listed the names of 26 persons from 21 nations who had been nominated for the design group. Harrison was to choose 10 of the 26 to take part in the actual work, while the other 16 would be given consultative roles.[15] The long list included the names of four Nordic architects: Edvard Thomsen from Denmark, Bunt Laugur Halldorsson from Iceland, Ragnar Hjort from Sweden, and Eyvind Moestue from Norway. Moestue was a major Norwegian modernist who, with the large open-air swimming pool *Ingierstrand Bad* (1934), created with his collaborator Ole Lind Schistad, had demonstrated that he understood the technology and style of the new era. In a letter of recommendation to the UN, Ambassador Finn Moe, who represented Norway's Permanent Delegation to the United Nations, praised Moestue for his "outstanding achievements in Norwegian architecture" and underscored that Moestue was the NAL's preferred choice.[16] Moreover, Moestue had been a member of the Norwegian committee for the Paris exhibition in 1937, a position that was viewed as qualifying him for the job in New York.[17]

Neither Moestue nor any of the other nominated Norwegian architects was included in the final working group, and probably none of them played any role in the ensuing activities. Sven Markelius, however, was chosen for the Board of Design, and was also given the task of decorating the chamber for the Economic and Social Council (ECOSOC). Arneberg was never considered for possible membership in the working group, but he received the commission for the Security Council Chamber long before Markelius and Finn Juhl, who designed the Trusteeship Council, were given theirs. How could that be?

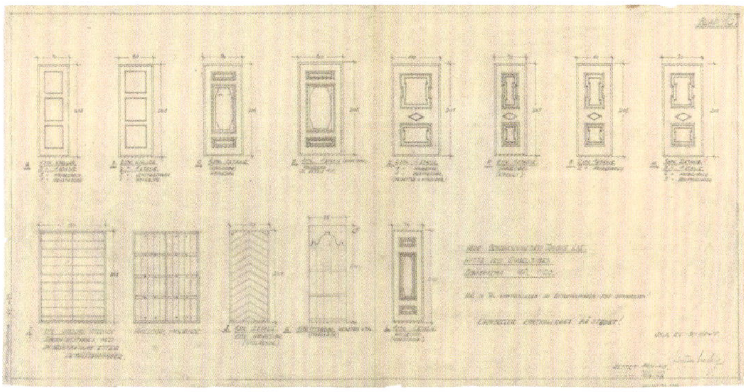

Before NAL and Moe recommended Moestue to the Board of Design, Lie was frank about which Norwegian architects might potentially take part in the prestigious collective. In a polite letter to Arneberg in December 1946 (which was marked "Private", although in the text itself he addressed Arneberg with the formal 'De' instead of the informal 'you'), Lie thanked the architect for having started planning work on the Norwegian people's gift to Lie – the construction of a cabin near Røros – and also proffered a moving expression of concern for young Norwegian modernists:

> Since I am writing to you now, I also want to mention that I have received an unusually large assignment to build the new headquarters for the United Nations in New York. It will be a sizable complex in skyscraper style, larger than Rockefeller Center. I would like to have one or two Norwegian architects on the so-called Advisory Design Committee. If you have any names to suggest, I would be grateful. I have given some thought to Engh, who was in the Norwegian Air Force in Canada during the war and who has also been educated here in America and speaks excellent English. I saw that he was among those who won the first prize in the competition for the new Östbane Station [a railroad station in Oslo]. What do you think of him? If you have any other candidates, please send me their names as soon as possible. I can pay from 7,000 to 10,000 dollars tax-free per year. It will doubtless be very instructive for a young Norwegian architect to be part of such an international assembly of architects, who will see this large building complex through to completion. I am not writing to anyone else about this, but will await your reply. I have nothing against your getting in touch with the Norwegian Architects Association about the matter, if you think that is necessary.[18]

Even though Lie assured Arneberg that he would not mention the matter to anyone else for the time being, he probably did just that. In a letter dated a couple of weeks later and sent from the Norwegian architectural firm Grimsgaard and Grevstad to the NAL, marked "Re: International competition – UN building", it is mentioned that the firm had been seeking "information about the matter in accordance with an agreement at our last board meeting", and that "secretary Dons" – who had just returned from the UN – believed that no competition would be held, because such a process would take too long. "From other sources, however," the letter writer added, "I have learned that the secretary-general has informed one of our representatives that an international architectural competition will be held."[19]

Arneberg's 1947 drawing shows the various doors of Trygve Lie's cabin, Lieset, near Røros.

But it didn't happen. There was no competition, and the NAL nominated Moestue, not Engh, to the Board of Design. Since I have been unable to find Arneberg's reply to Lie's proposal regarding Engh, I can only speculate as to what happened: Engh was a radical young modernist with a view of architecture that Arneberg probably did not share. Could it be that Arneberg made the case for himself by advancing the argument that the young should not always receive preferential treatment, and that competitions were not suitable for that purpose? It was on these grounds, in any event, that he later made certain that Per Krohg, also a veteran artist, would receive the commission to decorate the chamber with its central image (see p. 119). With Arneberg and Krohg on the team, Lie could feel safe. Unlike a young and inexperienced architect, Arneberg would finish the job on time, just as he had done countless times before when furnishing new and old buildings. All of this, however, belongs to the realm of guesswork. In his memoirs, typically enough, Trygve Lie never explains how Arneberg came to be granted the Security Council commission. Ingeborg Glambek, who has worked more with this material than anyone else, also assumes that the close relationship between the secretary-general and the Norwegian architect was decisive in the latter's being granted the commission. (see also p. 43).[20] Certainly, if you disregard today's bureaucratic contracting processes and look back to the 1950s old-boys' networks, it seems likely that the personal tie between Lie and Arneberg played an important role.

The friendship between them, to be sure, was in a sense a union of opposites. While Trygve Lie was one of the era's Labour Party standard-bearers, Arneberg was the preferred architect of the conservative upper classes. In the UN community in New York, however, Lie the Labourite managed to bring together powerful ambassadors and wealthy families – people from a range of political and social backgrounds – in a shrewd and effortless way (see pp. 106–108). In any event, a letter from Arneberg to Lie written in May 1949 bolsters the hypothesis that the latter personally and directly offered the Security Council Chamber commission to his architect friend. In the letter, Arneberg first describes how the work on the cabin near Røros is progressing ("I'm afraid the fireplace masonry isn't exactly as it should be.") and concludes by saying that he is now at work on the sketches for the Security Council Chamber. He is unreserved in his expression of gratitude (they have now, note well, moved from the formal to the informal 'you'): "Personally I must again thank you so much for this unusually interesting commission."[21]

There are many indications, then, that Lie himself chose Arneberg, and then introduced him to Harrison, who was responsible for the architecture of the entire UN complex. Even though Arneberg's earlier projects hardly seemed to fit into Wallace K. Harrison's concept of a "workshop for peace", Lie must have managed to talk Harrison into using him. As for Lie and Harrison, they got on well; Harrison was impressed by Lie's efficiency, and Lie trusted Harrison's professional judgement. Lie probably grasped the idea that the Security Council Chamber should stand out from the other two chambers, and likely wanted this room, with its particularly important function, to be more sober and refined than the others.[22] Perhaps Arneberg's neoclassical

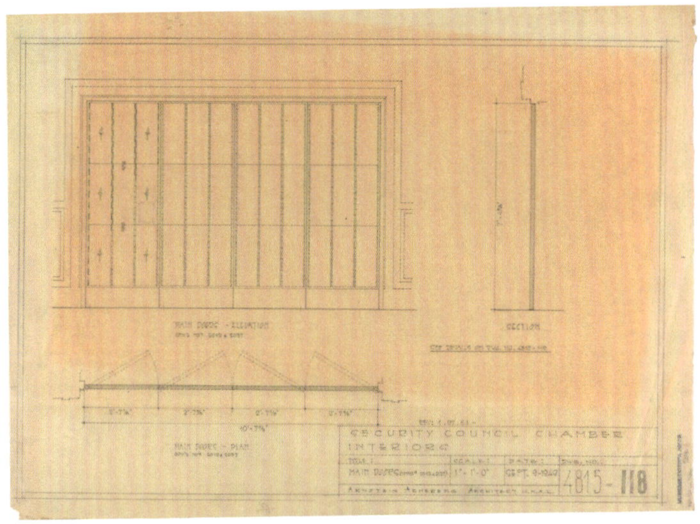

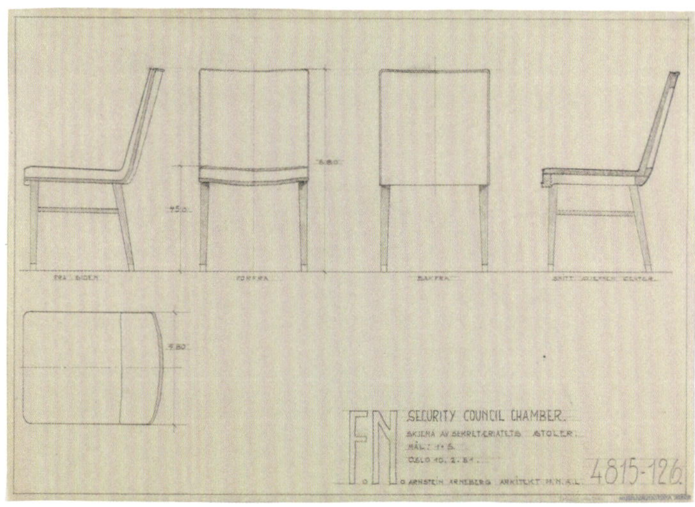

Current page:
The four-part main doors of the Security Council Chamber as they looked in Arneberg's 1949 drawing. The intarsia pattern is also drawn on the left-hand side of the sketch.

This 1951 schematic drawing of the Secretariat chair shows the chair from four sides and illustrates its simple but elegant configuration.

Opposite page:
This 1949 drawing shows how Arneberg wanted to place the points of light in the chamber's ceiling.

This 1949 drawing of the chamber's longitudinal section.

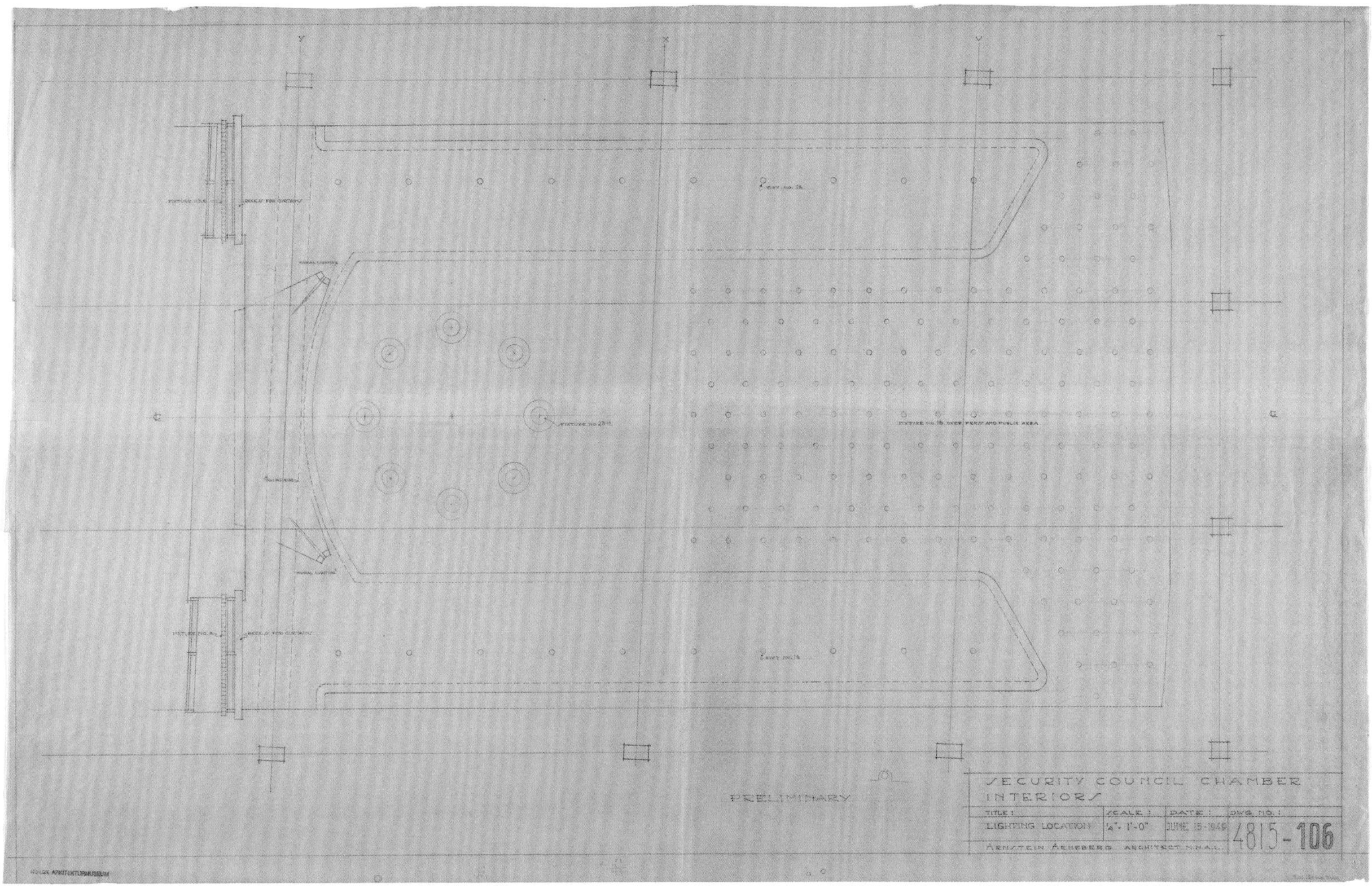
PRELIMINARY
SECURITY COUNCIL CHAMBER
INTERIORS
TITLE:
SCALE:
DATE:
DWG. NO.:
LIGHTING LOCATION
¼" = 1'-0"
JUNE 15-1949
4815-106
ARNSTEIN ARNEBERG ARCHITECT M.N.A.L.

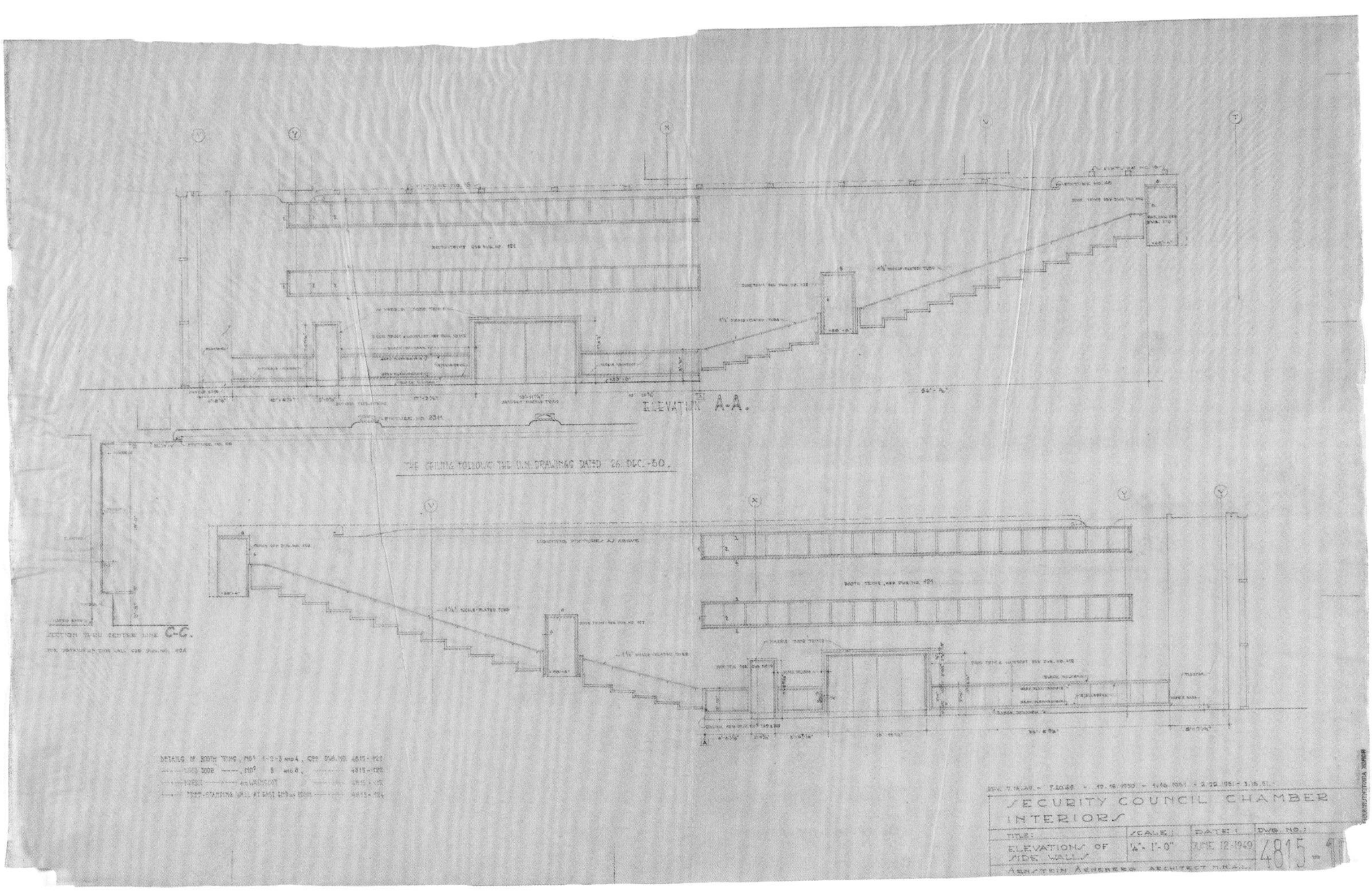
ELEVATION A-A.
SECTION THRU CENTRE LINE C-C.
SECURITY COUNCIL CHAMBER
INTERIORS
TITLE:
SCALE:
DATE:
DWG. NO.:
ELEVATIONS OF SIDE WALLS
¼" = 1'-0"
JUNE 12-1949
4815-
ARNSTEIN ARNEBERG ARCHITECT M.N.A.L.

project in Geneva lay somewhere in the background of all this? The conrrespondence among Arneberg, Lie, and Harrison suggests that Lie served as a middleman and resolved potential conflicts between the two architects. The plans for the Security Council Chamber advanced in this manner. Now and then Harrison put his foot down, however. For example, when Lie wanted pine panelling on the walls of his own – the secretary-general's – office, Harrison said no.[23]

Given Arneberg's plans to place a traditionally designed chamber inside a distinctively modernistic complex, there was doubtless much at stake, both for the architect and for the secretary-general. In a letter sent to Arneberg just before the chamber was completed, Lie all but begged his friend not to disappoint him now: "As you understand, an international competition is underway among the three Nordic lands here in the Headquarters and I would hate for Norway to lose."[24] Aware as he was of the sober nature of his architetural choices, he must have felt enormous pressure knowing he was performing on the same international stage as the greatest stars in the profession, and that he was creating a space that the world would evaluate with an eagle eye when it was finished.

In an interview he gave to the magazine *Interior* just after completing the chamber, Arneberg expressed his feelings about the project.[25] Being a polite, conservative denizen of Oslo's genteel west side, Arneberg expressed a degree of humility regarding his involvement in a working fellowship with some of the world's leading architects. At the same time, he seemed surprisingly resigned. He said he understood the criticism that had been levelled at his rather old-fashioned approach to the Security Council Chamber. He admitted that the process had been difficult, but he used what had really been an advantage – the fact that he had been handed his commission before the two other Nordic architects had gotten theirs – in his defence: He had been unable, he lamented, to work in sync with his Nordic colleagues during the planning phase. He maintained, moreover, that he had had few opportunities to visit the site in New York – even though he had, in fact, been there in April 1949 and several times in 1952.

Arneberg was at the end of his career. He had survived modernism's development during the first half of the twentieth century, and had established an architectural vocabulary that gave him the reputation of being an architect of uncommon integrity. In the same interview, having apparently conceded that the critics were right, he also insisted, rather paradoxically, that it was precisely his own formal language that best suited this type of assignment: "My understanding of the problem was to execute a room of good, durable materials with a character, in all simplicity, which represented not only a casual taste of today, but a character so neutral that it could withstand the test of time."[26]

And perhaps Arneberg was right. If the room did not comport with Harrison's notion of a peace workshop, neutrality, duration, simplicity, and timelessness were concepts that the United Nations could probably always agree on, and that would also stand the test of time.

The chamber today

Despite the apparent conflict between its underlying architectural ideology and that of the UN complex as a whole, the Security Council Chamber today feels like a representation of the complexity and verity of the modern movement. The design of the two precise rows of windows on each long side, from which the press originally witnessed the proceedings in the chamber, could just as easily have been part of any other beautiful modernistic interior. The warm woodwork that surrounds the glass, the play of hue and light on the wall textiles, the distinctive colour combinations in the furniture and the steel details in the railings, in combination with the intarsia fixtures on the doors, add up to a striking overall impact, whether the room is viewed from a distance or experienced up close.

The combination of the unusual richness of detail and the effectiveness of the total spatial experience can bring to mind the interior of the Oslo City Hall, not to mention certain other world-class modernistic spaces. Nor is the Security Council Chamber as different from Le Corbusier's and Oscar Niemeyer's work at the UN, or from the chambers designed by Markelius and Juul, as the critics in 1952 would have had it: the Security Council Chamber harmonizes surprisingly well, for example, with Niemeyer's General Assembly, where the powerful columns are decorated in green and yellow. A more significant divergence exists between Arneberg's rich, plastic work and Le Corbusier's tower block, with its smooth, uncontoured curtain wall. Then again, the high-rise as a form was not very typical of Le Corbusier. During the interwar years, he, like Arneberg, was preoccupied with the traditions of folk architecture – the rural, the rustic. After the war, his work grew heavier and rougher. He developed a colour palette with a set of distinctive combinations of pigments. Even if some of the combinations in the Security Council Chamber were not decided upon solely by Arneberg (see p. 73), there is little doubt that Arneberg, too, mastered the art of bringing together various hues and materials to create something that would surprise and enchant. Good modernistic architecture is rarely pure, white, and soulless. Moreover, like several other modernistic works that have stood the test of time, the Security Council Chamber remains beautiful, distinctive, and special.

With passing time, the Security Council Chamber has been increasingly recognized as an architectural achievement. Trygve Lie may have been correct when he wrote, in one of many letters intended to console Arneberg (who, in private, felt disheartened after the completion of the complex): "There is no reason for despair."[27] "I can comfort you with the thought that the Security Council Chamber looks excellent. (...) Right now the debate is raging as to which room is the prettiest – the Danish, which seems very modern and artistic; the Swedish, with its wood and steel; or the Norwegian, which most people say is more conservative in style. Personally I have no doubt that the Norwegian chamber will be the most beautiful in the long run, especially when we get Per Krohg's fresco painting in place."[28]

The General Assembly's meeting hall. It is the largest in the UN complex and can hold up to 1800 people. The hall is decorated by two abstract paintings by the Frenchman Fernand Léger and features a cupola-shaped ceiling above the delegate area.

The secretary-general

Trygve Lie (1896–1968) had a remarkable political career. His father abandoned the family early on, and Trygve Lie grew up in a home in Grorud, near Oslo, where he lived with his mother, Hulda, and his older sister, Ruth. His mother ran a café where she always had four or five workingmen as tenants. Lie became politically active at an early age. Despite his humble background, he managed to complete an education in the law. He also held a series of important posts in both the labour movement and in local Oslo politics before he was appointed, in 1935, at the age of 39, as Minister of Justice in the government of Johan Nygaardsvold. In 1939 he became Minister of Trade.

During the Second World War, Trygve Lie was Norway's Foreign Minister in exile in London. A gifted networker, he was quick to make political contact. At the UN conference in San Fransisco in 1945, Lie headed up the Norwegian delegation. In February 1946, after a nerve-wracking series of votes, Lie was, surprisingly elected as the UN's first secretary-general. He moved to New York that same year, and began to work out of a hotel room at the Waldorf-Astoria. Temporary offices were established and Lie effectively pulled strings to ensure both that the UN would make its home in New York and that the new international organization would have a practical and architecturally impressive headquarters.

After Per Krohg had worked on his picture for the Security Council Chamber for a year, a draft was rolled up and sent by ship to New York in the custody of his assistant Wilhelm Meling. Krohg followed by plane a few days later. The 1951 test mounting was witnessed by a prominent Norwegian delegation. From left to right in the photograph we see an unknown photographer, Ambassador Arne Sunde, Prime Minister Einar Gerhardsen, Trygve Lie, Per Krohg, Mrs. Werna Gerhardsen, and assistant chief of protocol Pierre de Meulemeester.

MUTUAL
MUTUAL
MUTUAL
WNYC

Guri Hjeltnes

Trygve Lie:
A Man of Action

In January, Trygve Lie had no idea that he would become the secretary-general of a complicated world organization. In March, in a military plane, he landed just south of New York City. By June, he had acquired for the UN a substantial fleet of cars – as he put it, "25 new Buicks, 3 Cadillacs, 15 Facecars, 10 Oldsmobiles, 40 Fords, 15 buses, and 8 station wagons. Moreover, I can get as many cars of other well-known brands as I want."[1]

The UN got down to business very quickly in March 1946, the moment it set up shop in the New World. The secretary-general moved into a hotel room at the Waldorf-Astoria and began working out of that room with his team. Trygve Lie appeared self-assured and invigorated, and got great press. The American media were impressed by this burly man who, with his rolled-up white shirtsleeves and broad suspenders, made things happen. He was a *doer* – a lawyer and experienced national and local politician, a crafty organization man and a gifted network-builder. He had been foreign minister during the critical years of the war, when he had close international contacts. Was he a world politician on a grand scale? Well, that is another discussion. However, he had been chosen to oversee the establishment of a prestigious organization – one in which an entire generation, in the ruins of the Second World War, placed its hopes. This 'organization man' fully embraced the challenge.

Today it is difficult to imagine the intensity of feeling surrounding the UN after the war – the optimism, the idealism, the sense of engagement, the hope for peace among the peoples and countries of the world. The idea that the UN could make a real difference was a driving force for Lie, the pioneer, who believed strongly in its founding goals and objectives. This conviction that the UN could change the world also motivated many of the people who applied for jobs with the world organization. Like a magnet, the UN drew to it a good many people and a great deal of attention.

For an organization that needed to provide space for the forthcoming meetings of the Security Council and the UN General Assembly, this attractive power was not a liability. The first minutes from the secretary-general's newly established office are dated Wednesday, 27 March 1946. On 30 March, Trygve Lie would hold a private inspection of a possible UN site, the Sperry factory, where he would "personally meet Mr. Moses to discuss the whole question".[2] This was a reference to Robert Moses, New York's legendary city planner, with whom Lie met six days after arriving in New York.

Page 92–93: Trygve Lie was guide during the 1951 test mounting. From right to left in the photograph we see Trygve Lie, Mrs. Werna Gerhardsen, Per Krohg, Prime Minister Einar Gerhardsen, Ambassador Wilhelm Morgenstierne, Ambassador Arne Sunde, Mrs. Sigrid Sunde, and assistant chief of protocol Pierre de Meulemeester.

Page 94–95: On 13 April 1947, the UN and Trygve Lie were officially presented with the East River site. The secretary-general spoke to the gathering on this occasion, and the microphones show that several of the local radio stations covered the ceremony. In the first row behind him sit notables, listening attentively. The third person from the left is the Archbishop of New York, Francis Cardinal Spellman. To his right sits Mayor William O'Dwyer, and to his right is Grover Whalen, who was chairman of New York's official UN reception committee .

Page 96: In October 1949, Lie and architect Wallace K. Harrison laid the cornerstone for the UN complex. The cornerstone rests on two documents, the UN Charter and the Universal Declaration of Human Rights.

"Now, you mustn't think that I'm going
to become secretary-general."

Who can see into the future? Trygve Lie himself pooh-poohed rumours that he might be named to the UN's top position. The man who would serve as the UN's first secretary-general during the next eight years had no idea that this task would fall to him.

On the contrary, in the run-up to the first UN General Assembly, in London in January 1946, Trygve Lie, who at the time was Norway's foreign minister, wanted to be considered for an entirely different job – namely, president of the UN General Assembly, a one-year position. After that possibility faded in the midst of a great-power political game, Lie was more preoccupied by the social and cultural life in the big city, where his family had spent five years in exile. In any case, this is what he told his own family.

"Now, you mustn't think that I'm going to become secretary-general", wrote Trygve Lie to two of his daughters in a letter from London dated 20 January 1946.[3] He wrote vividly, as he always did in his letters, about both political and private matters. Those chilly January days in "swinging London" were hectic. Trygve Lie and his wife, Hjørdis, had gone to see two shows that were "very nicely staged with... half-naked dancers, etc.". They had seen the 1945 film *Caesar and Cleopatra*, directed and produced by Gabriel Pascal and starring Claude Rains and Vivien Leigh. The very next day they went to see *Follow the Girls*, a musical that had been a hit on Broadway in 1944 and had opened on London's West End in October 1945. The Lies had also managed to secure tickets for the fully booked His Majesty's Theatre. In addition, they had attended "a number of lunches and dinners, so the days went quickly". Moreover, Lie added, jokingly, "I am now and then at the General Assembly". Shortly afterward, he wrote that he hoped they had heard his recent UN speech on the radio.

Trygve Lie was a power-happy and ambitious man. In the letter to his daughters, he turned quickly from japery to serious political matters. "I was not hurt by the defeat I suffered when I lost the presidency. I had expected to get only 8 or 9 votes", he wrote.

During the 1945 Christmas holiday, Trygve Lie had been with his family and close friends in the mountains, at Baastjernbu between Numedal and Hallingdal, when a telegram was brought to him by a vigorous skier. The telegram was from the Americans, who asked if he would be willing to run for president of the UN General Assembly if the United States nominated him.[4] With the support of his family – who had already spent many years abroad – and of Prime Minister Einar Gerhardsen and the government, Lie travelled to London on 8 January 1946.[5] At the UN's first General Assembly, however, an intricate political game was underway. In the end, it was the Soviet Union that proposed Lie for the presidency, with support from the Eastern Bloc. The Americans, for their part, sat perfectly quietly and did not mention Lie's name, as they had said they would.

After a secret vote was taken, the job of president went to Belgium's foreign minister, Paul-Henri Spaak, a politician whom Trygve Lie knew well from his years in exile as foreign minister in the Nygaardsvold government. Lie did not appreciate having been set up to run against

On 1 February 1946, Trygve Lie was – surprisingly – chosen to be the UN's first secretary-general. Here is Lie in Church House in London in January of the same year. He is welcomed by the president of the General Assembly, Paul-Henri Spaak, with Acting Secretary-General Gladwyn Jebb of the UK in the middle.

a European colleague whom he knew well.[6] However, as he told his daughters, "it was best that it went the way it did".

He then got right to the point: "Now you mustn't think that I'm going to become secretary-general. The matter is already decided. So far I haven't been about to publicly pull myself out of the running. But that job is too tough for me – yes, almost for anyone. The opposition between the peoples is too great. And the intrigues are too many. So take it with good humour, girls."

This was written on 20 January, however. The pressure on the UN's member countries and the delegates to agree on a candidate continued to increase – as did the struggle among the great powers over the top job.

In the debate as to who would become the first UN secretary-general, a number of leading international names were floated. Anthony Eden, who had been Britain's wartime foreign minister, was one of them. Eden had said he would take the job if asked. He would later state, "Mr. Trygve Lie was an enthusiastic protagonist on my behalf."[7] In London, Trygve Lie argued for Eden, whom he saw as "an ideal choice".[8] Many other UN delegates agreed.[9] However, Eden was unacceptable to Britain's new Labour government.[10] Another strong candidate was General Dwight D. Eisenhower. He was an enormously popular name in Europe: he had been Supreme Commander of the Allied Forces on the Western Front and directed the D-Day invasion. But Eisenhower was not popular with the Soviets. In any event, choosing an American secretary-general, even as the discussion was being held as to whether the UN should be headquartered in the US, was problematic.[11]

America's own favourite candidate for secretary-general was Lester B. Pearson of Canada, an unusually gifted diplomat who would later serve as his country's foreign minister and prime minister. Nevertheless, the Soviet Union strongly opposed the idea of a secretary-general from North America, and especially from Canada, a close ally of the US. Instead, the USSR suggested Yugoslavia's ambassador in Washington, Stanoje Simitch. Not a strong candidate, to be sure, but in any case a suggestion that reflected the need for a person who could occupy a more neutral position in the clash between East and West.[12] Among many other names that were mentioned were those of Britain's Gladwyn Jebb, who led the UN's preparatory commission; Eelco van Kleffens, the Dutch foreign minister; and Henri Bonnet from France, a former delegate to the League of Nations.[13]

Trygve Lie was the number-two candidate on the Americans' list. At the same time, he was in third place on the Soviet list – following Simitch and Wincenty Rzymowski, the Polish foreign minister. As it became clear that the USA and the Soviet Union could not support each other's top candidates, Lie began to look more and more like a shoo-in.[14]

Even though many people have said that it was evident from the start that the first secretary-general of the UN would have to hail from one of the smaller member states, the participants had to engage in quite a bit of diplomacy, politicking, and negotiating before arriving at this insight.[15] Nonetheless, it eventually became clear, in the buzzing hallway conversations, that a secretary-general from one of the "Big

Five" countries – the USA, the Soviet Union, Britain, France, and China – was out of the picture. The job could not go to one of the great powers; otherwise, there was a risk that the individual in question would use his position to the advantage of his own country or bloc. Thus, it became clear that the first secretary-general would have to come from a small country, preferably from one that had been under the Nazi heel. No matter who was selected, he would be a compromise candidate. Trygve Lie's name came up in speculations in the newspapers, and he received various private inquiries, but he kept a low profile after the election of the General Assembly president. The negotiations finally wound down and the great powers agreed on him. After receiving the offer, Lie flew to Norway to talk with his prime minister and his government about whether he should accept it.[16] Meanwhile, the tug of war went on in London.

Many sighed over the selection of the Norwegian Trygve Lie from the list of prominent candidates. There was "no consideration of who might be best qualified for the job. As they could not agree on a winner, the undistinguished choice of Lie was regarded by both sides as politically a safe bet", wrote Brian Urquhart, today the UN's Grand Old Man, then a young and very idealistic UN fan who went to New York as Lie's personal assistant.[17] Years later, to be sure, an elderly Urquhart reflected in his memoirs that Lie perhaps lacked "the ideal qualifications or the charisma for the job, but then who didn't? And, more relevant, who else could have been accepted by East and West?"[18]

Amid the oppositions between East and West, then, a Norwegian sailed into the top job. One of the UN's historians, Arthur W. Rovine, characterizes the choice of Lie more positively as "an encouraging sign of cooperation between the United States and the Soviet Union".[19] On 29 January 1946, the UN Security Council, with eleven member nations, unanimously recommended the 49-year-old Trygve Lie as the UN's first secretary-general. On 1 February 1946, the UN General Assembly chose Lie as the organization's first secretary-general by a vote of 46 to 3. The next day he took the oath.[20]

It was a far tougher office than Lie had been asked to take on at Christmastime four weeks earlier. Rather than a short-term position as president of the UN General Assembly, he had been chosen to be the first to helm the entire organization, serving a four-year term with the possibility of re-election. The position would mark the apogee of Trygve Lie's professional career. It would be fair to say that he stumbled onto the world stage almost by accident.

In his memoirs, he wrote, quite appropriately, "In this way, then, I was hurled into the position of secretary-general of the new international organization that would preserve the peace and ensure progress in a world full of unrest, poverty, and great-power rivalry. The whole thing exceeded my wildest dreams, but at the same seemed like a nightmare. I hardly dared think about what lay ahead of me. Instead I asked myself again and again how it could be that this fearsome office had fallen into the lap of a 'trade union lawyer' from Norway?"[21]

Lie went on to say that after the chaotic process was over, he had taken on the job of establishing the Secretariat and the UN organization with "a considerable degree of self-confidence". Trygve Lie knew administration. "To this extent, in any case, national administration can

On 16 July 1949, Lie took possession of the cottage at Røros, designed by Arnstein Arneberg. The media were in attendance when the gift was presented.

be compared with international", he wrote. "I had sat in the Norwegian government for many years, originally as Minister of Justice, but trade, industry and shipping were not unknown to me either. At the outbreak of war in 1939, I had been assigned the task of organizing Norway's supply service and later was given a similar responsibility for our merchant fleet. I even believed that I could handle bureaucrats."[22]

He had foreign-policy experience, too, having been one of the stronger ministers in the Norwegian government-in-exile, during which time he had met regularly with the representatives of other Allied governments and witnessed great-power politics close-up.

Which country?

In the archives of the UN, many metres of shelves are filled with boxes of files about all the wishes, plans, and visions of what the UN was to become and what it would be like. The very first big question was which continent, which country, which city should be the home of this new world organization? San Francisco? Geneva? Somewhere else?

The watershed San Francisco conference got underway in April 1945, while the war was still underway. It was to this conference that the news of peace in Europe was communicated in early May, and it was to this conference that the first shocking pictures of the concentration camps were relayed after their liberation. The common sentiment among the delegates was simple: "no more war". Fifty countries signed the UN Charter in late June. When Poland, which had not been represented in San Francisco, signed the Charter later, the total of nations rose to 51.

The close of the San Francisco conference marked the beginning of the meetings of the UN's preparatory commission, whose task it was to set up the whole thing – to plan what the new organization would look like and how it would work. The commission's work got underway in London on 16 August, only a few days after the atomic bombs fell on Nagasaki and Hiroshima, and continued until 24 November.[23] The leader of the commission was Sir Gladwyn Jebb, a member of the British Foreign Ministry, who established a base for the commission in Church House, Westminster, London. Perhaps suitably, the UN's General Assembly met for the first time in London, in January 1946. However, no one envisioned the British capital as the permanent home of the world organization.[24]

During the last phase of the war, Trygve Lie, who was then still serving as Norwegian foreign minister, discussed with his Norwegian advisors in London the question of whether the new international organization would not be best served by being headquartered on American soil, "so that the idea of international collaboration could, so to say, measure its power against the arch-enemy, isolationism, on its home turf".[25] The thought was not unnatural after five years of war. What would happen if a new great war broke out, if Europe were again to be entirely occupied? In that case, a European headquarters for the UN would be totally cut off from democratic countries on the other side of the ocean. One thing that the world did not need was another isolated and powerless organization such as the League of Nations.[26]

For his own part, Trygve Lie's wartime experience had strengthened his sense of the importance of future European-American cooperation, and of the need to restructure Norway's transatlantic policies (a process that had been shelved at the end of the war).[27] He believed very strongly that the US had to be a part of the new international organization.[28]

Conversations started up at once about where the UN headquarters might be located, and this question became one of the chief preoccupations of the preparatory commission. Later, China's ambassador in Washington, D.C., Wellington Koo, pointed out that the matter had been under discussion "day and night" for almost six months, from the minute the preparatory commission started its work in August 1945 to the last meeting of the first General Assembly in the winter of 1946.[29]

That autumn, Trygve Lie advised the members of the Norwegian delegation that took part in the preparatory commission that if it was, in fact, decided to place the headquarters in the US, they should try to secure an appropriate site on the East Coast.[30] The European members of the commission, such as France, the Netherlands, and Britain, eagerly supported Geneva. The British cabinet minister Philip Noer-Baker – who had taken part in the founding of the League of Nations and had been one of Fridtjof Nansen's close collaborators – made an emotional plea in favour of Geneva, and rejected the argument that the Swiss city would serve as a reminder of the failures of the past.[31]

Soviet ambassador Andrei Gromyko argued strongly for a site in the US. It was conveniently located between Asia and Europe. "The Old World had it once, and it is time for the New World to have it."[32] Where in the US? That was something the American government could decide. It probably disappointed many people in Western Europe that the Soviet Union, from the very outset, was in favour of locating the headquarters in the US. The acting head of the American delegation to the preparatory meetings, Adlai Stevenson, declared that his government was neutral on the issue, even though many Americans hoped that their country would win out. Stevenson privately advised a group from Chicago that they should try to get the UN to settle there. London, as it happened, was crawling with Stevenson's countrymen, "all of them well versed in the fine art of back-room politics and convinced that their hometown would be the ideal place....Let it be said that there were many magnanimous hosts in the bar in Church House", Lie commented.[33]

Some never gave up on Geneva. It was Switzerland itself that squelched the idea. After a good deal of back and forth, and expressions of hospitality toward the UN on the part of the Swiss government, it was made clear that this traditionally neutral country had certain well-defined scruples. Switzerland's message was as follows: it would gladly welcome to its territory all of the UN's organs and allow them to work there. However, should the Security Council find it necessary to order the use of military force, neutral Switzerland would demand that such resolutions be made outside the proposed headquarters in Geneva – that is to say, outside Swiss territory.[34]

There were other European alternatives. Brussels, Paris, and London were mentioned, as well as the three Nordic capitals. Proposals were made, evaluated, and discarded. It seemed clear, wrote Trygve

Lie, that an "entirely new world, which once had been just the parade grounds for an empire, had grown up and acquired power and distinctiveness." London was out; time was not on its side. World power was moving westward.

Influential figures in the General Assembly wanted to locate the UN permanently in Philadelphia or San Francisco, where the founding conference had taken place in 1945. President Truman offered the Presidio, the old Spanish fort in San Francisco, free of charge. However, the Soviets and Britons rejected the city by the bay because it was too far from Europe. Somebody proposed White Plains in Westchester County, north of New York City. Fairmont, Connecticut, was also mentioned. Suggestions poured in.

The pendulum swung back and forth between Europe and the US. The preparatory commission voted, and by a vote of 30 to 14 decided that the UN's permanent headquarters would be located in the USA. The actual difference of opinion on the matter was much smaller: not long before that vote was taken, a proposal recommending Europe had been rejected by a vote of 25 to 23, with two abstentions. It was then proposed by Noel-Baker, a supporter of Europe, that the choice of the US be made unanimous.[35]

On 22 December 1945 – after having "managed to stem the flow of delegations from American cities" – the preparatory commission decided that the headquarters would be located in the eastern USA. A committee was put to work to study the many proposals and sift out the most unsuitable ones. A group travelled around on an inspection tour and offered the suggestion that the UN's permanent headquarters should be located in the North Stamford/Greenwich area in Connecticut, north of New York City, with a temporary headquarters in the big city itself.[36]

However, it did not turn out to be so simple. Many of those who attended the General Assembly meeting in January 1946 were anxious about the committee's report. How did Americans look upon the idea of acquiring new neighbours? How did they really feel about the UN? According to the governors or state legislatures in Connecticut, Massachusetts, Rhode Island, and New York State, the attitude of the people in their states was positive and welcoming.

In London in January 1946, the committee discussing this issue divided into two factions. One of them, consisting of supporters of a headquarters in Europe, wanted to put off the choice of a location until the autumn. However, the idea of delaying a decision was rejected by a vote of 19 to 19 – an indication that the idea of placing the UN in Europe still had its strong champions.[37] Delegates from Australia, Egypt, Syria, and Iran spoke against New York and for San Francisco. On the same day that officials in Westchester County in New York voted to welcome the UN, protests against this invitation took place in two cities in that county, Greenwich and Stamford, with the participants calling for a referendum on the subject of building a UN headquarters in their midst. Meetings and conflicts took place throughout the region. Would the area around the new headquarters become "too European"? Others feared that homes and properties would be expropriated, and thought that the process of choosing a location for the headquarters was "un-American and unfair".[38] At this point, the idea was that the

UN headquarters should consist of a restricted international territory measuring up to 100 square kilometres.[39] There were also dreams of a UN located in its own peaceful city, far from the madding crowd, far out in the American countryside.

After a long period of conflict, the committee presented its recommendation on the last day of the General Assembly, 14 February 1946. It was then unanimously decided that the permanent headquarters would be located near New York City, either in Westchester County in New York State or in Fairfield County in Connecticut. The temporary headquarters would be established in New York City. Thus the ball was passed to the newly elected secretary-general. Trygve Lie himself was well satisfied with the decision to have a temporary headquarters in New York.[40]

Twenty-one days to go

Now it was a race against time. The period between the conclusion of the Security Council session in London and its next meeting in New York on 21 March was 21 days.[41] After his selection, and during the period when the General Assembly had been in session, Trygve Lie had put together a personal staff consisting of several Norwegians with whom he had worked in London during the war. The General Assembly had also decided that the UN Secretariat would be organized into eight departments, each led by an undersecretary-general. These people would make up the secretary-general's 'cabinet'. A new tug of war now took place as to who should be given these eight positions, and the great powers definitely wanted a say. The political and geographical calibrations and compromises that took place are beyond the scope of this essay.

Within the period of three weeks – 21 days – a temporary headquarters had to be set up, a space prepared for Security Council meetings, and a Secretariat established, with its various obligations. A tough task, but Lie's people managed to pull it off. It helped that New York's mayor, William O'Dwyer, and his staff, were very sympathetic. Soon, however, finding a site in midtown Manhattan began to seem hopeless. After World War II, there was a precarious housing shortage and a lack of office space in the city, as hundreds of thousands of New Yorkers, many of them in the armed forces, were returning home from all over the world.[42]

Together with his undersecretaries, Lie worked out of scattered hotel rooms at the Waldorf-Astoria, as well as a few additional offices at Rockefeller Center. The hopeless and impractical working situation sometimes caused Lie and his colleagues to dissolve in laughter. One day the Chinese undersecretary, Victor Hoo, arrived too late for a meeting. He had been summoned to a meeting at 610 Fifth Avenue in Rockefeller Center, but had misunderstood and had instead gone to room 610 at the Waldorf-Astoria. Hoo knocked on the door, and an elderly woman opened it, looked him over quickly, and said, "No thank you, I don't have any laundry today." Hoo took it in good humour, and made his way to Rockefeller Center.[43]

The UN quickly shifted into full operation in rented spaces all over

New York City. Beginning on 21 March, its temporary headquarters was located at Hunter College's Bronx campus (now Lehman College), far from midtown – 30 minutes by car and subway – and rather impractical. There was no air conditioning, and what should have been offices were classrooms that were too large and that were not easy to partition. Hunter was a women's college that had been used by the Navy during World War II and that would be occupied by students again in the autumn, so a number of other facilities were looked into.

New temporary – and also rather impractical – premises were kindly offered by New York City. The UN Secretariat and the councils would be housed at the Sperry factory in Lake Success, Long Island. The factory, which had been retooled for war production, was now empty – and was 45 minutes away from the city. However, there was not room there for everybody. The UN General Assembly would be given space in Flushing Meadows Park in Queens, where the 1939–40 World's Fair had taken place. Since the fair, the large park had stood empty. Moreover, the annual meetings of the UN General Assembly, the first in October 1946, would be held in the part of the facilities that had been an indoor skating rink.

On 25 June 1950, nine members of the Security Council voted for the American proposal for a ceasefire in Korea. The meeting was held in the Security Council's temporary space at the UN site in Lake Success on Long Island. The delegate area is very much like that in the permanent Security Council Chamber in Manhattan, with a horseshoe-shaped meeting table with a table for the Secretariat in the middle, plus a press gallery along the side walls. From right to left around the table sat Tingfu. F. Tsiang of China, Carlo Blanco of Cuba, Jose Correa of Ecuador, Fawzi Bey of Egypt, Jean Chauvel of France, Secretary-General Trygve Lie, B.N. Rau of India (behind Lie), Security Council President and Assistant Secretary-General Konstantin Zinchenko, who counted the votes, Arne Sunde of Norway, Terence Shone of the UK, Ernest Gross of the US, Djuro Nincic of Yugoslavia, and, on the far right, John M. Chang, Korea's ambassador in Washington, who was a guest at the meeting. The empty chair belongs to the Soviet delegate, who did not attend the meeting.

It was a combination of workplaces and meeting spaces that was not propitious in any sense, but at least there was room for the UN to do its work. New York authorities blasted, bricked up, and converted gyms and swimming pools into a Security Council Chamber at Hunter College, divided classrooms to make offices, furnished meeting rooms at Lake Success, and transformed Flushing Meadows into a site for the General Assembly.[44]

The establishment of the UN was an enormous undertaking. As secretary-general, Lie was the person with primary responsibility for hiring what the General Assembly had estimated at 2450 people over the course of nine months.[45] There were many aspirants, whose applications exuded idealism and optimism – "peace" and "hopes for peace for all time" were recurring phrases. The employment process had to happen fast, and the employees also had to find housing. The majority of administrative employees were, naturally enough, American citizens, and there were many Americans among Lie's closest advisors. Hiring was carried out quickly, and by the end of November 1946 it was stated at one of the secretary-general's regular meetings that there were now 3,014 employees on the payroll.[46] Later there would be staff reductions and, eventually, a redistribution of jobs in accordance with geographical and other considerations.

Where would all these people live? The hotels in Manhattan took in delegates and journalists, but what about the employees? Thanks to the mayor and city planner, the UN was able to secure 1,612 apartments in New York and Long Island, with an average rent of $20–25 a month.[47] Those who got jobs in the Secretariat tended to live some distance outside of the city and had to travel to and from the various facilities that the UN was using – which involved tiresome road trips from Lake Success to Flushing Meadows to Manhattan.

American attitudes toward the UN shocked some employees and delegates. When they drove around in cars marked with UN plates, taxis honked at them, bus drivers gave them a downturned thumb, and other motorists tried to rip off the UN logo. Neutral-minded Americans did not hide their feeling that a supranational organization such as the UN had no place in the US. Even the areas that had offered to house the UN, such as Westchester County in New York and Fairfield County in Connecticut, eventually turned against the UN. Nasty letters poured in from vocal UN opponents in New York.[48] It was an unpleasant situation. A permanent location for the UN now had to be settled on as soon as possible, and Lie pressured the city, giving it a late 1946 deadline.

A 96-hour deadline

Over the course of 44 years, Robert Moses, New York's legendary city planner, had built and restructured the entire city. He had constructed parks, sports arenas, playgrounds, streets, highways, and bridges; he had torn down entire neighbourhoods and built them anew. When it came to planning and building, Moses had wielded immense power through the administrations of five successive mayors and six different governors. Under his leadership, the seven years between 1946 and 1953 became one of the most intensive periods of public building in the entire history of the metropolis. Moreover, the United Nations was one of the biggest projects of them all.[49]

Moses wanted the UN to be in New York, and he worked closely with Mayor William O'Dwyer in his campaign to persuade the UN to make the city its home. O'Dwyer shared Moses's sentiments: the idea of a New York-based UN triggered his ambitions. "I felt that this was the one great thing," he said, "that would make New York the center of the world."[50]

However, there were a number of other places in the USA that also wanted to be the centre of the world. In addition, many of them had money. New York did not. O'Dwyer asked Moses to head up a committee to generate revenue. Moses brought in a number of big names, among them two members of the Rockefeller clan, Winthrop W. Aldrich and one of John D. Rockefeller Jr.'s sons, Nelson.[51]

For the mayor, the city planner, and everyone else who wanted the UN to be in New York, the challenge was demanding: the city did not have a site in midtown that was large enough for the purpose. The UN delegates and their staffs, as well as the organization's several thousand employees, would demand both good public transport and plenty of parking space. The delegates would want to be exempted from city taxes, and they needed residences for themselves, their staffs, and the Secretariat. These many demands from a new, ambitious organization were tough to satisfy at the same time that the city's inhabitants themselves needed schools, hospitals, libraries, sewers, and much else.[52] When the delegates to the General Assembly met for the first time in October 1946, it turned out that they disliked the place the city had placed at their disposal. Flushing Meadows was too far away.[53] They wanted to be in Manhattan.

In the autumn of 1946, it happened. Almost daily, the UN's many troops marched over to the mayor's office to get an answer. At the same time, San Francisco's mayor quietly came to New York and offered the UN a large site. Boston mobilized a team, including the city's mayor, the governor and the lieutenant governor of Massachusetts, who offered the UN both a good location and a guarantee to build both its headquarters and its residential facilities. Many delegates, meanwhile, strongly favoured Philadelphia.[54]

Secretary-General Trygve Lie, however, himself an experienced politician at both the municipal and national level, knew how to use friendly locals to sneak his way into the city's power circles. He was on good terms with the mayor, networked at baseball games, and grew chummy with Robert Moses over the course of several meetings in 1946. He was particularly impressed by the city planner's ability to get things done. In any event, he had a steadfast belief that the UN's future lay in Manhattan. That was where his loyalty lay.[55]

Yet it was far from a done deal. On 9 November, the UN General Assembly told the headquarters committee to look to other cities. On Friday, 6 December, Lie left a committee meeting and picked up the phone. At the time, Philadelphia was so sure it had won the competition for the UN headquarters that it had begun to condemn land for the purpose.[56] The secretary-general phoned Mayor O'Dwyer and Moses and warned them that "unless they came up with a new and better proposal, the whole thing would be over as far as New York was concerned. I had done all I could".[57] He also explained that a final decision in Philadelphia's favour could be expected on the following Wednesday, when the headquarters committee would be meeting again.

Secretary-General Trygve Lie looks out from his office window at the UN in Manhattan.

On the same day, O'Dwyer received another phone call, this time from the real-estate magnate William Zeckendorf. For a couple of months, Zeckendorf had been buying up land in Turtle Bay, which from the time of the Civil War had been an area of slaughterhouses, featuring enclosures for animals, packing plants, and so on. Zeckendorf had succeeded in buying up a large area in the middle of the old slaughterhouse district, part of which had now been converted to slums. He had been thinking of building large blocks of flats here, but neither the plans nor the financing was in order. It was a unique piece of land, located along the East River between 42nd and 48th streets. The UN could have it, said Zeckendorf. He was willing, in short, to sell to the UN the largest piece of land that had been available in the city in a quarter of a century.

O'Dwyer promptly reported this news to Trygve Lie, who replied, "Turtle Bay ... even now, could turn the tide."[58] But what about the financing? The name of Rockefeller was mentioned. Years ago, the wealthy oil clan had provided support for the League of Nations. O'Dwyer had no connections to the Rockefeller family, but Moses did. He had been cultivating a friendship with Nelson for a long time, and had worked closely with Nelson's father, John D. Rockefeller, Jr. The family was contacted.

In any event, there was a sea of bureaucracy to cut through, and a team of lawyers worked feverishly to complete official papers that were necessary to gain possession of Zeckendorf's site, plus some adjoining land that he did not own. Trygve Lie later described Saturday and Sunday, 7 and 8 December 1946 as the most exciting days in his entire term as secretary-general.[59] There were intense meetings involving the mayor, the city planner, the secretary-general, Ambassador Warren Austin, who led the headquarters committee, and Wallace K. Harrison, the architect and close friend of the Rockefeller family, as well as other people who were eager to see the UN settle down in New York. A process that would ordinarily have taken months was now completed within the period of a few days.[60] There were negotiations and preparations behind the scenes, with the older Rockefeller being worked on by his sons.

Zeckendorf was unaware that so much hard work was underway. He was at a birthday party at the fashionable Monte Carlo restaurant when Wallace K. Harrison walked in with a map of the buildings in the area. "Would you sell it for eight and a half million?" he asked. Zeckendorf said yes. Early the next day, while the magnate was nursing a hangover, the phone rang. Nelson Rockefeller said, "We've been up all night patching up the details, but it's going to work. The old man is going to give $8.5 to the UN, and they're going to take your property. See you soon. Good-bye."[61]

On the same day – only minutes later, in fact – the headquarters committee met. Ambassador Austin took the floor and announced the Rockefellers' gift to the UN. Three days later, the UN's General Assembly accepted it. A key factor in this decision was Mayor O'Dwyer's promise of residences – a promise that Moses kept by overseeing the construction of a large apartment project reserved for UN personnel.[62]

Eight days after the phone call to the mayor about the slaughterhouse sites, a surprised Zeckendorf was able to declare that the General Assembly had formally approved New York City as the headquarters for the United Nations.[63] The headquarters committee also accepted, rather quickly, a suggestion from New York City and the American government to put Wallace K. Harrison in charge of the planning work. Harrison had been one of the chief architects for Rockefeller Center and a number of other prominent building projects. "He and his wife became my good friends", writes Trygve Lie.[64]

For Trygve Lie, the six years that passed between the awarding of Rockefeller's gift and the completion of the complex in 1952 were a joy. "The planning and building of this large set of structures [was] one of the UN projects that was closest to my heart."[65] Lie himself writes that the story of the construction of the UN building is a story of "a team at work". In this work, unlike most of the other work underway at the UN, which involved "depressing indirect dealings and dead ends in international politics", there was a clear mandate and, not least, "an extraordinary helpfulness and goodwill at every turn".[66] During the six years of construction, there were informal meetings every Monday at the mayor's residence, Gracie Mansion, where Wallace K. Harrison, Byron Price, O'Dwyer, Robert Moses, various experts, and Trygve Lie himself were present.[67]

To be sure, given how elaborate the plans for the UN complex were and how difficult some of the architectural challenges were, it was impossible for the secretary-general to micromanage it all. Besides, the Cold War conflicts of the late 1940s demanded his full attention. Nevertheless, Lie was a man of action who could be counted on to ensure that the UN be provided with a suitable physical plant.

He was a man who rolled up his sleeves and went to work. The Americans around him noticed this and responded to it positively. "The Americans liked Trygve Lie", recalled the journalist Arne Skouen, who in 1945 and 1946 worked for the Norwegian Foreign Ministry's informa-

On 25 March 1947, Trygve Lie accepted a gift of $8.5 million to purchase the UN site from Rockefeller. From the left sit city planner Robert Moses, New York Mayor William O'Dwyer, Trygve Lie, and John D. Rockefeller III, who handed over the check on behalf of his father.

tion office in Rockefeller Center and helped introduce Secretary-General Trygve Lie to the US. "He had a flair for surrounding himself with skilful people and choosing good advisors. His staffers were good at language, made sure his correspondence was error-free, and had diplomatic talent and flexibility."[68]

Arthur W. Rovine emphasizes the enormous forces that were in play when the UN Secretariat and headquarters were established. The conflict between East and West was growing, presenting the world organization with challenges it could hardly handle adequately. "Into this stepped Trygve Lie ... who from his election in 1946 to a forced resignation in 1953, made a great contribution in terms of constructing and building an Organization and Office of secretary-general, and seeing them through the early period of their harshest trials."[69]

The hypermodern building of glass and marble that still looms today above the East River was Trygve Lie's work. He secured a permanent headquarters for his new organization, providing it with a set of beautiful spaces that are still prized for their quality and distinctiveness. However, the journey to the completion of this splendid complex in midtown Manhattan was a demanding one. Almost at the very second that the secretary-general oversaw its opening in November 1952, he threw in the towel and resigned. By that point, McCarthyism had caused a good deal of turmoil and anxiety in the corridors of UN power, and had "cleansed" the Secretariat of questionable employees. At the same time, because of his intervention (on the UN's behalf) after the outbreak of the Korean conflict, the secretary-general was repeatedly stymied in his attempts to take action by vetoes and boycotts on the part of the Soviet Union and Eastern bloc. In the early 1950s, the UN Secretariat was under pressure from every direction, and the secretary-general quit.[70]

However, the building complex he left behind still stands today.

The painter

Per Krohg (1889–1965) was one of the leading Norwegian artists of his time, know not least for his large decorative commissions. Among these were frescos at the University of Oslo and Kunstnernes Hus in Oslo – and, not least, the decoration of the Oslo City Hall, where he collaborated closely with Arnstein Arneberg.

Krohg grew up in Paris among artists from around the world. His artistic style was rooted in the Paris school and was inspired by Henri Matisse. He was also influenced by Picasso and cubism, but most of his work was figurative. In the beginning, the UN complex's Board of Art Advisors in New York was somewhat sceptical about the choice of the Norwegian painter, but under pressure from Trygve Lie, and after a tour of Krohg's atelier in the Oslo City Hall, they changed their minds.

Krohg's decoration of the City Hall shows great compositional freedom and creativity. In the Security Council Chamber, the composition is far more stylised. With a pictorial field that can bring to mind the structure of a comic strip, Krohg's painting in New York does not exhibit the organic expression in many of his previous works. Formally, the painting resembles a classic altarpiece, except that the religious symbols have been replaced by secular symbols of peace.

In the autumn of 1952, Per Krohg's painting in the Security Council Chamber was officially unveiled. In his memoirs, Krohg writes that on the opening day he had put on a blue suit and his finest white shirt. He strolled down to the UN and sat next to Peru's delegate at the table. The hall was dark. In the middle, in front of the picture, sat Trygve Lie and Prime Minister Torp together with the individual who was president of the council that month. Torp was presented and delivered his speech. The picture was unveiled, the lights turned on, and the entire chamber applauded. But nobody mentioned that the artist himself was in the room, Krohg recalled. The next day, to his disappointment, he read in a New York newspaper that the artist had not been present.

51.11.09.

Oslo 28/9-1951.

Herr Arkitekt Arnstein Arneberg

Jeg har av Dem, fått beskjed om at Arkitektkontoret ved de forente Nationers nye bygning i New York, mener at den spesielle takbelysning på mitt store billede til sikkerhetsrådets sal, ikke behöver å installeres får efter at billedet er plasert på veggen –

Jeg synes dette er meget beklagelig da jeg ikke kan nå å få billedet ferdig malt og satt på plass får like inn på den dato da den store höitidelighet skal finne sted i Oktober næste år og hvor billedet også vil bli avslöret.

Installasion av lyset bår derfor, efter min mening skje nu, får rummet blir ferdig, så kan man alltid instille lampene i riktig vinkel og bestemme lysets styrke når billedet er plasert –

Jeg vil be Dem Herr arkitekt Arneberg om å insistere overfor F.N. byggets arkitekter på at dette blir gjort –

Ærbödigst Per Krohg

Vibeke Waallann Hansen

Per Krohg's UN Painting: An Altarpiece for Peace

"If it is not desired that the picture be placed in this room, I consider it most appropriate to resign as the architect for the room", wrote Arnstein Arneberg in a letter to UN secretary-general Trygve Lie on 12 June 1950.[1] The room he referred to is still one of the world's most important, and the commission to design the Security Council Chamber held high status and prestige for both the architect himself and the nation of Norway. Nonetheless, in the midst of the process, Arneberg considered withdrawing from the assignment if Per Krohg's painting were not hung in the location that he had chosen for it from the outset. The background for the 1950 letter to Lie was that the committee responsible for the artistic decoration of the UN complex had changed its mind underway, and now – about six months after Krohg took on the job – the committee wanted no painting at all hung in the Security Council Chamber. As we know, the conflict was resolved in Arneberg and Krohg's favour: Lie intervened, and the room was completed in accordance with the original plans.

There is no way of knowing, of course, whether Arneberg actually would have quit had the picture been removed from the chamber, but the correspondence about the commission shows clearly that he considered it imperative from the very start that Krohg's artwork be included. In this essay, we will look more closely at the decision-making process and the diplomatic activity concerning the work of furnishing the Security Council Chamber. First, we will take an excursion into the form and content of Krohg's picture.

From idea to sketch

It is not clear from the correspondence about Krohg's commission whether he was given any guidelines in regard to the creation of the picture, other than the measurements.[2] The picture measures 50 square metres and by virtue of its dimensions is an absolute eye-catcher. The reason for its size is that is placed in front of a large window that Arneberg wanted to cover, preferably with a fresco or a mosaic-decorated wall. In the chamber of the Economic and Social Council, the architect responsible for designing the space, Sven Markelius of Sweden, chose to block light from an equally large window with a textile that was specially designed for the purpose.

In his choice of subject for the fresco, Krohg took into account the most important issues that would be discussed in the Security

Page 112–113: The central panel in Krohg's painting is entitled "Peace". The theme is carried over from his 1940 painting of the same name. Here, he painted himself and his happy family surrounded by wildflowers. The phoenix spreads its wings and leads people from the underground up to a world full of peace and progress. In the group of people in the middle we see the blue ribbon and UN flag. In the foreground, prisoners in chains are being welcomed. To the right we see the symbol of peace, the rearing white horse.

Page 114: Letter from Per Krohg to Arneberg: "Oslo 28/9-1951 / Dear Architect Arnstein Arneberg / I have received from you the news that the Architectural Office at the United Nations' new building in New York believes that the special ceiling lights in my large picture of the Security Council Chamber do not need to be installed until after the picture is in place on the wall. / I feel this is very regrettable, since I cannot get the picture completed and put in place before the date when the big ceremony is set to take place in October of next year and where the picture will also be unveiled. The installation of the lights should therefore, in my view, take place now, before the room is completed. The angle and brightness of the lamps can always be adjusted after the picture has been put up. / I ask you, Mr. Architect Arneberg, to insist to the UN building's architects that this be done. / Yours truly, Per Krohg"

Council Chamber. The picture can be read as an allegory of the UN's central document, the Universal Declaration of Human Rights, which had been signed on 10 December 1948, a year before he was given the assignment. In his 1966 memoirs, he recalls working for a long period on various sketches and drafts before the final composition came into focus.[3] It had not taken him long, by the way, to complete a conceptual design study:

> The core of the idea is to give an impression of light, of safety, and of happiness (...). The world we abandoned cannot be erased just like that, but one can build a bridge over the adversity and from that journey a new society, a state as clear as day with the rule of law and with no deviousness. (...) To this new world will stream all of those who have suffered under inhuman and brutal conditions we are leaving behind us. (...) They will mix with new crowds. (...) Together they will create a harmonic entity when the last group of war criminals is driven away. In such a way will the UN's and the Security Council's deeds sprout into new and precious life.[4]

As we can see from this account, Krohg, in his work on the picture, was very attentive to the Security Council's delegated purpose. This first written explanation is dated 20 February 1950. A few weeks later, the Norwegian Foreign Ministry, which had commissioned Krohg's work, sent this text and five painted sketches to Norway's UN delegation in New York and tasked them with showing the material to Secretary-General Lie and Wallace K. Harrison, the architect who was in charge of the artistic decoration of the UN complex.[5] Krohg described the theme in the following way:

> The columns that support the new world rise up amidst the ruins of the old. One sees in the sketch, in the foreground, how anguished, indifferent, dull people settle in dark caves or the remains of dwellings. They are without initiative, sceptical, but among them there are also many who find the power to break loose from the misery. We see them here, streaming in toward the centre of the picture, from the dark foreground and from the pale, cobweb-like, dead ruined cities in the background. In the sparkling crystal-clear light, they meet and unite and divide into crowds as they head toward the ideal state of the future, which rises in arches up to the sun.[6]

The five sketches from the first phase are today unknown, but it turns out that the description of the picture's theme that Krohg provided here corresponds to one of Arneberg's sketches for the space (see p. 78–79). It may have been Krohg who drew the part of the sketch that corresponds to the wall painting. Alternatively, perhaps Arneberg drew it in accordance with Krohg's instructions. Unlike Arneberg's other early sketches, this one is neither dated nor signed. This, in addition to the fact that some of the figures and details bring to mind previous works by Krohg, suggests that it was the artist himself who drew it. A comparison of the completed work with this first description and Arneberg's sketch shows that Krohg made major changes along the way. Nevertheless, he retained the core idea, which was to give expression to the hope that the UN represented a brighter future. In the picture, war and "the darkness" are a stage people have put behind them as they head toward a new world of "light, security, and joy".

An alternative to peace

About a year after this first shipment to the UN, the painting was complete. The foreign minister and his entourage were invited to the City Hall atelier[7] to examine it.[8] Now there was a new description of the meaning of the various scenes:

> Up out of the old world's piles of ruins, therefore, rises the new, well-ordered society, whose goal is peace and happiness. (...) The soldier has impaled the dragon of evil with his sword and prevented its attempt to tear down the new society's foundations. He then sets down his weapons and enters into the people's fellowship. So do the woman and man, who are being rescued from the swamp of despair. The black and the white prisoners of war who are brothers in degradation and in liberation, and the whole of the large, grey, tired mass of humanity that is streaming, under the wings of the phoenix, through the portal that leads into the new world, where all people meet with open hands and outstretched arms under the UN's banner.[9]

When Krohg worked on the UN painting, he needed a large studio. Therefore he was allowed to use the City Hall atelier. The canvas for the oil painting measured 5.48 x 8.84 metres. It was set up in the atelier and scaffolding had to be used to reach it.

The principal message, as we see, is that the founding of the UN offers hope for an international community dominated by peace and freedom. In order to clearly communicate this positive message, Krohg placed the image of peace at the centre of the completed composition. The picture's oval middle field is entitled *Peace*, and the image brings to mind a nuclear family. A man and a woman face each other, kneeling. They are physically connected in that each is holding the other's right arm. Surrounding the couple are four children and a fruit tree. The boy in the upper part of the picture strikes an angelic pose and seems to be hovering over the adult couple. But the boy has no angel wings, and upon closer inspection, one can see that he is resting on one of the tree's branches. In Krohg's view, the family represents the foundation of peace: respect, love, and togetherness. In addition to this, the picture's middle section is dominated by the phoenix. This is the picture's only conventional symbol and breaks with the highly realistic narrative style that characterizes the composition as a whole. The phoenix symbol underpins the picture's principal narrative: the hope that something good will grow out of evil and destruction.

In the side panels, the themes are equality, freedom, and brotherhood. *Equality*, at the upper left, is represented by a group of men and women who weigh and share grain in equal portions. *Freedom* is illustrated in the panel on the right, symbolized by a prancing white horse. While working on the painting, Krohg said that he had tried to avoid the "prevailing symbols"; about using a white horse as an image of freedom, he said, "One gets the impression of freedom when the horse takes the bridle and, receiving a friendly departing slap gallops out onto the green fields with a fluttering mane and tail."[10] The representation of *Brotherhood* extends across two panels and is placed on each side of the middle panel, *Peace*. Four young men and women are entwined by a blue band, which shows that they are connected and mutually dependent in their work for peace. The colour of the band is UN blue, and in the panel to the right Krohg has made the UN's significance for the international brotherhood explicit by depicting a UN flag waving above the crowd. Solidarity and optimism for the future are symbolized by a large group of people who are expressing joy. The group of men, women, and children with different skin colours and costumes represent various cultures and parts of the world, and they move forward together, toward the sun and the light. The two oblong panels in the upper part of the composition show all the art forms in harmonic union. The argument for including a representation of the art forms was that it was the artists, in Krohg's view, who would "interpret and advance" the events to come.

Krohg's UN painting has been aptly described as an "altarpiece for peace".[11] In this picture, the belief in peace and freedom has replaced religious belief, the Universal Declaration has replaced the Bible, and the UN is presented as the 'saviour' of modern times, with a message of a better future. The division of the picture into distinct panels, each of which illustrates an ideological concept, recalls the Christian tradition of altarpieces.[12] Of Krohg's monumental paintings, this is the only with such a unified compositional framework. The inspiration from the Christian artistic tradition can be found in several of his earlier works. The stylized tree root on the short wall in the eastern room in Oslo City Hall is a variation of the rose window of church architecture; the concentration camp motif in the same wall decoration mimics the Bible's representations of Hell, and images of the Holy Family are a recurring element in Krohg's pictorial universe.[13] The fact that a mandorla encircles the Holy Family, that is to say, the peace motif in the UN painting, makes it clear that Krohg had Christian symbols and the Christian pictorial tradition in his thoughts. He chose to employ a visual vocabulary that was well established in Western culture, and he combined this with his own symbols for freedom, equality, and brotherhood. Krohg's own explanation of the picture, written in 1951, was published in reworked form after the picture had been hung in the room. Here he reflects over his own process:

> Now that I was going to render my hope for the future, it could be done with the use of some great symbolic figures, but I feared that in the long term they would seem stiff and theatrical. A richer and more natural configuration would be more appropriate to my view of this composition. In order for the whole thing not to seem chaotic, which would be the opposite of the picture's meaning, I divided it up into panels that would fit together from both an intellectual and a purely decorative perspective – in other words, into a polyopticon.[14]

Krohg's *UN Painting* is realistic and detailed, and as we can see from his reflections, it was an artwork that entailed conscious work with the means of expression during the process of creation.

The Eastern Hall on the first floor of the Oslo City Hall is decorated with Per Krohg's mural. It is an organic, imaginative, and lively composition. A reference to church decoration can be seen on the short wall above the door. A woodcut of a tree root, viewed from below, brings to mind rose windows.

"The fastest case processing in Norway."

How did it happen that Per Krohg, of all people, was chosen for this important assignment? Was the direct awarding of the commission a manifestation of Arneberg's personal preferences, or was the choice based on an agreement that Krohg was the leading Norwegian monumental painter of the era, and thus the one who could assert himself most impressively in an international context?

From the very beginning of the project, Arneberg wanted an artwork that would be integrated into the space. He made the following proposal to the UN's building committee: "In order to obtain a continuous harmony of the room, it is suggested that the section between the two large windows should contain a mural in the form of either a mosaic or a fresco. It is also important that this work be made by a prominent artist."[15] The question is whether he already had Krohg in his thoughts. The concept for the room was approved, but at the same time, he was informed that the budget would not cover artworks. In November 1949, therefore, Arneberg applied to the Norwegian Foreign Ministry for financial support:

> As a salute to our land, a Norwegian architect has been entrusted with the work of designing the interior of the Security Council Chamber. (...) It is important that this interior represent Norway in a worthy manner. (...) If this room is to stand out in comparison with the others, further artistic decoration is necessary. However, this will not be paid for by the UN.[16]

He went on to advise against holding an open competition for the job and justified his position as follows: "You're not going to get the older artists to take part in public competitions." Arneberg emphasized that the construction of the buildings needed to be completed within a relatively short time, and that it was therefore important to find an artist who was known to be capable of pulling off such a major task.[17] Therefore, he made it clear that he did not want a competition, and at the same time he took the liberty of making a specific proposal: "One of those who could take on this assignment in an outstanding manner and complete it in good time is Professor Per Krohg. He would be able to perform this job of decoration in harmony with the spirit of the building."[18]

Arneberg had gone a step further: "Without making any promises, I have conferred with him about his conditions. The picture, which is very large, about 50 square metres, will have to be measured here, put up on the wall, and be completed on site. For the picture itself the professor requires an honorarium of 60,000 kroner."[19] Arneberg also suggested that the sculptor Emil Lie be hired to create some marble reliefs,[20] but summed up by saying that it was especially important to secure economic support for the painted wall panel: "Norwegian artists today have broad experience and are well equipped to solve a task such as the present one in what is, for the country, an honourable way."[21]

On 9 January 1950, a message was sent to Arneberg from the foreign minister's office: "I hereby authorize you to enter into negotiations with Professor Per Krohg and sculptor Emil Lie regarding the completion of those works that are described in your letter of 17 November last year."[22] As we have seen, Krohg had his first draft ready in February 1950. It was sent to New York, and by mid March it was made clear that he had received the commission: "it is the fastest processing of a case that has ever occurred in this country,"[23] Krohg himself told *Dagbladet*.

The ministry's reason for granting the money had essentially been summed up by Arneberg, Much weight, unsurprisingly, was placed on the fact that the nation would profit from the arrangement: "The Foreign Ministry finds it desirable that the Norwegian state pay for the proposed artistic decoration so that the interior of the Security Council Chamber may represent Norway in a worthy fashion."[24]

Oslo's "Michelangelo"

The design of the room was well underway in the spring of 1950. The press was also informed about the important commission that had been given to Arneberg and Krohg. In March 1950, *Aftenposten* wrote, "Norway's offer to decorate the Security Council's chamber approved."[25] The headline in *Morgenposten* read, "Security Council Chamber will be Norwegian".[26] However, in the early summer the UN's newly created Board of Art Advisors sent out a surprising message to the contrary. After further discussion, the committee had concluded that it was not desirable to have pictorial art in the meeting hall:

> The Board of Art Advisors ... concluded that in none of the working chambers should there be any murals, believing that such pictorial representation would become controversial, in addition to being a distraction from the deliberations of the Council which will use the room. They considered the Council Chambers and major Conference rooms as the most important working areas and recommended that all art work be omitted from these spaces. ... In line with this policy, we are suggesting the possibility of omitting the mural which you had planned for the Security Council Chamber and perhaps using something by Mr. Krohg in some other area of the Headquarters at a later time.[27]

On 7 June, Arneberg sent a letter to Wallace K. Harrison and reminded him that the Norwegian government had appropriated funds for just such an artwork, and that this sum would probably be withdrawn if Krohg's work were placed in a room other than the Security Council Chamber. Some days later Arneberg wrote to Lie and asked for help: "In my plan for the room, there has always been an expectation that there would be a large decoration. On the basis of the drawings that I showed you over a year ago in New York, the working sketches for the room have been drawn up with the picture as the centrepiece."[28]

The case then became a matter of diplomacy, with both the Norwegian foreign minister and the Norwegian UN ambassador pitching in to work out a solution.[29] Lie proposed that the committee be invited on a tour of the Scandinavian capitals in order to become acquainted with these countries' art and design and to meet their collaborators there. Arneberg informed Krohg about this proposal in a letter:

> This committee, "the Board of Art Advisors", has almost concluded that there should not be decorative embellishment in the meeting halls. In an attempt to straighten the situation out, Trygve Lie proposes that a committee consisting of the architect Harrison and Robertson and Carlu from France should come to Scandinavia and here to Oslo around 15 August to discuss the matter.[30]

He writes further that it is important for Krohg to be present, and in late August 1950, the delegation arrived in Oslo to see Per Krohg's work in person.

After their trip to Oslo, the members of the delegation agreed to stick with the plan to let Krohg decorate the large wall.[31] They chose, then, to reject the Board of Art Advisors' decision not to have art in the meeting rooms. This principle had, at least, been the official explanation as to why the committee wanted to remove Krohg's picture from the room. Nevertheless, it is important to note that the committee made its decision after Krohg's first sketches had been submitted, causing some committee members to question their artistic quality.

Perhaps the committee regarded Krohg's style as conservative in relation to the overall modern look of the UN complex. Indeed, a letter from Arneberg to Foreign Minister Skylstad makes it clear that the committee reacted with scepticism to Krohg's sketches: "I would like to inform you that Secretary-General Lie has told me that the 'Art Committee's' members have not been particularly enthused over Professor Krohg's sketches." Arneberg also wrote that Lie was not pleased with the situation, and that he would attempt to resolve it 'to everyone's satisfaction'."

Lie himself wanted to be able to take part in the committee's visit to Oslo, and hoped that it would be possible "to get it to change its opinion when it gets to see Professor Krohg's decorative works in Oslo".[32] On 22 August 1950, *Morgenbladet* carried the headline "UN's chief architect will study the City Hall in Oslo", and further down in the article we read, "Now it looks as if the impression the Americans get of the City Hall will be decisive as to how the Security Council's chamber ends up looking." The idea, then, was for the committee to be convinced of Krohg's brilliance by being shown one of his most impressive works: the eastern gallery of the Oslo City Hall.

Morgenbladet followed up on the story and reported a few days later that the UN architects had been convinced by Krohg's City Hall decorations. At the press conference, it was stated that the committee, before its visit to Norway, had been inclined not to want any painting in the Security Council Chamber because it would be almost hopeless that they would be able to find something suitable. They said that Per Krohg's draft, however, had turned out to be brilliantly appropriate: "We have found Oslo's Michelangelo", the French architect Jacques Carlu is supposed to have said.[33]

There is every reason to believe that Krohg's wall paintings in Oslo City Hall impressed Carlu and the rest of the delegation. But Michelangelo? Carlu hardly believed that he had found the equal of the Renaissance genius, although he may have felt, at least, that he had met *Oslo's* Michelangelo. It is known, in any event, that the committee definitely encountered some Krohg enthusiasts in Oslo, so that their decision to let him complete the assignment was apparently the result of successful diplomatic work. As Lie put it in a letter to Krohg, Arneberg had been able to "straighten everything out".

Per Krohg – a natural choice

When Arneberg requested the Foreign Ministry's financial support for artistic decoration and at the same time expressed scepticism toward the idea of a competition, he argued that established artists would not take part in such a competition. He was probably referring to Krohg, Alf Rolfsen, Henrik Sørensen, and Axel Revold, who together were known as the "fresco brothers". Arneberg knew Krohg from his work on the Oslo City Hall, but the same applied to Rolfsen and Sørensen. Why he selected Krohg specifically for the task is unknown. Perhaps it was important to him that Krohg was a professor at the country's most important institute of art education. It may also have been a kind of compensation for Krohg's having been given one of the more peripheral rooms in the Oslo City Hall. Or else the choice was simply based on the success of Krohg's many earlier wall paintings.

Per Krohg was one of Norway's leading artists in the first half of the twentieth century. The son of two artists, Oda and Christian Krohg, he grew up in Paris, and was thus part of the international art scene. As a young man, he had been a student of Henri Matisse, but he also drew on ideas from both cubism and surrealism. Krohg was distinctly curious, and this is reflected in the diversity of his *oeuvre*. He was probably the closest thing there was to a Picasso in the Norwegian art world of his generation. Like that great master, he was playful in his approach to art and had a tireless willingness to experiment; but perhaps most striking is the fact that he had something of the same ability to balance humour and seriousness.

When Per Krohg was awarded the prestigious commission to provide a painting for the UN, pictures were taken for a report in *Aktuell*. Here the artist sits with his sketchbook in his studio in December 1950.

Krohg was also in the habit of referring to Picasso as a role model: "I pondered Picasso and his significance. My admiration was great, but I understood that I didn't have to follow his working method."[34] Krohg is best known for his monumental paintings, the most notable of which include his frescoes for the National Library and the Physics Building at the University of Oslo. There is no doubt that, when seen through Norwegian eyes, he was an important artist at the time of the UN assignment. If one wanted a *prominent* artist to create a mural or a mosaic, and this artist was to be Norwegian, it would make sense to think of Krohg.

Nor does it appear that there were significant protests against awarding the commission to Krohg. Henrik Sørensen cleared himself out of the City Hall atelier so that Krohg could have room to work on his 50-square-metre picture. After the dedication of the Security Council Chamber in 1952, *Dagbladet* ran an article headlined "Norwegian spirit in world art": "Arnstein Arneberg, who was given the task of decorating this hall, felt it should be adorned with a monumental Norwegian painting and got the Norwegian government to donate it. Quite naturally, it was Per Krohg who was commissioned to attend to the artistic aspects of the painting."[35] Writing about a 1965 Per Krohg exhibition in Bergen, journalist Henning Sinding-Larsen also seemed to agree that it was 'natural' for Krohg to be selected directly for the job:

> ... speed of thought and action was a consequence of solid skills and a broad horizon. That was why he could reach the top of the stairs in three steps. It was just as natural that he should be given the honourable commission to decorate the Security Council Chamber in the UN building, as it was inexplicable that he was given the worst room when the Oslo City Hall was to be decorated. Perhaps it was understood that nobody else would be able to master the job.[36]

Reflecting in 1952 upon Krohg's work, Arneberg expressed satisfaction with his contribution to the space: "For the large wall panel between the windows, Per Krohg was commissioned by the Norwegian Foreign Ministry to produce a decorative picture. It was framed and recessed in marble, and creates an excellent overall impact in the room."[37] Although Arneberg states that Krohg was given the commission by the Norwegian Foreign Ministry, it would be closer to the truth to say that the ministry, without debate, accepted Arneberg's choice of artist.

The combination of Arneberg and Krohg resulted in a room heavy with symbols, and it is possible that the two men encouraged each other to move in this direction. The Arneberg sketch in which Krohg's first thematic proposal is included gives us reason to believe that the two of them were in close dialogue about the design of the picture. The UN painting lacks Krohg's characteristic balance of seriousness, humour, and playfulness, which marks so much of his other work. Perhaps it was the collaboration with Arneberg that led Krohg to produce such an atypical work. Perhaps the solemn responsibility of fulfilling the Security Council's mandate led Krohg to have specific intentions about communicating the UN message.

The first art at UN headquarters

Questions have been raised as to whether Arneberg and Lie involved themselves in Krohg's choice of themes. How did Arneberg, and possibly Lie, contribute to Krohg's decision to create an ideological altarpiece about peace for the Security Council Chamber?[38] It is very likely that Arneberg and Krohg had discussed the themes, but this does not necessarily mean that Arneberg was involved at the level of detail. Krohg's view of art was well known to Arneberg, and by choosing Krohg, he guaranteed himself a partner with attitudes that were in line with his own. Krohg's art had changed character after the war, and he had become more preoccupied with preserving tradition and conveying an edifying message in his pictures. As for Lie, he was far from an art expert, but he also had resolute opinions on the subject. He reputedly expressed a distaste for Picasso, and in general, he took a dim view of abstract art.[39] Lie made it obvious that it was in his interest for Krohg to receive the commission, but it is less clear whether he had any influence on Krohg's work.

Then again, the UN painting is one of the least formally experimental works Krohg ever created. His first draft (in Arneberg's sketch) was a simplified symbolic representation of a world society on its way from evil to goodness. The small sketch suggests a formal language that is reminiscent of Krohg's earlier monumental paintings. Krohg himself reflected afterwards that he had moved away from the idea of using "large symbolic figures" and had instead sought out a "richer and more natural design". Perhaps the involvement of both Arneberg and Lie had helped him decide upon a more descriptive and figurative kind of representation? We know for a fact that Lie, via Arneberg, encouraged Krohg to make the picture, in general, on the bright side.[40]

As for his selection of theme, Krohg was far from the only artist represented in the UN complex to have chosen war and peace. To a preponderant degree, the artworks that have been added to the complex over the years have focussed thematically on the organization's founding pillars – peace, international justice, and human rights. For the 1952 opening, it had been arranged for nine artworks to be integrated into the complex; one of these was Krohg's picture. These works were put in place during the building process or were completed shortly after the opening.[41] The largest of these is a painting that was installed in the lobby and that is in two parts. The work of a Brazilian, Cândido Portinari, it was a gift to the UN from the Brazilian government.[42] One of the two parts of Portinari's picture is about war and is painted in dark, somber shades. The other part is about peace and is done in warm, bright hues. The colour symbolism, then, is the same as in Krohg's *UN Painting*.

The human struggle for peace and freedom is also the theme of José Vela Zanetti's wall painting, which was a gift from the Dominican Republic, and which was accepted by the Board of Art Advisors in June 1952. Here, too, the horrors of war are depicted alongside symbols of peace and freedom. War and suffering dominate the left-hand side of the composition. In the middle sits a gigantic male figure who is in the process of installing the UN emblem, while symbols of justice, reconstruction, and human rights dominate the picture's right-hand side.

Portinari's, Zanetti's, and Krohg's monumental works, as we can see, are relatively complementary in content and theme. Formally, however, Krohg's painting is distinguished from the other two by its realistic and relatively detailed style. The UN painting is one of Krohg's late monumental paintings. Simplification, stylization, and a greater degree of experimentation with visual effects mark his earlier works, such as those for Sjømannskolen and Kunstnernes hus in Oslo. The UN painting is illustrative, time-bound, and specific in its particulars. Details such as clothing and hairstyles anchor the work in the decade during which it was created. By contrast, the pictures by Portinari and Zanetti are distinguished by simplification and abstraction. The people do not have as much individual character, but function more as representatives of the masses. Alongside these works, Krohg's picture in the Security Council Chamber seems more of a traditional history painting in the sense that it tells of an important historical event of modern times: the establishment of the UN.

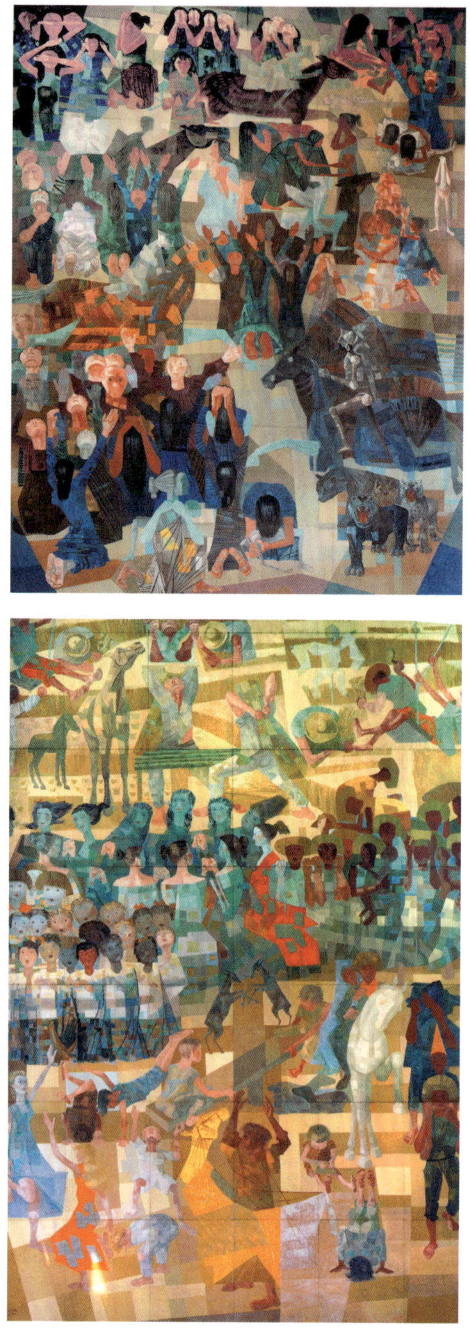

Brazil's gift to the UN consisted of two paintings entitled *War* and *Peace*. They were presented in 1957 and painted by Cândido Portinari. The pictures hang outside the delegates' lobby in the General Assembly building.

José Vela Zanetti's mural painting was a gift to the UN from the Dominican Republic. Zanetti was originally Spanish, but had emigrated during the Spanish Civil War. The painting bears the descriptive title *Mankind's Struggle for a Lasting Peace*. Here, too, the UN's blue colour and emblem are central elements.

A gift to the UN from the Norwegian state

It was not just the Norwegian delegation that was eager to see its country presented "in an honourable" way in the UN's headquarters. Almost from its inception, the organization received offers of gifts of art. Shortly after the complex's design was made public in 1947, the various delegations began to push for greater influence in the design of the headquarters.[43] In response to all this generosity, Secretary-General Lie formed the Board of Art Advisors.[44] Krohg's picture was the first artwork to be approved by this committee. Even though it was Lie himself who had set up the committee, we have seen that he did not heed their recommendation in the case of Krohg's picture. It was obviously more important for him to ensure that Norwegian art receive prominent exposure than to listen to the professional art experts he himself had appointed. Today, it may seem surprising that an artist who was relatively unknown beyond Norway's borders was given such a prestigious international commission. Then again, Lie had been elected secretary-general of the UN in 1946, and with this action Norway moved from the periphery to the centre of international politics. With political power comes cultural power, and this developed into a matter in which diplomacy trumped the opinion of the art committee.

It also turned out to be strategically wise of Arneberg to have at an early stage secured financial support from the Norwegian Foreign Ministry. Later, when the committee responsible for the artistic decoration in the UN complex took a principled stand against having pictures in the meeting halls, it became difficult to reverse the decision pertaining to Krohg's contribution because it had already been approved as a gift from the Norwegian government to the UN. To refuse a gift is always difficult, but perhaps it was especially difficult in this case, since the gift was being given by the home nation of the construction project's supreme commander, Trygve Lie.

51590.

UNITED NATIONS NATIONS UNIES

NEW YORK

CABLE ADDRESS · UNATIONS NEWYORK · ADRESSE TELEGRAPHIQUE

FILE NO.: 120-10-6-1

17 May 1951

Mr. Arnstein Arneberg,
Ovre Vollgate 7,
Oslo, Norway

Dear Mr. Arneberg:

..... I am enclosing for your information a sample of the olive ash natural finished, for the Security Council table. We hope you like the appearance of this finish. The table is now constructed complete and looks extremely beautiful.

Very best personal regards,

Sincerely,

Abel J. Sorensen

Abel Sorensen
Headquarters Planning Office

The process

The correspondence between Arnstein Arneberg and the construction office in New York during the work on the Security Council Chamber was extensive. The letters show traces of disagreement, misunderstanding, and frustration. In the first drawings of the chamber that were received by Arneberg, there was a large wall panel between the windows facing the East River. Arneberg felt that the wall was begging to be decorated. Later in the process, the wall panel was replaced with windows, By that point, Arneberg had already secured financing for Krohg's painting from the Norwegian government.

Compromises and time pressure influenced many of the decisions. But Arneberg did have greater control over several of the design elements. The chairs for the delegate and the wooden doors with intarsia patterns, for example, were completed in accordance with Arneberg's design and produced by Norwegian carpenters. He also chose most of the textiles, patterns, and colours. The blue-striped material for the delegates' chairs was by the textile artist Birgit Wessel. The Biri wallpaper was designed by Klare Schee, while Else Poulsson designed the wall textile. All of this was produced in Norway and transported piece by piece across the Atlantic.

On 17 May 1951 – which happened to be Constitution Day in Norway – Abel Sorensen of the Planning Office in New York sent Arneberg a sample of the wood that would be used for the delegates' table. The table was made of American ash wood and manufactured in the US, and there is some uncertainty as to the identity of the designer. We know that Arneberg decided on the material. When the Planning Office designed the Secretariat's table so as to be able to order it at the same time as the main table, it was up to Arneberg to approve the design.

OLIVE ASH
1
2
4
45
3

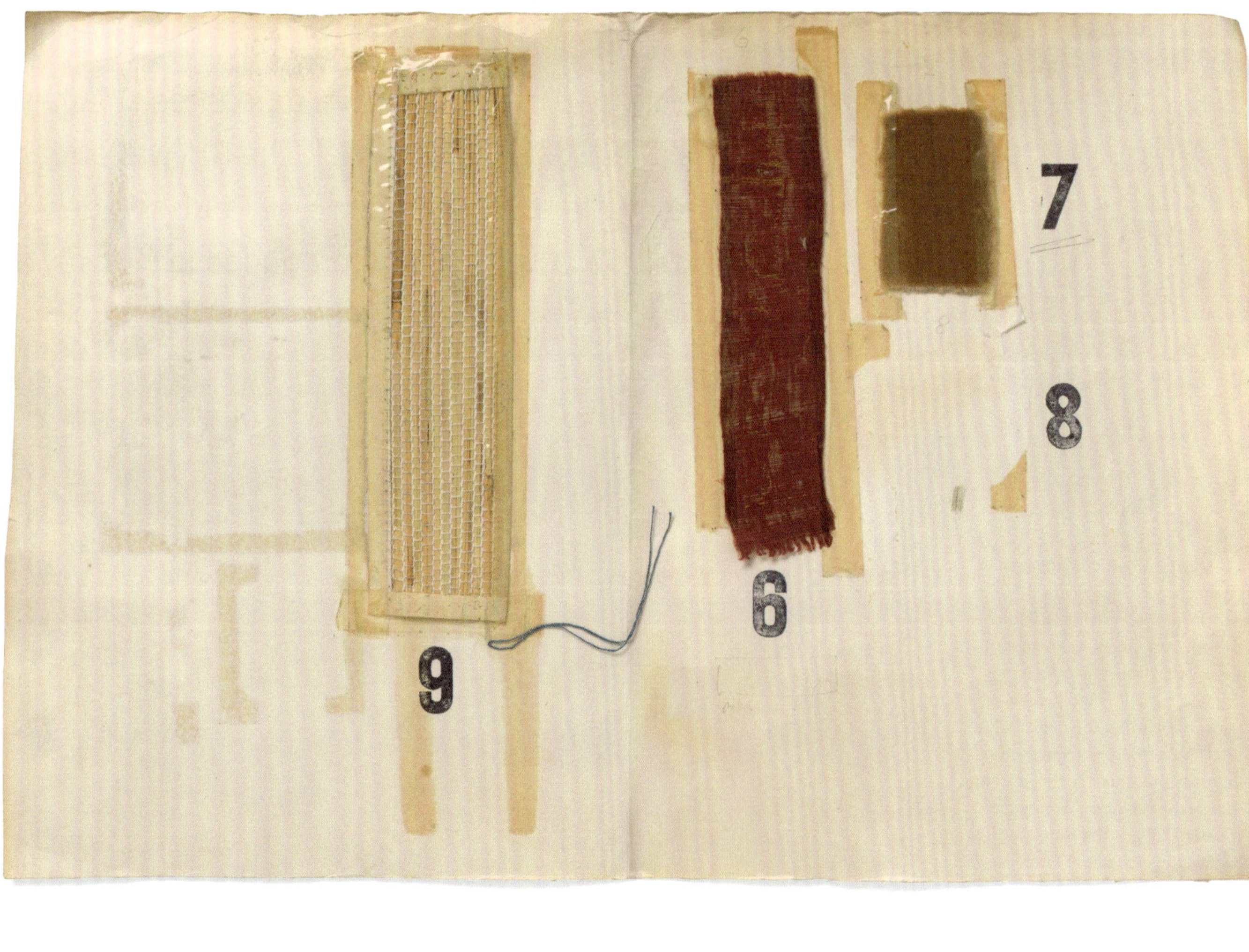
7
8
6
9

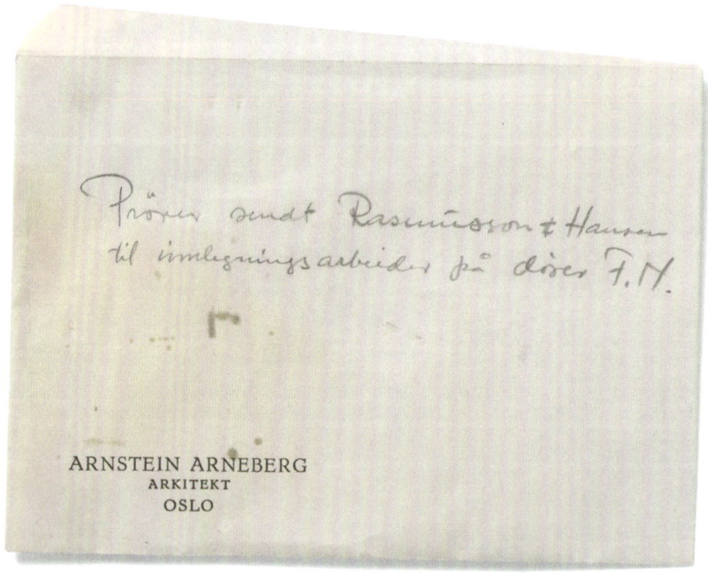

Left: In Arneberg's archive there is a large variety of material samples that were part of the work on the Security Council Chamber. Not all of them were used, but the samples illustrate the nature of the working process and communication process. On 23 November 1950, Arneberg sent a letter to New York in which he described the 9 numbered samples: 1 "veneer sample of olive ash for all the woodwork", 2 "Colour sample for wall fabric", 3 "Colour sample for carpet", 4 "Colour sample for advisory chairs", 5 "Colour sample for delegates chairs", 6 "Colour sample for observers chairs", 7–8 "Colour samples for press and public chairs", 9 "Straw tapestry".

Right: The doors of the chamber are decorated with walnut and metalwork. On the envelope it says: "Samples sent to Rasmusson & Hansen for the intarsia on the doors U.N.".

F. N.

54 INCH

WINDSOR CORDUROY

TEX-CELO Inc.
40 EAST 34th STREET
NEW YORK 16, N. Y.

Sales Agents for
Crompton Upholstery Corduroys

Ashes of Roses 1738 | Yellow 5633

Shell 1738 | Citron 1738

Pomegranite 5633 | Olive 5633

New Blue 248 | Green 5633

Strand Rose 117 | Periwinkle 5633

Steel 5633

QUALITY

Mauve 5633 | Sage 5633

Turquoise 3655 | Scarlet HW

Coral 5633 | Chestnut Brown

Brown 3655 | Globe Turquoise 117

Gotham Blue 117 | Plum 5631

Forest Green

Also Black

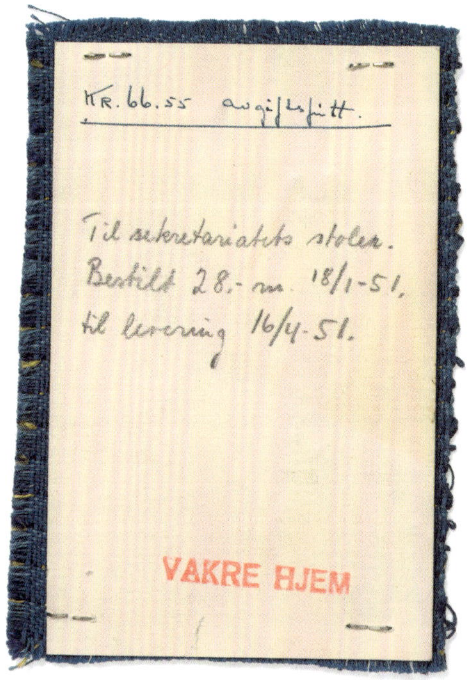

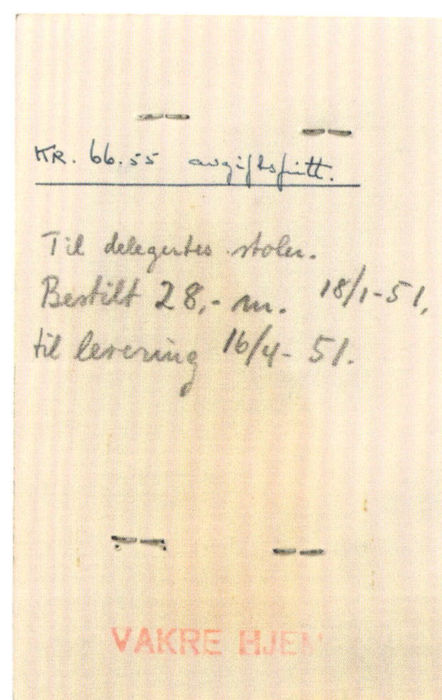

Left: Arneberg received a folder containing corduroy colour samples. In a letter to New York, he writes that New Blue no. 248 could be nicely suited for the advisory chairs. Shortly thereafter, in another letter, New York responds that they haven't been able to find a material that resembles sample no. 7 in Arneberg's collage. They therefore propose that he use the color Green 5633, which resembles sample no. 8 in Arneberg's collage, for the press and audience chairs. Arneberg agrees to this suggestion, and the green audience chairs in the chamber ended up being upholstered in this colour.

Current page: The blue material samples were ordered on 18 January 1951 by the manufacturer *Vakre hjem (Beautiful Homes)*. The sample at the top was for the Secretariat's chairs, while the sample at the bottom was for the delegates' chairs. The pattern was designed by Birgit Wessel.

Herr

Arkitekt Arnstein Arneberg!

For mitt arbeide med farveforslag og diverse alternativer til tekstiler i Sikkerhetsrådets sal beregner jeg følgende honorar:

Tegning av Veggstoff, i naturlig störelse	–	Kr. 800 =
Tegning av Gardinstoff i naturlig störelse med arbeidstegning på ruter	–	Kr. 800 =
Tegning av forskjellige förslag til möbelstoff hvorav 2 benyttes	–	Kr 200 =
Tilsammen		Kr. 1800 =

Tegningen vil fordyre Gardinstoffet med ca 9 – Kr pr. m.
" ——— " —. Veggstoffet med ca 2 35 Kr pr m.
Efter 90 – m. lengde for gardinstoffet og
840 – m " ——" veggstoffet.

Ærbödigst

Else Poulsson

Oslo 20/10 – 49.

50
5100

The textile artist

Of the leading figures who contributed to the design of the Security Council Chamber, it is clearly Else Poulsson (1909–2002) who has received the least attention. It was difficult for a textile artist and a woman to make a name for herself in a male-dominated art world.

But for Arneberg, Else Poulsson was a key collaborative partner. They had worked together on the design of the royal yacht and the Oslo City Hall. At the City Hall, Poulsson was responsible for most of the textiles. As for the Security Council Chamber, Arneberg would later emphasize Poulsson's role. In a 1952 issue of *Byggekunst*, for example, he noted that she had designed beautiful red curtains to cover the muted blue walls. She had also put together designs for all the materials. But because time turned out to be too short, her specially designed contributions never saw the light of day.

Even as a student Poulsson excelled, and at a young age she was taken on as head of the Norwegian Craft Association's textile studio. Under the inspiration of German textile artists, and in a manner reminiscent of the Bauhaus school, she modernized the association's patterns and revitalized its designs. Her decorative textiles, however, were more in line with the national romantic movement.

Letter from Else Poulsson to Arnberg: "Mr. Architect Arnstein Arneberg / For my work on colour suggestions and various alternatives to the textiles in the Security Council Chamber I have calculated the following fee: / Design of wall material in natural size – kr. 800.- / Design of curtain material in natural size with working design on squares – kr. 800.- / Design of various proposals for furniture materials, two of which were used – kr. 200.- / Total kr. 1800.- / Cost of curtain material will increase by ca. 9.- kr. pr. m / Cost of wall material will increase by ca. 2.35 kr. pr.m / [Calculations based on] 90 m length for curtain material and 340 m length for wall material. / Yours truly / Else Poulsson / Oslo 20/10–49"

Else Poulsson's textile was manufactured in royal blue with yellow pattern elements. The wheat, anchor, and hearts symbolize faith, hope, and love. It was woven by Joh. Pedersen AS and manufactured in rayon satin damask. In 2015, this original textile sample was presented as a gift to Cooper Hewitt, Smithsonian Design Museum in New York and is today part of its permanent collection.

E HYRDE GIR
SITT LIV FOR
FÅRENE

Sarah A. Lichtman

Uncovering Else Poulsson: Norwegian Textile Designer

The United Nations Security Council Chamber numbers among the most remarkable interiors of the twentieth century. Why then is Else Poulsson (1909–2002), the designer of the decorative blue and gold textiles that help define the chamber and give the space its distinctive character, so little known today? In his 1949 review of the Applied Art Association's annual exhibition in Oslo, designer and editor Arne Remlov named Else Poulsson one of the most notable textile designers in Norway.[1] Head textile designer for the Norwegian Home Craft Association (Den Norske Husflidsforening) from 1929 to 1954, Poulsson designed textiles for the Oslo City Hall (1950) and worked on a wide variety of other projects including textiles for churches, the Norwegian Royal Yacht (1947), and postwar model homes. Her designs were also shown at national and international exhibitions. The surprising lack of research on Poulsson's life and career likely results from a combination of factors such as her gender, the status of textiles within design history, and her work on behalf of an organization. The 2013 restoration and redesign of the United Nations Conference Building and its interiors, however, coupled with feminist historians' longstanding efforts to diversify the design pantheon, has prompted further research on the building's textiles and the women who designed them. Through a contextualizing overview of Poulsson's life and work, this essay recognizes, reevaluates, and recovers the designer of the United Nations Security Council Chamber textiles whose notable career spanned more than six decades.[2]

As a woman designer, Poulsson faced challenges distinct from those of those of her male counterparts. She acknowledged "discrimination against female artists" and although Poulsson was professionally trained and experienced, she recalls receiving very low pay – "teeny tiny wages", in her words – for her work. More than fifty years after the opening of the Oslo City Hall, Poulsson vividly recounted the insult women designers working on the building endured when the reception organizers instructed them to attend alone while they welcomed the wives of politicians and their male colleagues. Nevertheless, Poulsson possessed a strong sense of self, and work remained central to her identity. She continued to use her given name professionally after she married and, as is the case with many working women, noted the importance of having a supportive, and employed, spouse.[3]

In addition to her gender, Poulsson's profession as a textile designer and weaver may have accorded her a lesser status. As design historian Pat Kirkham explains, design is the "site of gendered work"

Else Poulsson in front of her altar rug "The good shepherd" as it was displayed at the Norske Husflidsforening's 1950 exhibition in Lillehammer. In her hand she holds a cloth that is intended to cover a baptismal font.

and in the hierarchy of the arts, textiles have been closely aligned with "women's work" and the sexual division of labor.[4] T'ai Smith, who has written on Bauhaus weavers, argues that textiles have traditionally been "denied a meaningful place in mainstream art history and art theory."[5] Likewise, Elissa Auther in her research on women and craft has enumerated reasons for the marginalization of fiber art. These include social hierarchies and gender bias; the devaluing of supposed "rote, nonintellectual craftwork"; and the association of fiber with the domestic sphere and decoration.[6] Embellished, traditional, and craft-based, Poulsson's designs, although possessing modern qualities, fall outside of a doctrinaire modernist aesthetic promoted in dominant design historical narratives.[7] Furthermore, although Poulsson was mentioned in period newspapers and design magazines, the majority of articles appeared in women's periodicals, sources sometimes overlooked by historians. Finally, Poulsson's decades long affiliation with the textile department of the Norwegian Home Craft Association (Den Norske Husflidsforening), may have also overshadowed her individual accomplishments as a designer.

Born in Tinn, Norway, Poulsson grew up in Rjukan, hailed from a creative and cultured family, and enjoyed access to a wide range of educational opportunities. Her father, Jens Jørgensen Poulsson, an engineer, was an accomplished amateur painter and her uncle, the architect Magnus Poulsson, co-designed the Oslo City Hall.[8] Poulsson credits her interest in textile design to her studies at the State Women's Industrial School, Oslo, (1925–1927), a school for women to learn textile arts, sewing, patternmaking, and weaving, as well as gain employment within the craft industry and teach craft.[9] Poulsson continued her education at the National College of Applied Art and Craft (SHKS) (1927–1929) and studied with painters Martin Enevold Thømt and Eivind Nielsen. She also studied weaving at Tavastehus School for Weaving, Finland, and Johanna Brunson's Weaving School in Stockholm and, in 1931, at the National College of Applied Art and Craft. In 1929, the Norwegian Home Craft Association (Den Norske Husflidsforening) hired Poulsson, then twenty-nine years old, to work in the textile studio and three years later appointed her director where she remained until 1954. Poulsson found inspiration in travel and the Norwegian Home Craft Association funded several extended trips to Western and Eastern Europe, as well as the Nordic countries, where she visited museums, small shops, and rural villages in search of folk culture. During her tenure, she reinvigorated the organization through the promotion and implementation of traditional and modern textile patterns and techniques.[10]

Norwegian traditions

Husflid, or "home crafts", occupies a central place in Norwegian culture. With the increasing rise of industrialization during the 19th century, husflid declined as chemical dyes and mechanization began to replace plant-based pigments and handmade goods. Reformers and cultural institutions sought to promote what they considered to be an important and endangered national pastime. Defined as making

A sweater pattern designed by Else Poulsson for the Norwegian Crafts Association. The pattern draws in part on traditional patterns, but has an amusing figurative touch in the form of a skier in Norway's national colours.

handicrafts at home during leisure time for use or sale by individuals or family members, husflid traditionally served as a needed economic supplement for rural Norwegians and was thought to be an appropriately moral activity. Theologian and Sociologist Eilert Sundt (1817–1875) helped foster interest in husflid. Sundt wrote *Domestic Industry in Norway* (1867) (*Husfliden i Norge*), a well-read text based on his research with rural Norwegian populations. Rather than promoting the artistic merits of husflid, Sundt, saw the economic and moral value of home craft and its use in fostering self and national sufficiency. Other reformers, and the educated class, on the other hand, would promote the aesthetic rather than utilitarian merits of husflid and by the 1890s it became a resource for a new, national style during a time when Norway sought independence from Sweden.[11]

Under the urging of the Norwegian government, the newly founded Oslo Museum of Decorative Arts (1886) promoted handicrafts through exhibitions and published books on Norwegian folk art, enacted school programs, and conducted courses on woodworking, basket making, weaving, and other skills. It also established various organizations promoting the rejuvenation of folk art and home craft, which, in 1891, merged into the Norwegian Home Craft Association (Den Norske Husflidsforening). Its mission: to promote and develop Norwegian handicrafts by preserving and reviving styles based on old craft traditions and fostering new ones.[12] As an organization, it stressed education and the dissemination of handicraft through far-ranging pedagogical and retail networks. At a time of increased Nationalism, reformers considered textiles (and their rejuvenation) to particularly embody Nordic culture.[13] Rooted in the local, the handmade, and Norway's real and imagined medieval and Viking past, husflid assumed national prominence.[14]

As director of textiles, Poulsson worked in many areas of production and helped to disseminate the ideals of the Norwegian Home Craft Association to a broad public. She encouraged experimentation and helped the Norwegian Home Craft Association develop a range of new patterns, weaving techniques, and innovative yarn combinations, along with new types of weaving tools and looms. The Association also housed a collection of textile samples ranging from embroideries to utility weavings and fulfilled special orders for banners, state flags, and furnishings for public buildings.[15] It also produced quality patterns and hand-knitted goods such as mittens, hats, and sweaters featuring geometric, floral, and figurative motifs. Writing on the occasion of the 75th anniversary of the Association, Eyvind Engelstad praised Poulsson and associated her skills with Ingeborg Arbo and Marie Karsten, distinguished textile designers and co-founders of the Applied Art Association. Both women designed for the Norwegian Home Craft Association and drew heavily on traditional peasant designs. Like Arbo and Karsten before her, Poulsson's inspiration for cushions, portieres, and table runners, among other crafted goods, used distinctly Norwegian motifs such as stylized floral ornamentation and bands of geometric patterns, as well as abstracted figures found in old patterns and even garments such as damask shawls.[16]

Poulsson designed a wide range of textiles and cited her ecclesiastical work as among her favourites. She credits her interest in the genre to a 1930 trip to the National Exhibition in Trondheim where the city had just celebrated the St. Olav jubilee. Poulsson designed altar cloths and chasubles, as well as antependia in an array of colours and fabrics such as hand-woven silk and linen, and silk damask.[17] In 1937 the woman's magazine *Urd* noted Poulsson's contribution to Norwegian ecclesiastical design, enumerating the many colourful hand-woven fabrics the Association produced in a variety of colours such as vermillion, green, yellow, red, white, and olive. Throughout her career, Poulsson also designed over a dozen ryas for churches around Oslo, and expressed pleasure and pride in the quality and individuality of her patterns and how they represented "modern Norwegian ecclesiastic art and craft" at its best.[18]

Although rooted in folk motifs, Poulsson's textiles could also display bold geometric patterns indicative of the modern design she had seen throughout Scandinavia and Europe during the 1920s and 1930s. In 1930, she visited the Stockholm Exhibition, a landmark event in the history of functionalist architecture and design and one that, according to her recollections, affected her deeply. She also travelled to Finland in 1934 and met the designer Marianne Strengell whom she recalled as "sweet and helpful" and whose work she considered "truly modern".[19] While there, Poulsson attended classes at the Wetterhoff School of Weaving for two weeks and experimented with a variety of weaving techniques. The following year she travelled to Vienna where she found inspiration in the bold graphic style of the Wiener Werkstätte. Linear, textural, and devoid of representation, Poulsson's geometric designs for the Home Craft Association during the 1930s and early 1940s display what design historian Kjetil Fallan has termed "moderate modernism". They mediated and domesticated modern aesthetics for a broad array of middle-class consumers.[20]

Poulsson took leave from the Norwegian Home Craft Association from 1944–1945 after Nazis seized control of the organization. In 1942, Poulsson had married Per Reetz Moe, a teacher opposed to the German Occupation. The Nazis interned Moe for several months and during his confinement, Poulsson wrote him letters expressing concern for his welfare, as well as a deep and sustaining commitment to her work.[21] In 1945 Poulsson published *Rutemønster*, a knitting and embroidery pattern book featuring figurative, floral, and geometric motifs for sweaters, mittens, and domestic items. Poulsson's book would have appealed to Norwegian women at the time, many of whom engaged in complex domestic textile projects. In a 1938 *Milwaukee Journal* article, the author set about to explain this Norwegian phenomenon to American readers:

> The American woman who thinks she is doing well to darn a few socks or turn an occasional hem would be amazed to know that in Norway today many a housewife thinks nothing of hand looming a rug or a set of curtains for her home....The needle has become a symbol here, not of drudgery, but of woman's opportunity for artistic expression.[22]

In *Rutemønster* Poulsson encouraged women to customize and embellish the published patterns. As with her work for the Association, Poulsson wanted her book to contribute to the development of traditional Norwegian handicraft and hoped it could also be used as a teaching aid for schools involved in craft education and pattern drawing.[23]

Throughout her career, Poulsson participated in many exhibitions, both in Norway and abroad, that helped to disseminate Norwegian textile design. Her designs appeared in the National Exhibitions in Bergen (1928) and Trondheim, (1930), and in 1937 Poulsson showed pieces with the Association at an Applied Arts Association exhibition mounted in anticipation of Norway's contribution to the International Paris Exposition. The newspaper *Dagbladet* singled out Poulsson's designs as demonstrating a "daring artistry and an assured taste" as well as a fine colour sense and graphic boldness. "Else Poulsson", the caption beneath her portrait read, is "triumphant at the exhibition."[24] Critic Helen Engelstad also praised the colourful fabrics, and noted it was the first time that Norway exhibited modern hand-woven textiles abroad. During the Exposition, the Norwegian pavilion organizers filled an entire room with vibrantly coloured, geometrically pattered carpets and textiles and the Applied Art Association awarded a gold medal to Poulsson for her contributions.[25]

Poulsson continued to cultivate her relationship with the Applied Art Association (*Foreningen Brukskunst*), a progressive organization founded in 1918 by art and design professionals dedicated to promoting theories of good taste to the public through competitions and exhibitions.[26] In 1948, she addressed the annual meeting alongside such well-known designers as Arne Korsmo and Bernt Hieberg; in 1954, she served on an Association model home exhibition committee.[27] Poulsson also exhibited in several annual exhibitions. Writing in *Bonytt* – an influential design periodical founded in 1941 and, since 1947, the Association's official journal – editor Arne Remlov frequently singled out the quality of Poulsson's designs.[28] In 1953, industrial designer Tias Eckhoff cited Poulsson's textiles for their impeccable balance of tradition and modernity.[29]

In the 1950s, Poulsson's work with the Norwegian Home Craft Association was included in two North American exhibitions showcasing her designs and situating them within an internationally influential network of tastemakers. In 1951 designer Torolf Prytz and entrepreneur and *Bonytt* co-founder Per Tannum opened *Norway Designs for Living* in Chicago. A sales exhibition designed by Arne Korsmo and Birger Dahl, it featured ninety Norwegian manufacturers and craftspeople. The show was located at the Chicago Merchandise Mart and coincided with the second in the series of the *Good Design* exhibitions sponsored by The Museum of Modern Art. Like *Good Design*, *Norway Designs for Living* featured high quality, well-made household goods and furnishings and offered "good taste" solutions for daily life.[30] From 1954 to 1957, Poulsson's textiles travelled to twenty-four North American locations with *Design in Scandinavia*, a museum exhibition featuring decorative arts and handicrafts from Denmark, Finland, Norway and Sweden that attracted over 660,000 visitors.[31]

The post-war years in Norway necessitated the skills of designers like Poulsson. In *Norwegian Textile Art* (1951), Helen Engelstad noted that "above all there are thousands of homes to be restocked, reconstructed and built, all needing textiles."[32] *Bonytt* and writings published by other organizations contributed ideas for rebuilding affordable and functional standard dwellings by constructing model homes and advising on their decoration. Poulsson contributed textiles for the so-called "Standard Houses".[33] Furnished by the Norwegian Home Craft Association, the "clear colours and beautiful patterns of furnishing material, curtains and carpets", declared Engelstad, were crucial in making the "modern interior".[34]

In collaboration with the Norwegian Home Craft Association, Poulsson also designed textiles for hotels, resorts, and ship interiors.[35] In 1947, she provided textiles for the *K/S Norge*, the Norwegian Royal Yacht, launched in 1947 in honour of the King's 75th birthday. Collaborating with the interior designer Finn Nilsson and architect Arnstein Arneberg, she designed furniture fabrics for lounge chairs and sofas in the smoking salon, designed by Rastad & Relling tegnekontor, and the textiles for the King's sleeping and living room. Employing royal motifs such as crowns and griffins, Poulsson created a blue, gold, and red palette of striped and patterned materials to create a regal and vibrant interior environment. Poulsson also collaborated with the Home Craft Association on the ship interiors for the *M/S Oslofjord*, a Norwegian America Line cruise ship built in 1949. The *Milwaukee Journal* described her brightly coloured, geometrically patterned hand-woven rugs installed in the Leif Eriksson hall "pure primitive Norwegian" yet "modern in spirit".[36]

The City Hall and Arneberg

Among Poulsson's most notable contribution to postwar textile design was her work on the interiors of Oslo's City Hall, one of Norway's most important twentieth-century buildings. Architects Arnstein Arneberg and Magnus Poulsson first presented plans for the City Hall as early as 1918 but did not complete the project until 1950.[37] Through a combination of private commissions and competitions, Poulsson designed curtains and furniture fabrics for various rooms as well as table linens and napkins. In the Munch Room, named in honour of the 1910 Edvard Munch painting *Life*, Poulsson designed rust-coloured curtains decorated with city walls and interlacing vines. For the chairs, she designed "Tree of Life", a blue and gold textile punctuated by white leaves whose natural forms echo the centrally located tree in Munch's painting.[38]

Poulsson's best-known design for the City Hall is found in the Council Chamber, a room prized by Magnus Poulsson and Else Poulsson alike, who referred to the space as "my room."[39] Poulsson designed the upholstery fabrics for the chairs, sofas, wall coverings, and curtains as well as the monumental tapestry of St. Hallvard, the patron saint of Oslo, for which she completed several watercolour versions before settling on the final design. Located above the mayor's podium, the tapestry is a complex and vibrant image in a revivalist style designed with a rust-coloured floral border and blue background. Poulsson depicts the haloed Hallvard seated on a double lion-headed throne as two angels hold a blue crest of three silver arrows above his head. The saint is surrounded by his attributes of arrows, a millstone, and a woman lying at his feet, as well as the attributes of wisdom, medicine, architecture

In 1947, Poulsson was creating textiles for the royal ship *K/S Norge* in collaboration with Arneberg and interior architect Finn Nilsson. With a blue, yellow, and red palette, and with themes such as crowns and griffins, Poulsson supplied textiles for the smoking salon's furniture and for the king's sleeping cabin and salon.

This blue material with a rather abstract natural motif is a draft of material for furniture for the Banquet Hall in the Oslo City Hall. The motif was called *Livets tre (Tree of Life)*, but was not used for this room. Instead, it ended up being used for the furniture in the Edvard Munch room in the City Hall.

and the seven virtues. Poulsson also depicts old and new Oslo and flanks Hallvard with images of the new City Hall and the Akershus Fortress as well as scenes of workers and civilians in modern dress below. A large and technically complex work, the tapestry spans 3.3 by 5.5 meters, weighs 14 kilos, and took two years to make. It resulted from a collaborative and experimental process between Poulsson and master weavers Else Halling and Sunniva Lønning.[40] Lønning used natural plant dyes based on those found in Norwegian Renaissance tapestries and spun the wool from the Spelsau sheep – a distinctive, Norwegian, breed. Commonly found in Norway before industrialization, the short-tailed Spelsau was in danger of disappearing when nineteenth-century mills began importing other breeds whose wool they preferred. Strong interest in Norwegian handicrafts kept the breed going as weavers, such as Poulsson and Halling, prized its long haired, silken, thread and considered Spelsau wool to be superior to softer wools from Cheviot or Merino sheep, whose strands more easily covered imperfections and flaws and whose soft consistency left little range for differentiation in the woven material.[41]

The Council Chamber and its designs received positive reviews. In a 1950 article published in Oslo-based architecture journal *Byggekunst* the Council Chambers' architects singled out Poulsson's contribution as exemplary. Other contemporaneous articles extolled the "richness of details" and "harmonious" and "exquisite" colours and fabric designs and commented on the large format of the tapestry and the demanding technique and superior artisanship required to complete it.[42]

A central work in Else Poulsson's career is her St. Hallvard tapestry that hangs in the City Council chamber in the Oslo City Hall, behind the Mayor's chair. The upper part of the wall behind it is covered in Biri wallpaper, while the lower part is covered in a red textile that was also designed by Poulsson.

Poulsson's successful collaboration with Arneberg on the Oslo City Hall made her a natural choice to design the textiles for the United Nations Security Council Chamber. Initially Poulsson designed red window curtains and furnishing fabrics for the chamber that were to be offset by pale blue walls. Delays in the design approval process, however, complicated their production and Poulsson designed textiles only for the north and south walls and window curtains in a matching steely blue fabric woven with golden yellow thread depicting anchors, growing wheat sheaves, and hearts. Reminiscent of the decorative patterns found in her knitting and textiles designs, the symbols allude to the ambitions of the United Nations and represent faith, hope, and charity. Poulsson's textiles cover the large rectangular chamber in a broad and dramatic expanse, the golden thread picking up the light colour of the inlaid ash doors. Her floor-length curtains frame the monumental windows overlooking the East River. The curtains, usually closed to reduce glare – serve to set off Per Krohg's centrally located mural.[43] Poulsson's textiles define the interior and bestow a level of consistency, beauty, and dignity to the space.

Making and mounting the textiles, however, did not prove to be easy. Owing to cost and time constraints, the Norwegian Home Craft Association refused the commission, and Arneberg instead retained the Norwegian textile manufacturer Joh. Petersen, the same company that had produced some of the fabrics for the Oslo City Hall, to machine manufacture the needed 560 square metres in rayon satin damask.[44] Difficulty with fire safety regulations, however, plagued its installation. Correspondence between Arneberg, Michael H. Harris, of the United Nations planning office, and Secretary-General Trygve Lie reveals that the textiles initially failed a 1951 fire test despite the strict New York City fire codes that necessitated treating the fabrics with caustic fire retardants which caused sustained damage. Even when eventually treated correctly, however, Arneberg expressed frustration over excessive shrinkage caused by the chemicals and complained that the flame retardants had distorted and ruined the material.[45]

Often compared with the Economic Council and Trustees Council Chambers designed by the Swedish architect Sven Markelius and the Danish designer Finn Juhl, the Security Council Chamber, and Poulsson's textile, garnered lukewarm reviews. While *Architectural Forum* commented on the material's richness and the room's surface ornamentation, the magazine condemned the poor durability of the materials and found fault with the "monotonous" repetitive motifs.[46] Helen Engelstad, writing in *Bonytt*, describes Poulsson's pattern as "balanced and decorative", but criticized the ersatz material for its inferior quality and labeled it "too shiny and shrinking". She concluded that the mechanically loomed, synthetic fabrics were devoid of the beauty and quality of real silk damask.[47] As design historians have argued, hand-woven textiles of natural fibers help to mitigate austere Modernist spaces, such as those found in the United Nations buildings. Writing in 1950, Engelstad explained how handwoven textiles were, "necessary in an age of standardization", and in her research, Alexa Griffith Winton has noted the significance of hand-woven fabrics in the United Nations interiors. Such fabrics possess a rich tactility and human touch that Poulsson's mechanically produced, synthetic textiles seemingly lacked.[48]

Poulsson's designs for the UN Security Council Chamber were her last international and major public commission. In 1954, after twenty-five years as its director of textiles, Poulsson left the Norwegian Home Craft Association and for the next four decades continued to work and exhibit independently. During her long life and career, Poulsson designed distinctive textiles for public and private use that reached broad and varied audiences.[49] The recent renovation of the United Nations and renewed interest in the design of the UN Security Council Chamber is a welcome opportunity to reconsider Else Poulsson whose work ranks among that of other significant twentieth-century designers and warrants further inclusion, recognition, and research.

ENGLISH
FRENCH
EXIT

CHINESE
EXIT

EXIT

ENGLISH
EXIT

BOLIVIA
UNITED STATES

DIRECTOR
SWEDEN
UNITED KINGDOM

RESIDENT
UNITED STATES
BOLIVIA
CHINA

OCCUPANCY
BY MORE THAN
693 PERSONS
IS DANGEROUS
AND UNLAWFUL.

Michael Adlerstein

The Capital Master Plan – Restoring the United Nations Headquarters

Page 146–147: Arneberg's door design was used in the entire chamber. The walnut intarsia and metal work were made by Norwegian artisans and the doors were transported by sea to New York.

Page 150–151: The three different types of metal railings in the chamber were produced in Norway after designs by Arneberg. The quality of their handwork drew an enthusiastic response.

Page 156–157: The end wall is covered in Biri wallpaper after a design by Klare Schee at Semb Farm. She made creative use of straw, of which she had access to an ample supply, and in 1928 she began weaving it. Biri Tapet still manufactures straw wallpaper.

In the late 1990s, after decades of managing and hosting thousands of meetings and hundreds of high-level debates in a world organization that had tripled its membership and expanded its work force tenfold, the UN realized that its own house was over-stressed, inefficient, under-funded for maintenance and needed serious attention. After the attack on the World Trade Center just a few miles away, it was clear that a complete renovation of the headquarters was needed. The facilities were no longer adequately functional nor even safe in our ever more dangerous world. Initial studies and budgets were prepared and discussed. Following several years of debate on the scope and funding arrangements, in 2006 and 2007, the UN General Assembly approved a full renovation of the Headquarters, which it termed the *Capital Master Plan* (CMP).

The CMP was the largest renovation work undertaken in the history of the United Nations. In 2007, Secretary-General Ban Ki-Moon, announced that controlling climate change was one of his highest priorities and that leadership begins at home. From the beginning of the CMP, he supported every effort of my team to reduce the UN's own carbon footprint and make the UN more environmentally responsible – to lead by example. This was a once-in-a-century opportunity to adopt modern technologies, reduce power and water consumption, and greatly diminish our carbon footprint. Of course, aside from climate change, the major drivers of the CMP required the upgrade of the headquarters by modernizing its infrastructure, restoring the character-defining historic spaces, respecting and applying the host city's building, safety, and fire codes, and making the Headquarters more secure, energy efficient, and accessible.

Several additional factors added to the complexity of the CMP. The host city and country required that we retain the functionality of the headquarters site for all major functions due to security and traffic concerns. Every year the United Nations brings together over 120 heads of state and royal leaders. NYC has learned how to protect them, while keeping the city functioning. This requires keeping the UN functions within the UN parcel of land on First Avenue. They could not risk establishing a new security zone in another location. We had to gut-renovate the entire compound while retaining its functionality as a venue for high-level ambassadors and heads of state from every country of the world. And while we had to protect those special visitors from the normal assortment of threats, we had to additionally protect them from the two to three thousand construction workers that were needed at the site each day. The CMP team, along with UN Security and Operations, NYC and US security agencies, managed this multi-phase, highly complex project, with rigid but constantly changing UN zones, construction zones, and buffer zones.

The original planning and design of the UN Headquarters was led by an international team of the world's finest architects and planners in 1948. The first secretary-general of the UN, the Norwegian Trygve Lie, established a sponsorship program for specific Member States to provide detailed designs of the interiors of several of the most prestigious rooms. The secretary-general invited those Member States to select their best designer to lead the furnishings and fit-out design of each special room. Norway selected one of their finest architects, Arnstein Arneberg, to design the Security Council Chamber. The success of his masterpiece has been obvious to delegates and visitors for decades.

A unique room

The renovation of the Security Council Chamber presented unique technological and preservation challenges. The major complexity was due to the particularities of the Security Council itself – its importance in the UN system, with the ironclad requirement that it must constantly be prepared to host a meeting of its membership, 24 hours a day, every day of the year, and the insistence of its membership that the traditions, procedures, and appearances of the chamber must be fully respected. The many stakeholders in the Security Council from the Secretariat as well as the Member States considered the chamber to be a sacred, if not sacrosanct, room. However, my team was mandated to bring the tired, old technology for heating, air conditioning, broadcast, speakers, cameras, fire protection, video conferencing, security systems, and many other infrastructure systems from the 1950s to the state of the art today. We faced the conflicting demands of our CMP mandates and the traditions and protocols of history in many sensitive areas of the UN as the design work progressed, but never as intensely as within the walls of the Security Council suite of rooms.

In the complex discussions about design that preceded the work, our closest cooperator was the Permanent Mission of Norway. We also needed to coordinate closely with the Security Council Affairs Division and the Member States of each current Security Council, each year, to coordinate our work with their expectations. The scheduling of actual work was also a challenge. In almost all areas of the UN there are busy time frames mixed in with quieter days, like weekends, and relatively light work times, such as international holidays and the August holiday season, where the most noisy and intrusive construction work could proceed. In the Security Council, all days are potentially, relatively equal. Of course, there are regularly scheduled meetings. But the membership responds to serious crises as soon as possible, sometimes in the middle of the night on any given day. So, we needed to constantly adapt our work to their schedule. For construction, that is inefficient and expensive.

During the renovation phase of the project, most of the functions of the Conference Building were relocated to a temporary building constructed on the North Lawn of the headquarters complex. But following consultations with the members of the council and the security services, it was decided to relocate the functions of the Security Council to the large Conference Room 4 directly underneath the General Assembly Hall, on the basement level of the General Assembly Building. The council expected that even though they would be in these temporary quarters for no longer than two years, the feeling and visual arrangements of the chamber would need to be precisely preserved. So, we removed the tables and seating from Conference Room 4, and over the course of a weekend, we relocated the original horseshoe-shaped council table into its temporary space. In our efforts to satisfy the request of the council that its work environment be faithful to its permanent home, we created a digital reproduction of the Per Krohg mural, large but actually only 50 per cent as large as the original, fashioned on vinyl, and had it installed in a dignified frame behind the table. We were informed later that the Security Council members were very thankful that their deliberations could continue, undisrupted, in their temporary home. I was informed by staff that some delegates were not aware that they were in a temporary location. After all, not all delegates pay attention to architecture.

It was important for the Security Council to have a good temporary meeting space while the chamber was being restored. The table was refurbished and then put to use in the temporary space. A digital copy of Krohg's painting was printed and mounted in the room, and the rest of the temporary decor also resembled the original decor as much as possible.

We needed to preserve the original fabrics and material surfaces, the art and the artistic architectural features, and most importantly, the character-defining details of the room, known throughout the world, while providing its present and future users with the modern upgrades which are essential to its use. The restoration of the Security Council Chamber became the most complex preservation challenge of the CMP.

Cooling represents the major energy consumption of the chamber. All meetings are captured by video cameras, which, like a TV studio, require high-level, heat-producing lighting. The air conditioning runs all year. In order to provide for a more efficient system, and to improve sustainability, we decided that forced air should enter from under the floor rather than from the ceiling. Under-the-floor air conditioning is now known to be far more efficient than overhead ductwork. The chilled air is heavy and stays low in the room, while the hot air rises above the cool air. We need only to cool the bottom two meters and exhaust the very hottest air from above. To accomplish this, we first needed to remove all the contents of the chamber and install an elevated floor for the underfloor ducts. In some places, we brought the air in from the ceiling of the conference rooms on the floor below. We installed this much more efficient underfloor cooling system with minimal changes to the visible appearance of the room. This necessitated the actual installation of supply vents in the floor, but we preserved the highly visible ductwork on the ceiling for exhaust.

In the 1950s asbestos was one of the magical new materials, like formica and aluminium. The fibres within the asbestos stone, when ground down, made plaster stronger than the horsehair previously used. The same asbestos plaster was wrapped around steam and air conditioning pipes to better insulate the heating and cooling lines, and added to walls, like stucco, to improve sound absorption. Of course, the world later learned how dangerous asbestos can be. One of the CMP goals was to remove all asbestos from the UN buildings. By the end of the project we had removed enough asbestos-contaminated material to cover a football field up to a level of fifteen feet high.

In the Security Council, we removed the asbestos-contaminated wall plaster from behind the beautiful fabric wall coverings which adorn the north and south walls of the chamber, while installing new electrical, copper and fibre optic circuits, plumbing, and electronic controls for the new robotic cameras and automated lighting.

Searching for the right materials

The fabric on the north and west walls was originally designed by the Norwegian textile artist Else Poulsson. The beautiful symbols used in the fabric – the heart, the anchor, and the wheat – provide a subtle reference to the faith, hope, and charity that must be brought to the room by its working occupants, the diplomats who comprise the membership of the council. We worked with the Norwegian government to source the replacement material from the same Norwegian firm that wove the original fabric.

The west rear wall of the gallery of the chamber is lined with a material called Biri wallpaper which is made from oat straw and thread, designed by textile artist Klare Schee in 1938. Prior to the renovation, an earlier version of this material had been installed incorrectly on the vertical and not horizontal axis. Our friends at the Permanent Mission of Norway helpfully advised us that the renovation would be the opportunity to correct this.

The two pairs of main doors into the chamber are masterpieces of cabinetwork, with multiple species of wood highlighted by stainless steel inlays of torches and swords. The wood doors of the two other chambers, the Trusteeship and ECO-SOC Chambers, are equally ornate. We sent out the six pairs of beautiful wood doors for restoration and for safekeeping during the renovation work. Our security requirements mandated that the large council rooms have electronically controlled security doors. We quickly determined that the electronics would cause unacceptable impacts on the current highly decorated doors. The wood doors could not be fitted out with the required electronic security hardware without major surgery. So, we rearranged the hall space outside each chamber to create alcoves that allowed for metal security doors that would seal the room when needed, but be carefully hidden from view when the room was in use.

The UN system of simultaneous interpretation was a significant improvement in the 1950s over the far more limited languages available at international gatherings before the UN. At the League of Nations and at other international gatherings before WWII, speeches were normally sequentially translated into just one or two additional languages. The technology of simultaneous translation made communication into the six standard UN languages very efficient; however, the demand on the staff interpreters was significant. Over the years it was realized that they needed larger booths with better climate and acoustical controls. Many design hours were invested in enlarging the size of the booths and their glass windows into the chamber to meet the new international standards, while respecting the pattern and rhythm of the historic wall coverings.

A view of the delegates' meeting table from the side windows. Here are the translators in action in 1973.

The details on how to manage the famous horseshoe table provided much debate and discussion. Early discussions with the Security Council Secretariat clarified that the actual original table must stay. This is consistent with the best of preservation policy, but it is also complicated when the room is never 'closed'. The existing table was scratched, dented, in need of a complete refinish (the legs had been hit by thousands of vacuum cleaners), and new technology required the insertion of new fibre optic wires, speaker systems, and other electronics. We eventually convinced the Secretariat staff, and council members agreed to allow us to provide a temporary white Formica table for a very limited time frame.

In all the other conference rooms at Headquarters, we upgraded all the desk signage to an electronic signage system in order to provide provide an enhanced ability to change seating assignments. However, the Security Council members insisted on retaining the traditional slide-in, slide-out nameplates. So the Security Council remains the only large conference room with the old-fashioned name plates (as well as old-fashioned leather framed desk blotters).

New old colours

For almost 70 years, smoking in the UN rooms was normal. Only in very recent years has it been banned by a GA resolution. Of course, smoking not only injures humans, but it is also very damaging to architectural and art surfaces. In the Security Council, there were ashtrays available at every seat and most photos of the chambers reflect the popularity of smoking. The restoration of the Per Krohg mural on the wall behind the horseshoe table was undertaken by a specialized firm which diligently worked to remove the decades of nicotine and grime from the canvas. When it was reinstalled, the mural glowed and presented a dignified backdrop to the room. Over the years, users of the room had forgotten that the bottom of the painting depicted dark areas with people hiding in caves, victims of wars. They had slowly disappeared into the nicotine haze that was dense near the height of the council table. It was an amazing surprise to everyone, including myself, when the subtle light and colours of the painting were restored and the victims of wars were revealed.

The delegates' and advisors' chairs are shaped by the original wood frames, refitted with Naugahyde fabric in the exact shade of the original installation. Like aluminium and Formica, Naugahyde was the post-war modern material representing progress, rather than old-fashioned leather, which was out of style in the modern era.

One significant change was requested by the Security Council itself. Following consultations with members of the Council and DPA's Security Council Affairs Division, it was agreed that the staff seating in the well in the centre of the Security Council table was a distraction from their discussions, and should be moved. For years the Ambassadors were concerned that the discussions of the staff of "precis" writers were a distraction from the serious issues of the Council. Now there was a budget that could resolve the issue. We proposed relocating those seats to the side of the room. This is the only substantial change to the appearance of the room.

Per Krohg's painting was conserved during the major renovation project. After countless meetings and events, and exposure to an unimaginable amount of cigarette smoke, the surface of the painting was grimy. The clear, pure colours again became visible after the conservation. Here we can see the painting upon its re-hanging in 2013.

In this age of technology and teleconferencing, council members frequently receive briefings or testimony from individuals who are not present in the room. Instead of installing a large video screen like we did in the General Assembly Hall, as well as the Trusteeship and ECOSOC chambers, the council members wanted the technology to be subtle and less visible. In addition, because of the horseshoe-shaped table, the participants are facing every direction, and at least four screens would be necessary. We ended up providing individual iPads for the members and small screens which can be lowered from the ceiling for other guests in the chamber. In the process of eliminating the ashtrays, which were built into the conference room tables, we converted the locations to computer charging outlets.

The renovation of the Security Council is considered one of the gems of the CMP. This room has been called the most important room in the history of the modern world. The room is powerful, quiet, and awe-inspiring, as it must have appeared in 1952, and portrays the dignity and discipline worthy of the body that meets there throughout the year. I am very proud of the results of the CMP, but I am particularly pleased with the fully restored Security Council Chamber.

Restoration

In the early 2000s, after more than 50 years of wear and tear, it was recognized that the UN's buildings were in serious need of renovation. Improvements in security and technical upgrades were necessary. The UN's headquarters needed to be made more environmentally friendly, in part through a replacement of the entire air-conditioning system. In addition, the entire complex had to undergo asbestos removal. Approval was given, therefore, for a comprehensive renovation project, the Capital Master Plan.

Major upgrades and changes were implemented, but at the same time it was important to preserve the buildings' historic elements. What made the Security Council Chamber stand out from the rest of the UN complex was that the room had been preserved so well. Some maintenance and alternations had taken place since 1952, but for the most part the chamber still bore witness to the Arneberg era. Nonetheless, asbestos needed to be removed from all of the chamber's ceilings, floors, and walls. Therefore the interior was stripped down to the concrete, and then, between 2008 and 2013, was gradually and meticulously put back together so that it would be as close as possible to an exact copy of the chamber as it looked in 1952.

Page 168, 170–172: The Security Council Chamber during the renovation in 2011.

Linda Veiby

Norway's Role in the Restoration of the Security Council Chamber

In 2010, the Norwegian Consulate General in New York contacted Norway's Ministry of the Environment and requested professional help in connection with the restoration of the Security Council Chamber. The ministry referred the consulate to the Norwegian Directorate for Cultural Heritage, which became the UN delegation's advisor concerning those parts of the restoration that had to do with Norwegian materials and objects.[1] In a letter to the Norwegian consulate about the restoration process, the ministry wrote to the Consulate General: "We hope that further professional collaboration will help maintain the qualities that make the room unique and Norwegian."[2]

Such a restoration is rarely pure – in part because those who carry it out usually do not have a complete picture of what the object of restoration originally looked like. Generally speaking, the restoration process is characterized by many uncertainties and choices that occur in the field of tension between historical knowledge and the demands of the day. At the outset of a restoration, certain fundamental questions must be asked: What is important here, and what history needs to be told?

With the exception of persons employed by the Foreign Ministry, and politicians on business trips to New York, Norwegians tend not to be aware that one of the world's most important rooms was designed by a Norwegian architect and that most of the interior was produced in Norway. The Security Council Chamber never became an important destination for Norwegian architects, and in the context of Norwegian architecture, the chamber represented, in many ways, architectural ideals that were on their way to becoming passé. Nor was the interior discussed in connection with the 1950s' American enthusiasm for 'Scandinavian design'.

The restoration of the UN building, however, took place during a period when the value of postwar modernism, in terms of both aesthetics and cultural history, was of renewed interest.[3] The secondhand market for interior pieces from the 1950s and 1960s, for example, reached record prices both nationally and internationally. In Norway, the new interest in postwar architecture became particularly visible as a result of large-scale conservation projects.[4] At the same time, "the architecture of modernism" was discussed – and treated as a problem area – at several professional conferences on architectural preservation, some of them held in Norway and some abroad.[5] One of the major themes in the field of cultural heritage was how best to ensure the safeguarding of modern architecture's value as a part of our cultural heritage.

Naturally enough, when it became known that the UN complex was going to be restored, the news stirred interest. What method would be used? Would care be taken to preserve its aesthetic and the materials? Would emphasis be placed on the value of the experience or on authenticity? At bodies that focus on the preservation of modern architecture, such as ICOMOS and DOCOMOMO, opinions were divided. However, at the Directorate, we saw that there was little chance of saving the original, outdated building parts. For that reason, the value of the experience was given priority. Undoubtedly, the UN's restoration would send a strong signal as to both the current evaluation of the merits of postwar architecture and the choice of preferred method.

Gift to the UN

The Security Council Chamber is perhaps more interesting because of its political significance than as a groundbreaking work of architecture. From the perspective of Norwegian politics, the room is important as the expression of our nation's desire to contribute to the UN. From an international perspective, the space helps contribute to the national and cultural diversity that make the UN complex stand out as a place where, not only in content but also in form, the nations of the world unite into a single whole.

From a Norwegian perspective, the chamber is also interesting because it is one of the best preserved examples of a public room from the 1950s. With its symbolically heavy interior contained in a modernistic shell, the space communicates, in the clearest fashion, an era of upheaval in architecture, illustrating the way in which modernism and traditionalism lived side by side during that period.[6]

The fact that the space has maintained its original appearance to such a considerable degree underscores its significance and lends authority and a historical framework to the decisions that are made within it. At the same time, the space's immutability can be seen as bearing witness to a fear of reforms and of measures that might weaken the council's function.

The chamber has often been described as Norway's gift to the UN. This is true, but with an asterisk. Arnstein Arneberg was formally offered the job as the architect of the UN and would be paid through the UN system.[7] The costs of the interior were also to be covered by the UN, but there was no room in the budget to pay for works of art that might be placed in the room. At a meeting with the chief architect, Wallace K. Harrison, it became clear that if Arneberg had the opportunity to implement his ideas for the room, the Norwegian government would have to contribute financially. Arneberg described his vision to Secretary-General Trygve Lie, who did not comment on the interior design as such, but who made it clear that he wanted the Norwegian chamber to stand out from the other two. It was important to Lie that the room be the first to be completed, and that it be viewed as the most beautiful of the three (see also p. 88).

In his letters to Lie, as well as in exchanges with Norwegian politicians, Arneberg stressed the ways in which his design would help make the chamber a worthy space that would, indeed, stand out. "As a salute to our country, a Norwegian architect has been entrusted with designing the interior of the Security Council Chamber."[8] "If this room is going to be able to assert itself in comparison with Sweden, then further artistic decoration is necessary."[9] In line with this ambition, an application was submitted for a Norwegian government grant to pay for the artistic embellishment of the room; later, a second application was made for additional financing to cover marble, sculpture, and textiles, because the American budgets were insufficient to fully cover the costs of the materials Arneberg insisted on.[10]

Aside from these contributions, the UN paid for everything. The reason why the manufacturing took place in Norway was, above all, that the American dollar was strong in relation to the Norwegian kroner, so that the cost was halved, even when the price of transatlantic transport was included.[11] In discussions with Norwegian politicians, Arneberg emphasized that manufacturing the materials in Norway was important because it would give Norwegian design and Norwegian industry international visibility.

It is clear that Norwegian manufacturers considered a commission by the UN highly attractive. When Arneberg made inquiries, the interest was great. The producer of the Biri wallpapers was so eager to make an artistic contribution to the UN that she sent her business card to Arneberg not once but twice.[12] Arneberg already knew most of the manufacturers; indeed, his professional network and the considerable size of his architectural firm may have been one of the reasons why Lie had chosen him. Picking Arneberg meant playing it safe.

When the big restoration of the chamber began in 2011, we wanted the room to emerge from the process as a faithful tribute to the many strands of its history – to the legacy of Lie and Arneberg, to Norwegian industrial traditions, and, not least, to the almost sixty years of earthshaking world events that had taken place within its walls.

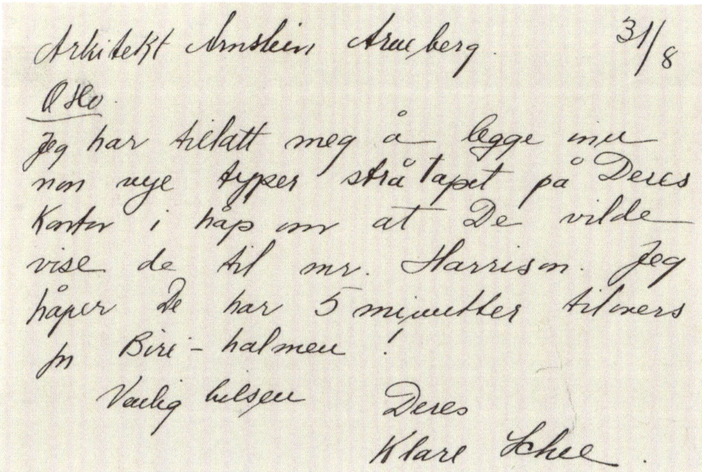
Arkitekt Arnstein Arneberg. 31/8
Oslo.
Jeg har tillatt meg å legge inn noen nye typer stråtapet på Deres kontor i håp om at De vilde vise de til mr. Harrison. Jeg håper De har 5 minutter tilovers for Biri-halmen!
Vennlig hilsen
Deres
Klare Schee.

Card from Klare Schee to Arnestein Arneberg: "Architect Arnstein Arneberg, / 31/8 Oslo / I have taken the liberty of leaving some new types of straw wallpaper in your office in the hope that you will show them to Mr. Harrison. I hope you have 5 minutes to spare for the Biri straw! / Yours cordially, / Klare Schee."

A joint transatlantic project

Although Arneberg was a seasoned architect, he found working on the Security Council Chamber challenging. When we read his communications with the UN, we can see that there was no shortage of misunderstandings and delays in the transatlantic dialogue. In his archives, there are telegrams and airmail letters, but much of the information and many of the materials were sent by ship. This long-distance relationship with the UN must have been demanding. Arneberg knew little about how far the building and planning process had advanced. He had to present his subcontractors with deadlines set by the UN, he encountered constant delays, he experienced budgetary uncertainties, and he was continually faced with the question of whether the things he proposed would in fact be approved by the UN. On 7 June 1950, he wrote to Harrison: "Under those circumstances I think it must be considered whether it is any idea at all to use a foreign architect for this work."[13]

Communication was also a challenge during the restoration process, even though we had technology on our side. Those of us in Norway did not have a "man in New York" who would be there to follow the project from day to day. Our role was to assist the UN as needed, and to ensure that questions related to Norwegian interests be raised. We had very little in the way of an overview of how the project was moving along and of what was being discussed when. We had no authority to request reports, but we did discover that our UN partners were eager to engage us in useful dialogue and were concerned that Norwegian interests be attended to.

Early on in the project, the UN Capital Master Plan (CMP)[14] made it clear that the space would retain its original form and feel. In other words, workers would dismantle, copy when necessary, and reassemble. Even in the most careful restoration projects, to be sure, new technical requirements or regulations that have consequences for the manner in which the project can proceed always turn up.[15] Since the Directorate was not exceedingly familiar with American requirements or regulations of this kind, it was hard to know what questions to ask. In our dialogue, we needed to draw on our experience in Norway to ask those questions that we felt needed to be cleared up. Would new demands for ventilation have consequences for the room's surfaces? Would there be new security needs that would impact the furnishings or something else? We received confirmation that no changes would be made at the expense of the surfaces or the furnishings, but we had no knowledge as to which new technical or security measures had been introduced. At a setting such as the UN, with all the security measures that such a place demands, it is natural that such information is not shared.

At the Directorate, our concern was initially focused on the conservation of Per Krohg's painting. How would it be safeguarded during the conservation process? We were also aware that it had sustained some damage and asked that it be repaired. In our judgement, the UN took these concerns very seriously, and the Directorate and the Ministry of the Environment received exhaustive documentation about the repair work.

We soon developed great confidence in CMP and the project heads, who were obviously approaching the process with great seriousness. The UN archives were scrutinized, and both American and Norwegian sources gradually made it clear that the room's surfaces had been changed several times over the years. If we wanted to return the room to the way it looked in 1952, then, we could not simply dismantle and copy the existing interior: extensive research had to be done to find out, in detail, how the room had looked in the beginning. What were we sure of, and what were we not?

Antiquarian judgements

When Arneberg planned the room, he was preoccupied with dignity. He had great respect for the task that had been vouchsafed to him, and he selected materials and symbols that would convey the seriousness of the Security Council's mandate. Of the original interior, the intarsia doors and the large marble panels were unchanged when our restoration began, although they had, to be sure, undergone a good deal of wear and tear. All the other original surfaces had been replaced at

The Security Council Chamber stripped naked. During the restoration, the circle in the middle was raised to be level with the rest of the floor.

some point.[16] The original textile wallpaper had been replaced two times, with the latest version being made of wool.[17] We did not know how the colours and materials had been selected, but we knew that the most recent commission had also been given to Norway, and that Statsbygg, the Norwegian government's key property manager, developer, and advisor, had been responsible for ordering the materials.

It became clear early on that it would not be possible to preserve the wool wallpaper after the room underwent treatment for asbestos.[18] In June 2011, members of the Directorate and the Ministry of the Environment travelled to New York to observe the dismantling of the room. What we encountered was a conference hall from which almost everything had been removed. All of the furniture was gone. The carpets had been taken out so that the raw concrete floor was visible. The textile had been taken down from the walls, but the old perforated surfaces, covered with an older layer of textile, were still up. Scaffolds had been erected for the initial work on the ceiling.

On one of the doors, we saw, under a piece of textile, a flap of another textile that we had not seen before. It was just a little flap, but was even brighter and more colourful than the textile sample that we had thought, until then, was the original. Which was the real original? The restoration architects at the UN went back to the archive and received confirmation that, yes, that little piece we had just discovered must be the original. Why was there no information about the textile having been changed at some earlier point? Was the piece we had found perhaps a sample that had never actually been used? Or had something gone wrong during the production phase that had made it necessary to produce the textile anew?

Back home in Norway, we had to return to the sources. Doing so, we discovered that there had been a problem with the flameproofing treatment of the textile when it was put up in 1952. Was this the reason why it had been replaced? We still don't know. What is certain is that the walls were originally covered in rayon, a wood-fibre material. Apparently, it had been delivered by Borregaard in Halden and woven at a weavery in Groruddalen on order from the Bryn textile factory. The rayon textile that we found was both stronger in colour and clearer in design than the 1997 wool version. Not least, it looked fresher than the smoke-damaged and filthy rayon textile that had been taken down during the previous restoration and that bore witness to a long period during which ashtrays had been important elements of the room's furnishings. If the colour selection in 1997 was the result of a misinterpretation based on the appearance, at that time, of the smoke-damaged wallpaper, we do not know. It may also have been the result of an aesthetic evaluation. Perhaps the restorers had simply not wanted to duplicate the original colours? We have not found a trace of an answer to this question, either in Statsbygg's or the UN's archives. In 2011, we had to ask ourselves whether we dared to return the room to its original colours. What would the reaction be?

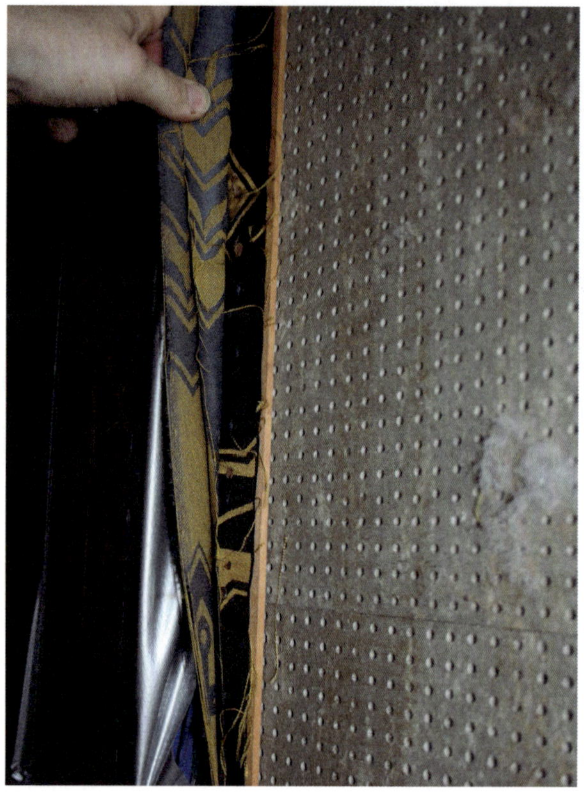

When the 1997 wool wallpaper was removed, two earlier layers of rayon wallpaper came into view. The original layer underneath the others was very colourful and shiny. In the picture we can also see the asbestos boards that were removed during the renovation.

Reconstructing colours

At first, the Norwegian Directorate for Cultural Heritage felt that when one carries out a comprehensive restoration, an effort should be made to recreate the original colours. In the great majority of projects in which antiquarian authorities are involved, surfaces are re-created based on the original colours, if they can be found. There are exceptions, however. When the modernistic restaurant at Ekeberg in Oslo was reopened, the original colours had been restored. Motivated by the widespread notion of modernism as a white style, the restorers chose to paint the outside walls white instead of recreating the original brown exterior. Prior to the UN restoration, we had had a discussion of the colouration of the exteriors of the Royal Palace in Oslo and of Stiftsgården, the royal residence in Trondheim. Both were Norwegian façades with a strong national symbolic value that had been reinforced over the years by countless images on television. On these buildings, the original colours were not re-created. Similar considerations became important in the work of returning the Security Council Chamber to its original 1952 appearance. From the UN's perspective, it was important to take the users of the room into account. Like the Royal Palace in Oslo, this is a place that has been well documented in the media for many decades, and that has established a strong politico-symbolic value. It is worth recalling, however, that in the decade of the 2010s there is a great fondness for grey and beige tones, and that antiquarian authorities often encounter scepticism and unwillingness on the part of clients when confronted with strong hues that do not fit into the colour schemes of their homes. The original wallpapers in the Security Council Chamber represented just such an unusual use of colour.

This is a sample of Birgit Wessel's textile that was used for the delegates' chairs. When Arneberg received the order from New York, they asked for 22 chairs. They were to be comfortable and upholstered and should have armrests. As for the Secretariat chairs that would surround the table in the middle of the room, they were to be upholstered but simpler in design and without armrests.

Still, since everything was going to be taken down, we believed that restoring the colours and materials of the 1950s would be the strongest way of capturing the UN's beginnings and the space's history. We do not know very much about how Arneberg came to choose the colours he did, but it is clear that his intention was to employ a diversity of hues – a palette featuring blue and yellow textile wallpapers, red curtains, blue chairs for delegates and secretaries, red fibrolite chairs for observers, and the grey-green corduroy coverings for the chairs for the public and press. On the back wall, there was to be a straw carpet and panel, and a painting framed in marble, while the ceiling was to be plastered in white.[19] Although for budgetary reasons, Arneberg never got his red curtains,[20] his use of colour tells of a period that must have had another meaning for the term holistic than we do today. We would have liked to have more knowledge about Arneberg's thoughts about colours and their role in creating a room.

Colours are certainly an important part of the chamber's character, and Arneberg himself emphasized that because "the room's very proportions are fixed, as is the height of the ceiling, so the work must depend to a great extent on the material – the impact and colours."[21] The use of colour was thus one of the most important elements of the original architecture. Fortunately, CMP supported our decision in this regard.

Production challenges

To produce a new rayon carpet that was as similar as possible to the original, and to produce it in Norway, would be demanding. After the Second World War, Norway imposed an import ban, and as a result, the national textile industry was large and flourishing.[22] In the 2010s, however, the situation was quite different. After the lifting of the import ban, the Norwegian textile industry had collapsed, and it was therefore very difficult to find suppliers that could take on the job of weaving a rayon textile. Not only are there few manufacturers of such materials in Norway, but the manufacturers that do exist have machinery suited to the production of textiles that are not the kind we needed. Thread count was a special problem. In addition, Norwegian weavery today is highly specialized, with a focus on wool and linen.

What we needed was someone who could manufacture rayon with a silky surface, shiny and dense, with a thread count in the warp of 44 threads per centimetre and a thread count in the weft of 30 threads per centimetre.[23] However, the closest a Norwegian manufacturer could come to this was a warp thread count of 30 and a weft thread count of 27/28.[24] If we wanted a higher thread count, we would have to go to another country. We decided that we would get good enough results with the highest thread count available in Norway, and that the slightly low thread count was more than made up for by the fact that we would, indeed, be able to retain the wallpaper's Norwegian identity.

Ordering the wallpaper – which was paid for by Foreign Ministry and arranged in accordance with the Directorate's advice – became a project in itself.[25] KRIVI Vev was chosen to supply the 840 square metres of textile. The material would be dyed while the fibres were liquid, and this process would be carried out by the subcontractors in Austria; the weaving itself would be performed at KRIVI's factories in Nordmøre, Norway, with the weavers following designs supplied by CMP. The Directorate monitored KRIVI's production to ensure that both the colours and the patterns came as close as possible to the original textile. The Directorate also wanted the individual pieces of wallpaper to be produced in the original width; but since, as it turned out, the textile had to be manufactured in a significantly larger width, and since this would not cause any problems when papering the walls, it was decided, for reasons having to do with resources, to go with the larger width.

As for the other textiles in the room, CMP ordered copies of them. CMP also ordered copies of the straw wallpaper that hangs on the back wall behind the press and audience area. The straw wallpaper is one of the most traditional of Norwegian industrial products for room interiors. The product was introduced in 1938 by Klare Schee, who first turned straw into wallpaper in the barn at Semb, his family farm. The straw must be cleaned by hand so that it has the proper lustre, and must then be sorted according to colour before it can be woven together. CMP contacted Biri, which is the only manufacturer of such wallpapers in Norway. In the order from CMP, it was stated that the wallpaper would be mounted horizontally. This turned out to be ambiguous, because if the wallpaper were to be mounted vertically, then the straw would lie horizontally. Which did we want? A vertical mounting

The newly woven wallpaper after the original designs were put back up in 2013. To sew the material together and get the pattern to flow nicely across the entire wall was a challenge, as it had been in 1952.

would mean changes in production and higher costs. On both sides of the Atlantic, we felt strongly that the results should be in keeping with Arneberg's original. In our first archival searches, we were unable to find pictures or descriptions that would enable us to answer this question. How to figure it out? One place to look for an answer might be the City Hall chamber in Oslo, which was designed by Arneberg and Magnus Poulsson at the same time that Arneberg was working with the UN (see also pp. 71, 142–143). The chamber has both textile wallpaper and straw wallpaper; but newer wallpapers have also been put up here, and it was unclear whether the original orientation of the wallpaper here had resembled that of wallpaper used in the Security Council Chamber. There are few pictures of the Security Council Chamber that show the public area, and it was therefore difficult to dig up documentation regarding the way in which the wallpaper had originally been oriented. After a good deal of searching, however, Jon Buono, CMP's gifted restoration architect, found a photo that shows the original 1952 mounting, and this led us to a final decision to go with horizontal straw.[26]

Cultural preservation is controlled change

The process of restoring the Security Council Chamber exposes some of the chronic dilemmas in the field of cultural heritage. When you want to tell a story, you always run the risk of misinterpretation. Posterity will tell whether those of us who worked on this project failed or succeeded. The restoration has involved replacing most of the surfaces, and the space, for that reason, is of diminished historical interest. On the other hand, all of the significant elements of the room have been maintained in the reconstruction – which has been carried out, moreover, with as much precision as possible. As a result, the Security Council Chamber, as it is experienced today, is still one of the rooms in the UN complex where one can most clearly feel the vibe of the 1950s.

When Secretary-General Ban Ki-moon reopened the chamber in April 2013, he said, "Standing here now, it is hard to imagine that at one point during the construction, this room had been stripped of everything. Only the bare concrete walls, the floor slab and the ceiling remained. Now it is whole again, and then some. We are back amidst the beauty and majesty of the Security Council Chamber. (...) If my predecessor Trygve Lie of Norway were with us today, I am sure he would feel quite at home in this renovated Security Council Chamber. Perhaps the only thing he would miss would be the ashtrays!"[27]

The room in use

When the Security Council Chamber was first put to use in the spring of 1952, the Council's president told its members that, after several years during which it had pitched its tents in many places around the world, the wandering was finally over. Prior to the opening of the chamber, the Security Council had held 573 meetings in temporary facilities – among them Paris, London, and various locations in New York. When the Council at last settled down into Arneberg's space, it was a moment of considerable significance.

Since then, the Security Council Chamber has been at the centre of world events on a great many occasions. All of the postwar era's most important world leaders have turned up here at one time or another. The Cuban Missile Crisis, the discussions of weapons of mass destruction in Iraq, and the more recent negotiations about the war in Syria are just a few examples of instances when the meetings in this room have played a crucial historical role. As the home of a body that requires an assembly hall that is available 24 hours a day, 365 days a year, the Security Council Chamber possesses a very special significance.

In 1964, Ernesto (Che) Guevara addressed the General Assembly in an effort to forestall the possibility of a US attack on Cuba. On 14 December he was photographed smoking, with Else Poulsson's wallpaper in the background, while listening to a speech by the American Ambassador to the UN, Adlai Stevenson. During Che's visit, Cuban exiles fired a bazooka toward the UN from the other side of the East River. Fortunately they failed to strike the headquarters.

UNDER SECRE
PRESIDENT
SECRETARY GENERAL

UNITED ARAB REPUBLIC
UNITED KINGDOM
UNITED STATES
VENE

SECRETARY-GENERAL
PRESIDENT
UNITED STATES

Loraine Sievers

The Security Council Chamber through the Eyes of Those Who Meet There

The Security Council held its first meeting in its official chamber on 4 April 1952. This was the council's 574th meeting, which means that for six years, since January 1946, the council had held 573 meetings in other, temporary spaces.

The excitement and awe in the Security Council Chamber at that inaugural meeting is tangible to those reading the verbatim record of the proceedings. Before taking up the political agenda for that afternoon, the council president for the month, Ahmed Shah Bokhari of Pakistan, invited his fellow council members to pause for a moment in order to "take note of our new surroundings" and mark the event of the first ever meeting in the chamber "in a manner befitting the occasion."

The council president pointed out that from 1946 to 1952, while awaiting the completion of its permanent home, the Security Council had "journeyed a great deal and pitched its tents in many places". Over that period, the council had held meetings in London, Paris, and several different locations in the New York City area. The president went on to say, "These wanderings are now over, or at least the Security Council has a permanent home from which to venture forth should duty call."[1] Thanking the government and people of Norway, and specifically the architect Arnstein Arneberg, the president affirmed that in the future, some of the inspiration of the Security Council

> will have its origin in the artists and craftsmen of Norway who were in their turn inspired by their belief in the noble spirit in which the Charter of the United Nations was conceived and inscribed. (...) Here we shall henceforth pursue the work which a war-weary and peace-hungry world, nervous yet hopeful, expects of us.

The president then invited Ambassador Arne Sunde of Norway to take the floor. Sunde affirmed that his government "felt deeply honoured by having been given the opportunity to assist in the setting up of the permanent meeting place for this august body, which plays such a vital part in the work of the United Nations to secure world peace." He added that Norway's contribution had been "inspired by the hopes which it entertains towards the fulfilment of the high purposes of the Security Council."

The representative of the United States, which had donated the land, then paid tribute to the process by which the location had been agreed on and a unanimous architectural plan achieved. After praising

Page 184–185: The Cold War and the Cuban Missle Crisis led to another important meeting in the chamber. Millions of American TV viewers sat glued to their TV screens in October 1962 when Adlai Stevenson presented his posters showing the upgrading of Cuban weapons. Stevenson said he had one simple question for his Soviet colleague: "Do you, Ambassador Zorin, deny that the U.S.S.R. has placed, and is placing, medium- and intermediate-range missiles and sites in Cuba? Yes or no – don't wait for the translation – yes or no?"

Page 186: US President George H.W. Bush (third from below) addresses the Security Council on 31 January 1992. In the upper left corner of the picture we can see Russian President Boris Yeltsin listening at the table. To his left sits Secretary-General Boutros Boutros-Ghali, while UK Prime Minister John Major takes notes.

the "magnificent design and the many appointments of this Chamber", Ambassador Warren Austin concluded by saying that, "The many contributions which have provided this inspiring structure symbolize the grand resolve written into the preamble to the Charter: '... to unite our strength to maintain international peace and security'."[2]

Each of the major design features of the Security Council Chamber contributes to create a special working atmosphere in the room. Various council members have commented on the overall cohesiveness of the chamber's design elements and materials. In their view, it is symbolically important that a body that, on a regular basis, must confront some of the most divisive issues facing the United Nations does so in an architecturally harmonious setting.

Another comment that delegates often make is that the Security Council Chamber seems austere, especially when compared to the meeting rooms of the other principal UN organs, which have some whimsical design elements. The story has been told among United Nations staff that the UN's first secretary-general, Trygve Lie of Norway, wanted to ensure that the council chamber would be designed with appropriate deference to the council's sober mandate under the UN Charter, and that consequently he personally involved himself in discussions about the materials and colour to be used.

A painting and a table

One element giving the chamber a particular note of solemnity is the large painting by Per Krohg. Some council members have said that they find the lower third of the painting portraying the sufferings of war and deprivation to be particularly grim. Yet these same delegates acknowledge that sitting below the painting, they are forced to recall both the important World War II origins of the council's mandate, and the seriousness of the issues before them.

The windows of the chamber on either side of the painting are soaring, and give a spectacular view of the East River. However, the curtains must always be closed for security reasons. One particularly pleasant day, the representative of one of the council's permanent members could no longer stand being deprived of the sunshine outside, and he walked over to open the right curtain. A security guard instantly appeared at his side. "Mr. Ambassador", the guard said. "With all due respect, you have veto power over everything having to do with the Security Council, except for these curtains."

Keeping the curtains in place to help block any shattering glass should the UN be attacked from the rear side is not just a theoretical precaution. In 1964, when Che Guevara was addressing the General Assembly, Cuban exiles fired a 3.5-inch bazooka at the United Nations from across the East River. Fortunately, the shell fell harmlessly about 200 yards from shore, merely sending up a small geyser and scattering a flock of seagulls. However, a later investigation determined that had the bazooka been properly aimed, it had sufficient range to send a projectile crashing into the UN building.

Besides the large painting, the other feature of the Security Council Chamber that is instantly recognized is its iconic table. From

The chamber as it looked from the audience seats during a 1952 Security Council meeting.

the outset, "the horseshoe table" quickly became a widely recognized symbol of the council. A book about the Council published in 2006 had as its title, *The Horseshoe Table*,[3] and "the horseshoe table" also figures in titles of some articles about the Security Council. It is impressive to think of the hundreds of representatives who have sat at the table since 1952, including many of history's most influential diplomats, some of whom later went on to become foreign ministers, or even heads of state or government. For that reason alone, it is likely that the Security Council's horseshoe table is the world's most famous piece of furniture.

The horseshoe shape of the Security Council table was adapted from the table configuration used by the Council of the League of Nations (1920–1946). The League's Council had only eight members, who sat at a semi-circular table. A semi-circular table was used at all the temporary locations where the new UN Security Council met from 1946 to 1952 (see photo p. 30).

The table that was installed in the Security Council Chamber in 1952 was made of American ash, in order to meet fire restrictions and be cost-effective. The table was a variation of the semi-circular shape previously used, because in this new design, the ends extended past the limited arc of a semi-circle.

The table, as first constructed, was made of 19 curved units. In 1965, when amendments to the UN Charter went into effect increasing the number of council members from eleven to fifteen, it was decided to preserve the original table by adding two more curved units to the table ends, for a total of 21 places.

The council president sits at the midpoint of the horseshoe table, with his or her back to the Per Krohg painting. A space is always reserved to the president's right for the secretary-general (whether or not he or she is in attendance), and a place to the president's left is designated for a representative of the Department of Political Affairs who assists with the conduct of meetings. There are two regular seats at either end of the table for any invited non-council member participants and, when necessary, portable microphones make it possible to seat a total of three non-council participants at each end.

The council members are arranged around the table in English alphabetical order, and every member moves one seat to the right each month when the council presidency rotates, also in alphabetical order. council members can get so accustomed to their particular place at the table that when rotation occurs at the start of a new month, there is sometimes a moment of uncertainty when a representative heads for the wrong chair, and then with a laugh, moves to the correct spot. The sense of disorientation can be particularly pronounced for the council member who reaches the last seat for members to the president's right and then, the following month, is catapulted to the opposite side of the table.

The traditionalism of the Security Council members towards their table is evidenced by the fact that unlike the other main UN organs, the Security Council members have never adopted the use of electronic nameplates. Rather, individually produced plaques mark each place at the table. The use of these plaques has led to some nerve-wracking moments when a mistake is spotted in the official title of a non-council member participant, or a speaker is added at the last minute and new plaques must be speedily manufactured before the start of a meeting.

Usually the monthly rotation of council members' nameplates takes place out of their sight, but that was not the case on 31 May 2010. That day, a flotilla of mostly Turkish ships tried to breach the Israeli blockade of Gaza. When Israel responded militarily, nine people were killed, after which the Security Council convened an emergency meeting. However, after an initial discussion, governments needed more time to develop their national positions before the council could adopt a decision, which resulted in a delay of several hours. While Council members waited, midnight arrived, and it became the month of June. At that point, the representative of Lebanon ceased to be council president, and the representative of Mexico took over. That was the moment when the council members waiting in the chamber saw the conference officers quickly move all the country nameplates over one place to the right to prepare for the moment when the Council members would be ready to adopt their decision, which finally occurred at 1:40 a.m.

Spending such long hours together in the chamber, or in the parallel Consultations Room across the hall, the council members find themselves often exchanging small talk and political opinions with those sitting on either side of them at the table. This can lead to the formation of friendships – sometimes unlikely ones – among council members who find themselves neighbours at the table owing not to the similarity of their views, but rather to mere alphabetical placement.

One of the very positive aspects of the table's round shape is that any member or invited speaker seated at the table can look at – and when they have the floor, directly address – anyone seated at the table.[4] This enhances the message that dialogue and negotiation are critical to the work of the Security Council.

At the same time, it is also symbolic that although representatives of non-Council Member States are frequently invited to address the council pursuant to Article 32 of the Charter and procedural rule 37, the seating of these temporary participants at either end of the table makes visually clear that they are not on an equal decision-making footing with the Security Council members. This impression can be even more pronounced during large open debates. At such times, representatives of invited non-Council Member States cross considerable floor space to reach their temporary seat at one of table ends, and then upon completion of their statement, they make the long trek back to one of the side seats. This can heighten awareness of which countries have the privilege of being members of the Security Council at a given point in time, and which do not.

At the time of the Capital Master Plan (CMP) to renovate the UN Headquarters, the council members were presented with two options concerning the table: to build a new table, or to renovate the existing one. Council members first feared that their table had been too damaged during decades of use and by the many holes drilled into it for successive sound systems. However, when they were assured that the original table could be successfully renovated, they decided overwhelmingly to preserve it.

The significance of the horseshoe table to the council members was highlighted when the CMP crews were preparing to disassemble the table in order to begin restoration. The UN's Department of Public Information designated this as a "photo op" for UN journalists, but one council member blocked this. A representative of that delegation quipped, "We do not want to see headlines in tomorrow's newspapers saying, 'The Security Council is coming apart, just like its table'." The council members did agree that the reinstallation of the renovated table in 2013 could be photographed.

On 16 November 2016, another incident occurred in the Security Council Chamber, which highlighted the reverence that some Member States accord to the council's iconic table. At a meeting on Kosovo, a representative of Japan advocated developing projects to enhance Kosovo's economic self-sufficiency, and he illustrated his point by placing on the table a bottle of wine from a successfully revived Kosovar vineyard. After completing his statement, the Japanese representative left the bottle on the council table. Almost immediately, a Russian representative raised a point of order and asked that the bottle be removed. In making this request, the Russian representative stated, "I would like to remind us all once again that this table is a sacred piece of furniture that should be treated with respect."[5]

In 2014, an issue arose regarding the need for propriety as concerns the Security Council Chamber as a whole. When producers of the Netflix drama *House of Cards* submitted a request to film one episode in the chamber, the proposal was put under a no-objection procedure for the approval of all 15 council members. The Russian representative broke the silence to state that "we consistently insist that the Security Council premises are not an appropriate place for filming, staging, etc."

Where history takes place

In its more than six decades, so much history has taken place in the Security Council Chamber. There was of course the dramatic, televised confrontation between American and Soviet representatives in 1962 over the Cuban missile crisis. In 2003, it was in the same chamber, with every seat taken, that the American Secretary of State Colin Powell presented evidence (which later turned out to be false) of the presence of weapons of mass destruction in Iraq.

The Middle East – including Palestine, Lebanon, Syria, and Yemen – Cyprus, the Balkans, Iraq, and Afghanistan are among the pressing issues which have brought the Council members again and again to the Security Council Chamber. In Africa, deadly conflicts in Rwanda, Liberia, Sierra Leone, Côte d'Ivoire, Somalia, the Democratic Republic of the Congo, Darfur, and South Sudan have dominated the Council's agenda at various times. However, although a number of longstanding intractable conflicts continue to challenge the Security Council, the council has had its successes, too. Many scholars believe that the important Council meetings on apartheid and its violent excesses, on the self-declared state of Southern Rhodesia, and on independence for Namibia helped convince the council, including its Western members, of the importance of taking decisive measures, including arms embargoes or sanctions, to end these situations. Moreover, 55 peacekeeping operations established by the Security Coun-

On June 8, 2017 Fatou Bensouda, Chief Prosecutor of the International Criminal Court (ICC), briefed the Security Council at its meeting on the situation in the Darfur region of Sudan.

cil have successfully completed their missions and then been able to withdraw.

What is striking is that the nature of conflicts on the agenda of the Security Council has changed radically since the inaugural 1952 meeting in the new council chamber. Classic interstate conflicts are now very rare on the council's agenda, while intra-state civil wars, the rampages of murderous militias, terrorism, sexual abuse and exploitation, and threats of nuclear proliferation increasingly demand the council's attention. Because of the insidiousness of these newer threats to international peace and security, the council has begun to meet more and more frequently on "root causes", with a view to devising overall guidelines and approaches to these complex situations. In addition, "cross-cutting, thematic issues" now regularly taken up by the council include women and peace and security, protection of civilians, rule of law, more robust peacekeeping, and suppressing trafficking in small arms.

A total of seven summit meetings, when Council members are represented by their presidents or prime ministers, have been held in the Security Council Chamber, the most recent one being the meeting convened concerning foreign terrorist fighters on 24 September 2014. United States President Barack Obama convened an important summit on nuclear non-proliferation in September 2009. Because Obama had been in office less than a year, he was a huge draw, and seats for observers in the council chamber had to be carefully apportioned, as many heads of state and government in New York for the General Assembly wished to be present. One could feel the power of having so many world leaders sitting in the Security Council Chamber at the same time, and security was very tight. Once the proceedings began, the chamber doors were closed and no one was to stand up or leave the room.

The council can also hold off-the-record private meetings in its chamber when an issue – including the appointment of UN secretaries-general – is considered too sensitive to be allowed coverage in the media. In the case of such private meetings, it is up to the council to decide whether other non-council members can be present in the chamber to observe, or whether only council members and any affected countries or briefers should attend.

A somewhat festive meeting – although under tense circumstances – took place on 31 December 2008. Fierce fighting between Israel and Hamas had entered its fifth day, and in response, the Security Council members convened an emergency meeting that evening, which happened to be New Year's Eve. This is probably the only time in the history of the council that a meeting was held in the chamber attended by council ambassadors wearing tuxedos.

The most poignant meetings held in the Security Council Chamber are when the council considers what happens to children in armed conflict situations. On several of these occasions, a former child solder or a conscripted child sex slave has addressed the council. It is amazing how poised these children have been as they have told the Security Council ambassadors the horrific stories of what happened to them. Such meetings are the quietest and most solemn of any proceedings held in the chamber, and the council's ambassadors have been visibly

On June 16, 2010 Special Representative of the Secretary-General for Children and Armed Conflict, Radhika Coomaraswamy (at left), addresses the Security Council at its meeting on that issue. Manju Gurung (at right), is a young Nepalese, who also addressed the Council, recounting her ordeal of abduction by Nepal's Maoists at the age of 13.

affected. One such occasion was when Manju Gurung spoke to the council members of her experiences as a kidnapped child soldier in Nepal. After her remarks, the American representative commented that Ms. Gurung's "courage and example are extraordinary", while the representative of Gabon called her testimony "deeply moving".[6]

At the time of the Capital Master Plan renovations, the Security Council members were consulted at various planning stages. The members sought a number of improvements with respect to their nearby private Consultations Room, where they meet informally, as well as the 'Quiet Room', where council delegates can converse with non-council representatives. Issues also arose with respect to the office suite for the council president and the secretary-general, the small caucus rooms for use in negotiations, and space for Secretariat staff and translators assisting the council. In this context, it is all the more noteworthy that as to the council chamber itself, no Security Council member raised any matter suggesting that the chamber was no longer appropriate for the way the council presently conducts its business.[7] This testifies to the wisdom and foresight of the original design, and its enduring suitability for the needs of the Security Council.

The importance of the Security Council Chamber's design is evidenced by the fact that during the CMP renovations, all other of the principal UN organs simply relocated to appropriately sized conference rooms elsewhere on the premises. However, both diplomats and the UN Secretariat felt that the council chamber was so important that a temporary replica – complete with a vinyl reproduction of the Per Krohg painting – should be created for the three years during which the actual chamber was being renovated. This suggests a universal acknowledgement that the Security Council Chamber itself confers a legitimizing effect on the proceedings conducted within its walls, and on the decisions adopted there.

The Security Council's temporary meeting space that was used during the renovation was located in the General Assembly building. The council held its meetings here for about three years while the work went on.

Media and press

The interest in the UN's impressive new headquarters in New York was great in the years leading up to its opening in 1952. While the construction was underway, the critics discussed and debated it in magazines and newspapers. There soon arose a kind of competition among the nations that were contributing to the decoration: which country's design would get the best notices? Arnstein Arneberg was extremely disappointed, then, when the opening of the Security Council Chamber was greeted with negative reviews.

Arneberg's defence took the form of a long article in the architectural journal *Byggekunst*. His frustrations over the complicated process can be read between the lines of the text. But he also criticized himself: the commission had been a big one, perhaps too big. Trygve Lie, for his part, reassured his fellow Norwegian: the secretary-general thought that the Security Council Chamber would, over time, come to be seen as the best of them all.

In the decades since, the world has become familiar with the chamber through countless newspaper articles and TV broadasts. For a great many journalists, the chamber is a workplace from which they continually report the news. All this activity has turned the Security Council, over time, into a modern icon – even though very few people know the names of the men and woman who created it.

From the very beginning, there was extensive TV coverage of the meetings in the Security Council Chamber. Here the UN cameras are in place during a Council meeting on 1 November 1953.

FUJINON
ARD
SONY

9/5 - 1952.

Herr generalsekretær Trygve Lie,
Granston Tower,
123 Greenway North,
Forest Hills, New York.

Kjære Trygve Lie.

Hjertelig takk for din store elskværdighet ved å sende meg platene av åpningstalen for Sikkerhetsrådets sal.

Som jeg forstår er det nokk dessværre delte meninger om denne. Jeg hörer "Time" skriver at salen er "expensively ugly". "Verdens Gang" ringte meg i den anledning og skriver: "Det er de yngre arkitektenes oppfatning som gjenspeiler seg der, sies det på FN hold."

Jeg forstår jo til en viss grad at Sikkerhetsrådets sal, som jo var det förste som ble utformet, adskiller seg kanskje vel sterkt fra bygningens övrige arkitektur,- men jeg syns jo at det vil være trist hvis Harrison skulle være direkte miss - fornöyet med rommet. Har du et inntrykk av dette ville jeg sette pris på å höre om det, f.eks. når du kommer hjem til sommeren.

Personlig tror jeg også at det henger endel sammen med glassveggen ut mot elven. Opprinnelig var det bare to smale vinduer på sidene, da jeg påbegynte tegningene og foreslo et dekorativt bilde på midten av veggen. Senere ble disse to vinduer noe utvidet og det dekorative veggpartiet ble stående igjen som en skjerm. Her har muligens Harrison strukket seg litt lenger enn han hadde lyst på, av hensyn til dekorasjonen.

- Her er det i öyenlikket etter noen regndager det vidunderligste, varme og friske vårvær og alt er grönt.

Med venlig hilsen til din frue og deg,

Siri Wolland

The Security Council Chamber in the Media

Page 196–197: At the Security Council meeting on 3 March 2014, the situation in Ukraine was discussed. Photographers and journalists follow the proceeding carefully from the room's side windows, which offer a view of the chamber and the delegates' table.

Page 198: "9/5 – 1952 / Mr. secretary-general Trygve Lie / Granston Tower / 123 Greenway North / Forest Hills, New York / Dear Trygve Lie, / Hearty thanks for your extraordinary graciousness in sending me the recordings of the opening speech for the Security Council Chamber. / As I understand, there are, unfortunately, mixed feelings about it. I hear that *Time* has written that the chamber is 'expensively ugly'. *Verdens Gang* phoned me about it and writes: 'It is the younger architects' perception that is reflected here, the UN says.' / I understand to a certain degree that the Security Council's chamber, which was the first to be designed, perhaps differs strongly from the rest of the building's architecture, but I think it would be sad if Harrison were to be directly dissatisfied with the room. If you have an impression of this, I would appreciate hearing it, for example when you come home for the summer. / Personally, I also think it has a lot to do with the glass wall facing the river. Originally there were just two narrow windows on the sides, when I began work on the designs and proposed a decorative picture in the middle of the wall. Later, these two windows were somewhat expanded and the decorative wall panel was left standing as a screen. Here Harrison has perhaps stretched himself a little further than he wanted to for the sake of the decoration / Here, at present, after several days of rain, we are enjoying the most wonderful, warm and fresh spring weather and everything is green. / With friendly regards to your wife and yourself, / [Arnstein Arneberg]"

During World War II, the Allies had called themselves the "United Nations" – thus creating a phrase that would outlast the war and give its name to the new world organization.

The UN was meant to be a force for peace and democracy in the world. In constructing its headquarters, it wanted, too, to democratize architecture and design. An effort was made to tone down individual perspectives and accentuate *the collective promise*. Among the objectives of UN architecture was to communicate culture, politics, and history – but not religion. The complex's functional design, it was hoped, would acquire its own symbolic beauty and triumph over the monumental.[1]

The architecture was also intended to reflect the UN's desired reputation. Such a reputation takes a long time to establish, and in the beginning, the UN received a good deal of negative press. In this essay, I will discuss the reactions to the Security Council Chamber that appeared in the Norwegian and American media in the years around 1952 – and later, in 2013, when the restoration of the chamber was completed.

The press in 1952

There was considerable debate in the media when it was announced that the UN complex would be built on New York's East Side. The buildings were constructed in record time, and in 1952, they were complete. One of those who wrote very negatively about the result was Lewis Mumford (1895–1990), the influential author, architectural critic, and expert on urban environments. For over thirty years, he wrote for *The New Yorker* as a commentator and critic; a professor of city planning at the University of Pennsylvania, he was an active proponent of rational urban design.

Mumford pointed out that 15 countries were represented on the Board of Design Consultants, chaired by the architect Wallace K. Harrison, and that not all of them spoke English. In addition, the group consisted of famous men with huge egos who were nevertheless expected to work closely with one another. Collaboration might be an essential element of the UN's spirit, but under such conditions, it would obviously be difficult to put into practice.

Mumford based his comments on the assumption that the UN buildings "should proclaim with a single voice that a new world order, dedicated to peace and justice, is rising on this site".[2] Structures with such a purpose, Mumford felt, should be loved as symbols in the same way as the Statue of Liberty – and, at the same time, should be powerful and impressive, like St. Peter's Basilica in Rome. In reality, Mumford found what he felt was an "absence of symbolism in the architecture! Plenty of unconscious symbolism!"[3]

Mumford further pointed out that the UN had leapt at the first opportunity to acquire a suitable plot of land, and the fact that it was Rockefeller who had donated the site made the situation rather dicey. For it was Rockefeller, and not the city of New York, that thus influenced the symbolism – it was Rockefeller's businesses and reputation that would give rise to the buildings' connotations. "Symbolically, these buildings are far from being an admirable expression of the idea of the United Nations," maintained Mumford, "and functionally they do not make the necessary provision for extensions, change of purpose and future development."[4]

That was not all: in addition, he felt that the UN buildings were made of the wrong materials. Glass, metal, and steel would not tolerate bad weather. Heat, sun, and reflections were not good for buildings, either. In addition, the General Assembly Building looked like a 1950s music hall. In short, the UN and New York needed a monumental set of structures, and this was no such thing. He did have one mildly positive thing to say: the lobby and lounges were fine.

Since he was most preoccupied with the UN buildings' placement, the Security Council's chamber was less important to him, and he had little to say about it. He mentioned only in passing that the Security Council's chamber was a gift from Norway.[5]

Another architect and city planner, Henry Stern Churchill (1893–1962), wrote in greater depth about the Scandinavian chambers in the journal *Architectural Record* in 1952.[6] To Churchill, the Security Council Chamber seemed surprisingly antique. Not old-fashioned, perhaps, he wrote – rather, the space reminded him of the decorations one finds in late medieval French architecture or late Gothic cathedrals. It was almost, Churchill commented acidly, as if the room had been restored by Eugène Viollet-le-Duc (1814–1879), the famous French architect and Middle Ages enthusiast (see also p. 81).[7]

Churchill found all three of the chambers to be superficial in form and insufficiently worked out. "It would be hard to find a better example of the uncertainty and irresolution that besets modern architecture outside the field of structural design", he wrote. "Striking as all three principal Council rooms are, they do not speak the same language; they lack a common accord of dignity. They are vibrant, thin; their attraction comes from and is on the surface, there is no depth. All three lack conviction; they are the expression of personal ideas of decoration. (...) There simply has not been enough time for the full expression of thought or for the revision necessary to fuse the parts into a thoroughly studied and consistent whole."[8]

In July 1952, the periodical *Interiors* published a rather long article that compared the three Scandinavian chambers. They were described as modern, if only because they contained no references to historic periods. That the three architects were Scandinavian should perhaps have yield more coherent results, argued *Interiors*, but such was not the case.

For the audience, the main entrance to the UN complex is on the north side of the General Assembly building. One steps into a large, airy, and bright reception area. The protruding balconies, together with the ceiling constructions, give the room an almost structural feel. The picture is from October 1952, shortly after the opening of the building.

Even though all three rooms were equal in area, they were quite different from one another. Arneberg was quoted to the effect that he felt he had been handicapped because he had submitted his sketches for the Security Council Chamber before the designers for the other chambers had been chosen. “My understanding of the problem was to execute a room of good, durable materials with character, in all simplicity, which represented not only a casual taste of today, but a character so neutral that it could withstand the test of time”, said Arneberg in the article.

Interiors went on to observe that the Security Council Chamber was as conservative as the City Council Chamber in Oslo, which was Arneberg's most famous work. It can seem that Arneberg wanted to defend himself against the argument that he was conservative.

The journal *Architectural Forum* wrote in April 1952 that there were two reasons why one would remember the conference building, in which the Scandinavian chambers are located. One reason was the interior of the public building; the other was the lovely terrace that added beauty to an otherwise shabby-looking stretch of waterfront. Nevertheless, the conference building was just a hyphen, wrote *Architectural Forum*. For obvious reasons, the conference building did not receive as much media attention as the other buildings, and during that period, the Security Council Chamber was rarely mentioned by name. This is not surprising; it had yet to become the setting of momentous political arguments and decisions, and the conflict level among its members was still low. The press was preoccupied by the major problems surrounding the UN, which at that point did not involve the council chambers to a significant extent.

Opinion

One task of the United Nations Department of Public Information (DPI) was to tell a public that was not necessarily cognizant of modern architecture about the new UN buildings' excellent qualities. DPI expected mixed reactions to the headquarters, and prepared information campaigns to explain the buildings. The public was to be made to feel welcome; the journalists had their own press area plus access to a TV studio and other facilities. Openness and availability were important attributes if you wanted to work at the UN. However, the message communicated by the UN via the press did not automatically elicit the desired opinions on the part of the general public. The complex's modern architecture was less popular than had been hoped. The war was over, people were less impressionable, and their interest in world affairs had given way to other preoccupations. Some weeklies felt that the UN's headquarters would be good for tourism, and that the top of the building could be a popular observation deck. A style magazine commented that the area would be terrific for fashion photography. The UN wanted to build its reputation quickly, so that it would have the power and influence it needed to effectively accomplish its postwar peace work.[9] This is understandable. Nevertheless, to try to legitimize one's activity through the press is always a risky endeavour, for the simple reason that the media have another agenda than to serve as a mouthpiece for the authorities, toward whom they can and should take a critical stance.

Reception in Norway

It is interesting to discover that when the UN complex was opened there were relatively few notices in the Norwegian media about the Security Council Chamber and the UN buildings.[10] The professional journals showed most interest in the event. In *Byggekunst* in 1952, architect Arnstein Arneberg briefly described the buildings and the three Scandinavian chambers. Among other things, he discussed his feelings about the room's functions, the obstacles and limitations that had to be overcome, and the choice of materials. As mentioned earlier, Arneberg felt that he had been labouring under a handicap because he had not had all the information about the chamber before planning its interior. Arneberg thus felt that the Security Council Chamber would be viewed as conservative in relation to the other two spaces.

The reports that appeared in the daily papers were brief. It seems almost as if many of them were based on a single source, presumably an item from a news bureau. The language was high-flown, and the project was hailed as an honourable commission for the nation. Per Krohg's painting received the most attention of all.[11]

In contrast to the American media, which discussed the UN buildings' placement, costs, architecture, and functionality, the media in Norway were preoccupied with the local perspective – the fact that this was a Norwegian gift and a Norwegian artwork. The real architectural debate or evaluation in the daily Norwegian press is striking by its absence.

The restoration

The Security Council Chamber has most often been described in the media indirectly, in evaluations of the UN buildings or coverage of the Security Council's handling of important issues. The space itself, and its architectural qualities, have rarely been a subject of interest. It is not well known, therefore, that a Norwegian architect and artist are responsible for this important room in the UN complex.

On assignment from the Directorate for Cultural Heritage, Retriever, a media analysis firm, has surveyed the media coverage of the Security Council Chamber in the Norwegian and American media from 2008 to the end of 2015.[12] The survey was conducted to identify differences and similarities in the coverage of the chamber in recent years. The Security Council Chamber was mentioned in 221 Norwegian media reports and 150 American reports between 2008 and 2015. Most of the Norwegian reports were in 2013 and 2014. In the American media, the chamber received the greatest amount of attention in 2009 and 2014.

The main finding is that the Norwegian reports tend to be about the fact that Norway was responsible for both the design and the financing of the chamber when it was built, in addition to the fact that the Norwegian government paid for most of the renovation before 2013, when the work on the chamber was completed. Several of the articles about the renovation concerned the contribution of Norwegian vendors. As in 1952, then, the Norwegian angle was paramount. The year

2014 stands out as the year in which most of the Norwegian media coverage of the chamber was about the political activity taking place within it. The reason for this is not immediately obvious. Through the entire period, 2008 to 2015, both Arnstein Arneberg and Per Krohg are mentioned.

The American reporting is primarily concerned with political and diplomatic activities, such as votes and resolutions. The United States, after all, has a permanent seat on the Security Council. The articles are most often about international politics, and the chamber as such is mentioned only briefly. The restoration is the subject of 15 articles, and it is the buildings themselves that receive the most attention, while the chamber itself is, again, usually referred to only in passing. There is no mention of Arneberg or Krohg in the American section of Retriever's report.

Best in the world

Many Norwegian articles from around 2013 are about the weaving of the wall material and the Biri wallpaper. "Grandma's wallpaper unites nations", writes *Aftenposten*. "Wallpaper made of straw is a hit abroad", reads the headline in *Nationen*, in which Ingeborg Semb, a third-generation manufacturer of the Biri wallpaper, talks about its history.

In *ArkitekturN*, the journalist and editor Ingerid Helsing Almaas writes in considerable detail about the work on the chamber both in the period prior to the opening in 1952 and around 2013, when the room was restored. *Dagens Næringsliv* published an article about the costs and said that it was a myth that the UN was paid by Norway. The gimmick of making a necktie out of Else Poulsson's old wallpaper material was covered in several articles. NRK reported that UN secretary-general Ban Ki-moon was given a necktie at the re-opening of the chamber in 2013, and that Norway had refurbished "the world's most important room".

"It is natural that Norway took responsibility for the renovation", said then Foreign Minister Barth Eide to the NTB news bureau. This was not entirely correct: Norway neither took nor was given the responsibility. But Norway paid NOK 47 million for the Security Council Chamber, and the Directorate for Cultural Heritage had an advisory role in the project (see also pp. 171–181).

"Newly refurbished Norwegian gift to the UN", wrote NTB in April 2013.Deputy Consul-General Henrik Width echoed the point that it was the most important room in the world and, at the same time, a distinctively Norwegian room – something Norwegians can be proud of, he said. "All splendour in this space" and "world's most conflict-filled building", read a major report in D2 in 2011. The article was one of the most extensive that has been written about the UN buildings and about the Security Council Chamber in the Norwegian press, and included a great many pictures of the refurbishing (see pp. 168–172).

On 16 April 2013, the Security Council Chamber was reopened after a long, costly, and extensive restoration process. Norway's Foreign Minister Espen Barth Eide addressed the council and presented a tie made of the old wallpaper to Secretary-General Ban Ki-moon.

The press as user of the room

The media are not only engaged in reporting on the Security Council Chamber – journalists from around the world are also among its most important users. I have interviewed several Norwegian and American reporters who work on news stories related to discussions in the Security Council Chamber. One American journalist in particular had strong views about the disadvantages of the strict security measures that are now in force in the chamber. In addition, it is problematic that the debates in the chamber have taken on a far more formal character over time. He says that the ambassadors read from their papers, and that the spontaneous exchanges of opinion have entirely disappeared. Most of the major media are represented here, but have little contact with one another. Technology enables reporters to follow the meetings from other parts of the complex, so they no longer spend much time in the chamber itself. However, the communications from the chamber do not make up for actual contact between journalists and ambassadors, which used to be far more extensive.

"It is a decrease in access", my source commented. Nevertheless, he still wanted to be present in the chamber to be able to provide a better picture of the events; he wanted to see what the ambassadors were doing, whom they were talking to, who was texting on his or her phone, and who was napping. The Norwegian media, for their part, are mainly in the chamber when the Norwegian ambassador is involved.

After more than sixty years of activity, the UN Headquarters and the Security Council Chamber have an extremely enviable international reputation. It is still the diplomatic activity and not the space itself that gets the attention – but that is exactly the way things should be. The differences between the press coverage of the space in Norway in 1952 and in 2013 are not major: the Norwegian media are still preoccupied with the fact that the chamber is Norwegian. Closeness to the event – either psychological or geographical – is, indeed, perhaps the most important criterion we have for news. UN news is clearly *closest* in the USA, but the Norwegian aspect of it all is *closest* in the Norwegian media. The Security Council Chamber was rather invisible in the press coverage in 1952, but today it enjoys the status of being (perhaps) the world's most important room. It took more than sixty years to acquire this reputation. Now it is only a matter of maintaining it.

It is rare for the chamber to be shown from this angle when meetings are being documented. Here we can see the audience and press gallery from a window box on the side wall during a 20 June 2017 meeting on the situation in the Middle East.

Appendix

Notes

Jørn Holme
Introduction – The World's Most Important Room

1 Mark Isitt and Åke E:son Lindman, *United Nations, The Story behind the Headquarters of the World* (Stockholm: Bokförlaget Max Ström, 2015), p. 19.
2 Trygve Lie, *Syv år for freden* (Oslo: Tiden Norsk Forlag, 1954), pp. 111–112.
3 Victoria Newhouse, *Wallace K. Harrison, Architect* (New York: Rizzoli International Publications, 1989), p. 114.
4 Lie, *Syv år for freden*, p. 118.
5 Lie, *Syv år for freden*, pp. 118, 120.
6 ARKDES, Stockholm, Sven Markelius' archives, UN Manhattan (169), undated transcript of telegram from the Swedish Embassy to the Foreign Ministry.
7 Isitt and Lindman, *United Nations. The Story behind the Headquarters of the World*, p. 35.
8 Isitt and Lindman, *United Nations. The story behind the headquarters of the World*, p. 48.
9 Lie, *Syv år for freden*, p. 124.
10 Letter from Trygve Lie to Arnstein Arneberg 26 December 1946. National Museum, Architecture Collection, Arneberg archive.
11 Karsten R.S. Ifversen and Birgit Lyngbye Pedersen. *Finn Juhl i FN: Et dansk mesterværk i New York.* (København: Strandberg Publishing, 2013), pp. 26–27.
12 Ifversen and Pedersen, *Finn Juhl i FN – et dansk mesterværk i New York*, p. 89.
13 ARKDES, Stockholm, Sven Markelius' archives, UN Manhattan (169) PM Norwegian Foreign Ministry, 11 April 1950.
14 Eva Rudberg, *Sven Markelius, Architect* (Stockholm: Arkitektur förlag, 1989), p. 131.
15 Ingeborg Glambek, "The Council Chambers in the UN Building in New York", in *Scandinavian Journal of Design History*, Volume 15 (2005): p. 15.
16 Isitt and Lindman, *United Nations. The Story behind the Headquarters of the World*, p. 100.
17 The sculpture was made by sculptor Henrik Starcke (1899/1973). Ifversen and Pedersen, *Finn Juhl i FN – et dansk mesterværk i New York*, pp. 90–91.
18 Glambek, "The Council Chambers in the UN Building in New York", p. 15.
19 In addition to the articles in this book, the introduction relies especially on these sources: Ingeborg Glambek, "The Council Chambers in the UN Building in New York" (2005); Karsten R.S. Ifversen and Birgit Lyngbye Pedersen, *Finn Juhl i FN – et dansk mesterværk i New York* (2013); Mark Isitt and Åke E:son Lindman, *United Nations. The Story behind the Headquarters of the World* (2015).

Ingeborg Glambek
The Security Council Chamber – from Idea to Reality

1 The article is a revised and shortened version of "The Council Chambers in the UN Building in New York", *Scandinavian Journal of Design History* Volume 5 (2005) by Ingeborg Glambek.
2 Trygve Lie, *In the Cause of Peace: Seven Years with the United Nations*, (New York: The Macmillan Company, 1954), p. 121.
3 UN archives, Security Council Chamber. RAG 1/Box31 File no. 120-10-6-1.
4 Undated letter from Arnstein Arneberg to Wallace K. Harrison, National Museum, Architecture Collection, Arneberg archive.
5 Letter from Wallace K. Harrison, 5 January 1949, National Museum, Architecture Collection, Arneberg archive.
6 National Museum, Architecture Collection, Arneberg archive.
7 Letter from M. Harris to Arnstein Arneberg, 17 March 1950, National Museum, Architecture Collection, Arneberg archive.
8 Letter from Arnstein Arneberg to G. Bennett, 22 December 1950. UN archives, Security Council Chamber. UN RAG 1/Boks 31 File nr. 120-10-6-1.
9 The National Archives of Norway. UD 1950–59 Box 1080, budget report S. no. 13 (1950).
10 The National Archives of Norway. UD 1950–59 Box 1080, press release 20 March 1950.
11 Letter from Arnstein Arneberg to Trygve Lie, 4 June 1952, National Museum, Architecture Collection, Arneberg archive.
12 Letter from Arnstein Arneberg to the Planning Office, 3. August 1950. UN archives, Security Council Chamber.
13 Linda Sue Phipps, "Constructing the United Nations Headquarters: Modern Architecture as Public Diplomacy" (Ph. D. Harvard University, 1998) p. 290, note 180.

Ulf Grønvold
Anstein Arneberg Between Past and Present

1 Per Krohg, "Under Fugl Fønix' vinger". *Dagbladet* 7.6.1951.
2 Carl W. Schnitler, "Arneberg og Poulssons raadhusplaner", *St. Hallvard* 1918.
3 The eastern tower is 66 metres high; the western is two metres lower because the terrain is higher there.
4 Letter from O. Seip and Knut Kvigne to Member of Parliament Rostad. The work appears to have been administered by Sverre Iversen, director of the Arbeidsdirektoratet.
5 Ann Katrin Pihl Atmer, *Livet som leves där måste smaka vildmark. Sportstugor och friluftsliv 1900–1945*, (Stockholm: Stockholmia förlag, 1998), p. 89.
6 Elisabeth Seip, *Norsk biografisk leksikon*, online edition, "Arnstein Arneberg". 13 February 2009. https://nbl.snl.no/Arnstein_Arneberg.
7 Andreas Aubert, *Norsk kunst og kultur*, Kristiania 1917, p. 204.
8 Arneberg made use of his artist friends from the Oslo City Hall: Reidar Aulie, Henrik Sørensen, Hugo Lous Mohr, Erik Werenskiold and Edvard Munch.
9 Kjell Lund in an interview with the author.

Nina Berre
Arneberg on the International Stage

1 Henry Stern Churchill, "United Nations Headquarters. A description and appraisal", *Architectural Record*, (July 1952).
2 See e.g. Siegfried Giedion, *Space, Time and Architecture. The Growth of a New Tradition*, fifth edition. (Harvard University Press, Cambridge, Mass., 1966), pp. 530–538.
3 NAL's archive showed that it asked for 40 programs, as opposed to the 30 that the administrators in Geneva first wanted to send. Based on notes and partly incomplete lists in NAL's archive, I can conclude that at the very minimum, the following architects ordered programs, for which they would pay five kroner apiece: Crawford Jensen, Harald Petersen, Finn Rahn, Finn Bryn, Blakstad & Munthe-Kaas, Lars Backer, Carl Michalsen, Nils Reiersen, Sigurd Sigmundsøn, Einar Foss, Leif Grung, Erling Gjone (on behalf of T.A.F.), Christian Skagen, Claus Hjelte, Arnstein Arneberg, Harald Sund, Ole Øvergaard, Gunnar Bjerke, Sverre Pedersen, Holger Sinding-Larsen. Norske Arkitekters Landsforbund. Series: Dbgb – 0003. Konkurranser fortløpende nummerering 1911–1930. Mappe Nasjonernes Forbund, 1928, Riksarkivet.
4 John Ritter, "World Parliament. The League of Nations Competition, 1926", *Architectural Review*, no. 136 (July 1964), pp. 17–28.
5 Ritter, "World Parliament. The League of Nations Competition, 1926", p. 17.
6 Via Siegfried Giedion, among others. *Space, Time and Architecture*, pp. 530–538. Ritter, "World Parliament. The League of Nations Competition, 1926
7 Sverre Poulsen, "Genève-komedien", *Byggekunst*, no. 4, (1928), pp. 62–63.
8 One of the Norwegian architects who submitted a draft, Holger Sinding-Larsen, requested that NAL ask the administrators in Geneva to publicize the competition, which NAL appears to have done. Sinding Larsen believed that the League of Nations could only overcome the scandal by publishing all the drafts: "This way, the competitors' reward for participation would be entirely negative the moment they are among the 360 non-winners." NAL archive, The National Archives of Norway.
9 Ritter. "World Parliament. The League of Nations Competition, 1926", p. 18.
10 Jens Christian Eldal, *Norsk kunstnerleksikon*, "Arnstein Arneberg". 9 January 2018. https://nkl.snl.no/Arnstein_Rynning_Arneberg,read 9.1.2018.
11 Ulf Grønvold, Nils Anker and Gunnar Sørensen, *Det store løftet. Rådhuset i Oslo*, (Oslo: Aschehoug & Co. 2000), p. 81. Arneberg and Poulssons "neoclassical period " is also discussed in Trond L. Schøning, *Det Norske Hus. Oslo Rådhus – en historisk sammenligning*, Thesis in art history, University of Bergen, 2001.
12 See, for example, *Swedish Grace. The forgotten modern*, ed. Peter Elmlund and Johan Mårtelius, (Stockholm, Axel and Margaret Ax:son Johnson Foundation, 2015).
13 John Ritter mentions a square-shaped neoclassical draft drawn by Christian Skagen from Bergen. From the NAL archive, we know that Holger Sinding-Larsen submitted the work. Aside from Arneberg's contribution, we do not know about any other Norwegians who participated, but it is likely

that there were many more than these three.
14 Press release for the exhibition, *A Home for U.N.O.: Must We Repeat the Geneva Fiasco*? Museum of Modern Art, New York, 5. February 5- March 3, 1946. https://www.moma.org/documents/moma_press-release_325505.pdf.
15 "Architects picked by nations for U.N." Special to *The New York Times*, 6.2.1947, UN archive, New York.
16 Letter from Finn Moe, "Norwegian Permanent Delegation to the United Nations", 29 January 1947. UN archive Fil G -833.
17 Ibid.
18 Letter from Trygve Lie to Arnstein Arneberg, 26 December 1946. National Museum, Architecture Collection, Arneberg archive.
19 Letter from Grimsgaard and Grevstad architectural firm to NAL, 9 January 1947. Archives of the National Association of Norwegian Architects. Dbgc - 0007. Competitions continuous numbering 1931–1084. File 8. Diverse 1. 1947. National Archives.
20 Ingeborg Glambek "The Council Chambers in the UN Building in New York", *Scandinavian Journal of Design History*, Volume 15, (2005): pp. 9–39.
21 Letter from Arnstein Arneberg to Trygve Lie, 21 May 1949. National Museum, Architecture Collection, Arneberg archive.
22 Andreas Vaa Bermann sugested this in a lecture held in New York in connection with the reopening of the chamber after its restoration.
23 "We are planning to use a Norwegian pine wood paneling in the secretary-general's offices. It is, however, difficult for us to obtain the proper information on these woods here in this country". Letter from Abel R. Sorensen of Harrison's office to Arnstein Arneberg, 14 July 1950. UN archive. Arneberg replies to Sørensen by referring him to the City Hall project, in which only 100% pinewood paneling was acceptable for the sake of "first-class workmanship". Letter from Arnstein Arneberg to Abel R. Sørensen, 8 August 1950. UN archive in New York.
24 Letter from Trygve Lie to Arnstein Arneberg, 24 August 1951. Arneberg's archive, National Museum.
25 I "An Unodious Comparison: The Three Council Chambers of the United Nations", *Interiors* (July 1952); pp. 46–67.
26 Ibid.
27 Letter from Trygve Lie to Arnstein Arneberg, 30 January 1952. National Museum, Architecture Collection, Arneberg archive.
28 Letter from Trygve Lie to Arnstein Arneberg, 1 March 1952. National Museum, Architecture Collection, Arneberg archive.

Guri Hjeltnes
Trygve Lie:
A Man of Action

1 Letter from Trygve Lie to Sidsel and Jens Halvard Bratz. Dated 12 June 1946, New York. Hjeltnes, unpublished manuscript.
2 Minutes. "Notes on Private Meeting in the Secretary General's Office 9.30 on Saturday 30th March 1946." S-0194-0003, Box 3, File 1 4 / 1946-8-1946. Trygve Lie.
3 Letter from Trygve Lie to his daughters Sissel and Mette. Dated 20 January 1946, London. Hjeltnes, unpublished manuscript.
4 Trygve Lie, *Syv år for freden*, (Oslo: Tiden Norsk Forlag, 1954), p. 14.
5 Lie, *Syv år for freden*, p. 16.
6 Lie, *Syv år for freden*, p. 21.
7 Anthony Eden, *The Reckoning. The Memoirs of Anthony Eden, Earl of Avon*, (Boston: Houghton Mifflin Co., 1965), p. 642; Arthur W. Rovine, *The First Fifty Years. The* secretary-general *in World Politics 1920–1970*, (Leyden: Sitjhoff, 1970), p. 209.
8 Lie, *Syv år for freden*, p. 23.
9 Rovine, *The First Fifty Years*, p. 209.
10 Ibid.
11 Ibid.
12 Ibid., p. 210.
13 Ibid.
14 Ibid.
15 Rovine, *The First Fifty Years*, pp. 209ff.
16 Lie, *Syv år for freden*, pp. 26ff.
17 Brian Urquhart, *A Life in Peace and War* (New York: W.W. Norton & Company, 1987), p. 99.
18 Ibid., pp. 100ff.
19 Rovine, *The First Fifty Years*, p 210.
20 Andrew W. Cordier and Wilder Foote, *Public Papers of the Secretaries-General of the United Nations*. Volume 1. Trygve Lie 1946–1953 (Columbia University Press, New York and London 1969), p. 33.
21 Lie, *Syv år for freden*, pp. 27ff.
22 Ibid., p. 53.
23 Urquhart, *A Life in Peace and War*, p. 97.
24 Stanley Meisler, *United Nations: The First Fifty Years* (New York: Atlantic Monthly Press, 1995), p. 26.
25 Lie, *Syv år for freden*, p. 63.
26 Ibid.
27 Guri Hjeltnes, "Tapte horisonter: Nordisk eller atlantisk: Striden om Atlanterhavspolitikken 1940–1945", in *Selvstendig og beskyttet: Det stormaktsgaranterte Norge fra Krimkrigen til NATO*, edited by Roald Berg (Bergen: Fagbokforlaget, 2008), pp. 61–76.
28 Lie, *Syv år for freden*, p. 63.
29 Wellington Koo in a speech to the General Assembly, autumn 1946. Quoted in Lie, *Syv år for freden*, p. 62.
30 Lie, *Syv år for freden*, p 67.
31 Carl Emil Vogt, *Fridtjof Nansen. Mannen og verden* (Oslo: Cappelen Damm, 2011).
32 Stanley Meisler, *United Nations: The First Fifty Years*, p. 27.
33 Lie, *Syv år for freden*, p. 66.
34 Ibid.; Meisler, *United Nations: The First Fifty Years*, p. 27.
35 Lie, *Syv år for freden*, p. 69.
36 Ibid., p. 70.
37 Ibid.
38 Ibid.
39 Ibid., p. 71.
40 Ibid.
41 Ibid.
42 Ibid., p. 73.
43 Ibid.
44 Ibid., pp. 73–75.
45 Ibid., p. 49.
46 Minutes. "Private Meeting in Mr. Lie's Office at Lake Success on 29 November, 1946, at 0930. A.M." S-0194-0003, Box 3, File 1 4 / 1946-8-1946. Trygve Lie.
47 Lie, *Syv år for freden*, p. 76.
48 Minutes. "Private Meeting in the Secretary General's Office on Monday 15th April at 9.30 A.M." S-0194-0003, Box 3, File 1 4 / 1946-8-1946.Trygve Lie; Lie, *Syv år for freden*, pp. 74ff; Urquhart, *A Life in Peace and War*, pp. 106, 111.
49 Robert A. Caro, *The Power Broker: Robert Moses and the Fall of New York*, (New York: New York Vintage, 1975), pp. 5, 7.
50 Ibid., p. 771.
51 Ibid.
52 Ibid., p. 772.
53 Ibid.
54 Ibid.
55 Caro, *The Power Broker*, p. 772.
56 William Zeckendorf and Edward McCreary, *Zeckendorf, The Autobiography of William Zeckendorf* (New York: Holt, Rinehart and Winston, 1970), p. 68.
57 Lie, *Syv år for freden*, p. 114; Caro, *The Power Broker*, p. 772.
58 Caro, *The Power Broker*, p. 772.
59 Lie, *Syv år for freden*, p. 116.
60 Caro, *The Power Broker*, p. 773.
61 Zeckendorf og McCreary, *Zeckendorf*, p. 71; Caro, *The Power Broker*, p. 774.
62 Caro, *The Power Broker*, p. 774.
63 Zeckendorf og McCreary, *Zeckendorf*, p. 71.
64 Lie, *Syv år for freden*, p. 118.
65 Ibid., p. 117.
66 Ibid., p. 118.
67 Ibid., p. 119.
68 Arne Skouen interviewed 24 January 2001 by Guri Hjeltnes.
69 Rovine, *The First Fifty Years*, p. 203.
70 Guri Hjeltnes, "McCarthyismens inntog i FN", *Arbeiderhistorie* (2004), pp. 32–53.

Vibeke Waallann Hansen
Per Krohg's UN Painting:
An Altarpiece for Peace

1 Letter from Arnstein Arneberg to Trygve Lie 12 June 1950. National Museum, Architecture Collection, Arneberg archive.
2 The painting is often described as a wall painting or fresco, but the technique is oil on canvas. From the beginning, Arneberg wanted a wall painting or a mosaic, but for practical and financial reasons it ended up being oil on canvas.
3 Per Krohg, *Per Krohgs memoarer: Minner og meninger* (Oslo: Gyldendal, 1966), p. 156.
4 Per Krohg, "Forklaring til utkast angående det store maleri på fondveggen i F.N.s sikkerhetsråds forsamlingssal", 22 February 1950. In the electronic archive of the Norwegian Foreign Ministry: Documents regarding the decoration of the Security Council Chamber. Protocol number: Dza 1080.3: 1950–1953, p. 245.
5 Letter from Norwegian Foreign Ministry, 30 March 1950. In the electronic archive of the Norwegian Foreign Ministry': Documents regarding the decoration of the Security Council Chamber. Protocol number: Dza 1080.3: 1950–1953, p. 245. It has not been possible to locate the sketches by Krohg that are mentioned in this letter. I have been in contact with Per Krohg's descendants, but they are unaware of the sketches.
6 Per Krohg, "Forklaring til utkast angående det store maleri på fondveggen i F.N.s sikkerhetsråds forsamlingssal", 22 February 1950.
7 Per Krohg understood that he would need a lot of room to make a picture measuring 50 square metres. It was arranged for him to use the atelier in the Oslo City Hall. At this point it was Henrik Sørensen who had his workplace there, but he now had to move out. Correspondence in the Foreign Ministry's office about this.
8 A note dated 16 March 1951 in the Norwegian Foreign Ministry's archive reveals that Krohg invited the Foreign Minister and his entourage to inspect the picture. In the electronic archive of the Norwegian Foreign Ministry: documents relating to the decoration of the Security Council Chamber. Protocol number: Dza 1080.3: 1950–1953, p. 143.
9 Per Krohg, "F.N. Billedet". The description is undated, but accompanies correspondence dated 29 March1951. In the electronic archive of the Norwegian Foreign Ministry: documents relating to the decoration of the Security Council Chamber. Protokollnr.: Dza 1080.3: 1950–1953 UD, p. 135.

10 Ibid.
11 Maria Veie Sandvik has provided an iconological analysis of the work. Veie Sandvik's conclusion is that the painting contains clear references to altarpieces. See Maria Veie Sandvik, *Iconology of a New World Order: Per Krohg's Painting in the United Nations Security Chamber in New York*. Vereinte Nationen: German Review on the United Nations. Volume 62, no. 4, UN and Art, (2014): pp. 156–162.
12 In 1920, with his colleague Axel Revold, Krohg was on a three-month stay in Italy to study historical frescoes. See Trygve Nergaard, *Bilder av Per Krohg* (Oslo: Aschehoug, 2000), p. 187.
13 Gunnar Sørensen, "Kunstnerisk enhet og fellesskap", in Ulf Grønvold, Nils Anker and Gunnar Sørensen, *Det store løftet: Rådhuset i Oslo* (Oslo: Aschehoug & Co., 2000).
14 Per Krohg, offprint of *Kunsten i dag*, no. 2, 1952.
15 Letter from Arnstein Arneberg to Wallace K. Harrison 30 March 1949. National Museum, Architecture Collection, Arneberg archive.
16 Letter to the Norwegian Foreign Ministry, 17 November 1949. National Museum, Architecture Collection, Arneberg archive.
17 Letter to the Norwegian Foreign Ministry, 17 November 1949. National Museum, Architecture Collection, Arneberg archive.
18 Ibid.
19 Ibid.
20 The sculptor Emil Lie received a commission to create marble reliefs for the room. Lie was to receive a grant of 15,000 kroner for these works. The proposal was withdrawn, however, while Lie was at work on the reliefs. Lie wanted to be represented in the room, and after it was dedicated he contacted the Foreign Ministry and, citing a statement by Arneberg that it would be good to have a bronze statue in the room, asked whether there was any money left in the budget to cover such a work. There wasn't, and so Lie is not represented in the room (letter to Norwegian Foreign Ministry from Emil Lie, 9 December 1953, digital archive). In a letter of 14 September 1951 Arneberg explains why Emil Lie's balustrades were out: "The architectural office in New York has decided to cancel these balconies mable reliefs for financial reasons."
21 Ibid.
22 Letter from the Norwegian Foreign Ministry to Arnstein Arneberg 9 January 1950. In the electronic archive of the Norwegian Foreign Ministry: Documents relating to the decoration of the Security Council Chamber. Protocol number.: Dza 1080.3: 1950–1953DU, p. 318.
23 *Dagbladet*, 29 March 1950.
24 Ibid.
25 *Aftenposten*, 18 March 1950.
26 *Morgenposten*, 20 March 1950.
27 Letter from Wallace K. Harrison to Arnstein Arneberg 5 July 1950. National Museum, Architecture Collection, Arneberg archive.
28 Letter from Arnstein Arneberg to Trygve Lie 12 June 1950. National Museum, Architecture Collection, Arneberg archive.
29 Norway's UN ambassador, Arne Sunde, was also drawn into the matter. On 14 July 1950, a letter was sent to Sunde from Skylstad at the Foreign Ministry. Sunde was asked to discuss the matter with secretary-general Lie, and to do what he could to find "a reasonable solution to the difficulties that have arisen".
30 Letter from Arnstein Arneberg to Per Krohg 3 August 1950. National Museum, Architecture Collection, Arneberg archive.
31 Letter from Wallace K. Harrison to Arnstein Arneberg 20 September 1950. National Museum, Architecture Collection, Arneberg archive.
32 Letter from Arnstein Arneberg to Secretary Skylstad 24 July 1950. In the electronic archive of the Norwegian Foreign Ministry: Documents regarding the decoration of the Security Council Chamber. Protocol number: Dza 1080.3: 1950–1953 UD, p. 325.
33 *Morgenbladet*, 2 September 1950.
34 Krohg, *Per Krohgs memoarer*, p. 194.
35 *Dagbladet*, 12 August 1952.
36 Henning Sinding-Larsen, *Per Krohg 1889–1965*, catalogue for exhibit at Bergen Art Association 12–28 March 1965.
37 *Byggekunst*, no. 10 (1952): p. 201.
38 Sandvik, *Iconology of a New World Order*, p. 39.
39 Linda Sue Phipps, *Constructing the United Nations Headquarters: Modern Architecture as Public Diplomacy* (Cambridge, Mass.: Harvard University, 1998), p. 290. In *The New York Times* of 7 March 1948, George Barrett reported that Picasso had offered to create a wall painting for the building. Footnote in Phipps, p. 180.
40 Letter from Trygve Lie to Arnstein Arneberg 1 March 1952. National Museum, Architecture Collection, Arneberg archive.
41 Jacob Baal-Teshuva, *Art treasures of the United Nations* (New York: Yoseloff, 1964).
42 This was planned from the beginning, but not carried out until 1956.
43 Phipps, *Constructing the United Nations Headquarters*, pp. 287–88. Phipps writes: "The Organization was continually obliged to placate powerful delegations by employing both individuals and materials from non-American member nations. The inconsistent use of stone throughout the complex – Vermont marble on the Secretariat, but English Portland Stone on the General Assembly – resulted from such pressures. Harrison continued to plod, diplomatically, through an endless sea of special interests."
44 Ibid. The committee was appointed on 1 March 1950.

Sarah A. Lichtman
Uncovering Else Poulsson: Norwegian Textile Designer

1 Arne Remlov, "Merkbar fremgang," *Bonytt* (October 1949): p. 179. In her *Aftenposten* obituary, Nils Anker, refers to Poulsson as "one of the country's most significant applied artists." Nils Anker, "Else Poulsson Moe," *Aftenposten*, March 18, 2002.
2 Pat Kirkham and Lynne Walker, "Women Designers in the USA, 1900–2000: Diversity and Difference," in *Women Designers in the USA 1900–2000: Diversity and Difference*, ed. Pat Kirkham (New York and New Haven: Bard Graduate Center and Yale University Press, 2000), 75 and 50; Alexa Griffith Winton, "A Striking Juxtaposition: Hand-Woven Textiles in the United Nations Conference Building Interiors," *The Journal of Modern Craft* 8, No. 2 (July 2015): 181.
3 Vibeke Hollekim, "Dette er liksom 'mitt' rom," *Aftenposten*, November 16, 1999. Poulsson's raise wasn't refused for lack of merit but, she was told, because she lived with her uncle and, therefore, didn't need the money. Else Poulsson interview, conducted by Tone Rasch and Kari-Anne Pedersen, November 3, 1998. Norsk Folkemuseum, Oslo.
4 Kirkham, Women Designers in the USA, 62.
5 T'ai Smith, *Bauhaus Weaving Theory: From Feminine Craft to Mode of Design* (Minneapolis: University of Minnesota Press, 2014).
6 Elissa Auther, *String, Felt, Thread: The Hierarchy of Art and Craft in American Art* (Minneapolis: University of Minnesota Press, 2009), pp. 98, 100.
7 The association of Scandinavian design with modernism is strong. Charlotte Ashby identifies Scandinavia as, "a region associated with modernity: modern design, modern living and a progressive welfare state." Charlotte Ashby, *Modernism in Scandinavia: Art, Architecture and Design* (London: Bloomsbury, 2017), p. 1. Likewise, Kjetil Fallan has discussed the strong modernist bias found in design historical discourse in general and Scandinavian design discourse in particular. See Kjetil Fallan, *Designing Modern Norway: A History of Design Discourse* (London and New York: Routledge, 2017), p. 1. See also Christina Zetterlund, "Just Decoration? Ideology and Design in Early-Twentieth-Century Sweden," in *Scandinavian Design: Alternative Histories*, ed. Kjetil Fallan (London: Berg, 2012), 103–116.
8 Her cousin, Vibeke Poulsson (1915–1980), was a well-known fashion designer. More information on Vibeke Poulsson can be found in the Else Poulsson Archive, Norsk Folkemuseum, Oslo.
9 I.S., "Våre kvinnelige tekstiltegnere: Else Poulsson i Den Norske Husflidsforening," *Urd*, 41 (1937): 145. The 1866 dissolutions of the Norwegian guilds removed the legal impediments keeping women from establishing commercial craft trades. The cultural barriers to receiving formal training and apprenticeships, however, problematized such endeavors. Established in 1875, the Women's Industrial School, aimed, initially to be a place where women could learn the design skills necessary for industrial production. By 1888, however, headmistress Sophie Borchgrevink reoriented the curricula away from industrial methods and toward traditional craft techniques rooted in folk traditions. Borchgrevink forged strong relationships with museums and the Norwegian Home Craft Association. The school, then, became a place for women to learn traditional craft skills and gain employment within the craft industry rather than a progressive organization advocating for modern opportunities for women. Kjetil Fallan, *Designing Modern Norway*, 18–19; Tone Rasch, "Den kvinnelige industriskole sett innenfra," *FORMakademisk*, vol. 5, 2 (2012): 1–3. 1. URL: https://journals.hioa.no/index.php/formakademisk/article/viewFile/508/496; Kristen Røvig Håberg, *Fra skyggetanter til yrkeskvinner*. (Drammen: ABM-media, 2012).
10 In 1931 Poulsson spent three months in Germany. She also traveled in Hungary, Czechoslovakia, and Poland to study Folk Art and textile collections. In Italy in 1932, Poulsson found the art of the primitive painters captivating and especially relevant for the applied arts. In 1935, she hiked through Norway and visited farms in search of traditional textiles. The following year Poulsson travelled to Denmark. I.S., "Våre kvinnelige tekstiltegnere," 154; "Hadde vi bare den svenske linen!," *Tidens Tegn*, October, 1937, Else Poulsson Archive, Norsk Folkemuseum, Oslo. For an overview of Poulsson's life and career, see the Else Poulsson interview conducted by Tone Rasch and Kari-Anne Pedersen, November 3, 1998. Norsk Folkemuseum, Oslo.

11 Marie Lien, *Norwegian National Organization for the Promotion of Home Arts and Crafts* (Oslo: Fabritius & Sønner, 1946), 13. Ingeborg Glambek, "Norway," in *International Arts and Crafts*, eds. Karen Livingstone and Linda Parry (London: V&A Publications, 2005), 288; Fallan, *Designing Modern Norway*, 20. The goods appealed to middle class buyers and tourists alike who purchased articles sold in hotels and shops. Eyvind S. Engelstad writing in *Bonytt*, described shopping in the stores as a "pure delight. A place where traditions from centuries past still live on in the present, through the craft of the hand." Engelstad, "Husfliden jubilerer," 256.

12 A 1902 Norwegian survey reported on large numbers of abandoned and broken looms and carpenter's benches, reinforcing reformers fears of the loss of Norwegian peasant culture. Lien, *Norwegian National Organization for the Promotion of Home Arts and Crafts*, 18 and 24. Eyvind S. Engelstad, "Husfliden jubilerer," *Bonytt* (September 1966): p. 254. Helen Englestad, *Modern Norwegian Textile Art*, in *Norway Arts and Crafts*, ed. Conrad Hofgaard (Oslo: Norges Eksportråd, 1950), 28. The decline and promotion of home craft was a pan-Nordic phenomena and across the Nordic countries reformers formed organizations and created museums to preserve folk traditions and national heritage. Elisabet Stavenow-Hidemark, "Scandinavia: 'Beauty for All,'" in *The Arts & Crafts Movement in Europe & America*, ed. Wendy Kaplan (London: *Thames and Hudson* in association with The Los Angeles County Museum of Art, 2004), 184.

13 Stavenow-Hidemark, "Scandinavia: Beauty for 'All,'" 179 and 184.

14 Fallan, *Designing Modern Norway*, 19–21. As Stavenow-Hidemark has argued, Norway, along with Finland, most fervently sought out their national identity in their history. Both of their causes were bound up in the quest for independence. Stavenow-Hidemark, "Scandinavia: Beauty for 'All,'" p. 179.

15 Den Norske Husflidsforening gjennom 60 år (Oslo: Morten Johansens boktrykkeri), 1951, p. 103; Lien, Norwegian National Organization for the Promotion of Home Arts And Crafts, 89.

16 Engelstad, "Husfliden jubilerer," 256. I.S., "Våre kvinnelige tekstiltegnere," 137 and 154. For more examples of Poulsson's work for the Association, see Jo Lunde, "Den Norske Husflidsforening: 60 år i brukskunstens tjeneste," *Bonytt* (September 1951): p. 149–153.

17 With the Norwegian Home Craft Association, Poulsson exhibited an embroidered altar cloth at the Nidaros exhibition in Trondheim, and designed linen altar cloths and red and gold woven chasubles for the Todal Church. "Mere kirkekunst til Nidaros," *Dagbladet*, 7 May 1930; "Nytt kirkeutstyr," *Aftenposten*, 5 January 1932.

18 The additional churches include Namsos, Slemmestad, Manglerud, and Parish Hall, Lamberster and Abildsø. See Else Poulsson, Artist Statement, Norsk Folkemuseum, Oslo; I.S. "Våre kvinnelige tekstiltegnere," 144. Poulsson was also involved in choosing the new altar cloth for Gransheard Church in 1951. Aaste Nisi, Kjetil Tjønnås, and O.A. Quamme, *Gransheradsoga* (Notodden: Notodden Kommune, 1977).

19 I.S., "Våre kvinnelige tekstildesignere," 154.

20 Fallan, *Designing Modern Norway*, 86. Fallan draws on the work of Kristina Wilson, *Livable Modernism: Interior Decorating and Design During the Great Depression* (New Haven: Yake University Press, 2004). For further examples of Poulsson's modern style, see Halvor Vreim, *Norwegian Decorative Art Today* (Oslo: Fabritius & Sønners Forlag, 1937).

21 Per R. Moe, "Den våpenløse kamp." Dagbok, brev og erindringer fra læreraksjonen 1942. Ms.4° 4470: 2. Private archive of Per R. Moe, unpublished closed manuscript. Monte Sol. Villa Joyosa, February 6th, 1978.

22 "Norwegian Women Revive All Ancient Textile Arts," *Milwaukee Journal*, 1938.

23 Else Poulsson, *Rutemønster for strikking og broderi* (Oslo: J.W. Cappelens Forlag, 1945). For another period home knitting book, see Annichen Sibbern Bøhn, *Norwegian Knitting Designs* (Oslo: Grøndahl & Søn, 1952).

24 "Kanskje vi blir en av de beste i Paris….," *Dagbladet*, 11 January 1937.

25 Helen Englestad, "Til Paris V. De håndvevde tekstiler," *Vi selv og våre hjem*, 5 (1937), 33; I.S. "Våre kvinnelige tekstiltegnere," 144. For more on the Norwegian contribution to the 1937 Paris Exposition, see *Beretning om Norges deltagelse, den internasjonale utstilling i Paris, 1937*, and *La Norvège à Paris: Catalogue du Pavillion de la Norvège à L'Exposition Internationale de Paris 1937*.

26 From 1930, the association sponsored touring exhibitions around Norway and established a permanent exhibition space in Oslo. Kjetil Fallan, "Visionaries and Weathercocks: Norwegian Furniture Design c. 1920–1965," 102–103; Fallan, *Designing Modern Norway*, 40–46; Knut Greve, "The Norwegian Association for Applied Art and Industrial Design," *Bonytt* (April–May 1951): p. 61–63.

27 "Årsmøte i foreningen brukskunst i Oslo," *Bonytt* (May–June 1948), viii; Arne Remlov, "Feriehus og ferieutstyr på utstilling," *Bonytt* (July–August 1954): p. 138–143.

28 Arne Remlov, "Kvalitetsarbeider: osloforeningen brukskunsts årsutstilling", *Bonytt* (May–June 1949): p. 103; Arne Remlov, "Foran gjenreisningen: en utstilling i foreningen brukskunst i Oslo", *Bonytt* (May–June 1949): p. 157; Arne Remlov, "Merkbar fremgang," *Bonytt* (September–October 1949). Remlov was also the Secretary of the Applied Art Association chapter in Oslo, co-founder of the Association of Interior Architects (1945), and the director of FORUM (1956–1982). Poulsson's work also appeared in Norsk Brukskunst in Gothenburg and Copenhagen (1951). Odd Hølaas, "Norsk Brukskunst en introduksjon," in *Norsk Brukskunst*, (Röhsska Konstslödjmuseet, Göteborg and Det Danske Kunstindustrimuseum, København, 1951).

29 *Bonytt* was an important outlet for the Applied Arts Association in disseminating modern ideas. Fallan, *Designing Modern Norway*, 8–9 and 74–86; Fallan, "Visionaries and Weathercocks," 106; Tias Eckhoff, "Brukskunsts høstmønstring 1953," *Bonytt* (Christmas 1953): p. 196. See also "Håndvevede tekstiler i Brukskunst," *Morgenbladet*, November 12, 1935; Ole Moelne, "Det kvinnelige element spiller sterkt inn," *Dagbladet*, 1935. Else Poulsson Archive, Norsk Folkemuseum, Oslo.

30 Per Tannum and Torlof Prytz brought "Norway Designs for Living" to Chicago. Tannum opened Norway Designs A/S in Chicago after the run of the exhibition, but closed the store in 1953 due to financial difficulties. Tannum took over the rights to the name and in 1957 he opened the company in Oslo, turning the store into an international business selling high quality design and crafts. See Per Tannum, "Norway Designs for Living," *Bonytt* (April–May 1951): p. 64; Anne Douglas, "Norway Shows City Her Finest in Furnishings," *Chicago Tribune*, May 27, 1951. For more on "Norway Designs for Living," see Kjetil Fallan, "Love and Hate in Industrial Design: Europe's Design Professionals and America in the 1950s," in P. Lundin and T. Kaiserfeld, eds., *The Making of European Consumption: Facing the American Challenge* (Springer, 2015), 50–53.

31 Norway was praised for its "colorful domestic crafts and woven goods." Gotthard Johansson, "*Design in Scandinavia*," in *Design in Scandinavia*, ed. Arne Remlov (Stavanger, 1954), 20; Jørn Guldberg, "'Scandinavian Design' as Discourse: The Exhibition *Design in Scandinavia*, 1954–57," *Design Issues* 27 (Spring 2011): 42. For the idea of Scandinavian Design as a cultural construction, see essays in Widar Halén and Kerstin Wickman, eds. *Scandinavian Design Beyond the Myth: Fifty Years of Design from the Nordic Countries* (Stockholm: Arvinius Förlag / Form Förlag, 2003). Also see Fallan, *Designing Modern Norway*, 113–133.

32 Englestad, *Modern Norwegian Textile Art*, 25; Helen Engelstad, "*Norwegian Textile Art*," *Bonytt* (April–May 1951): p. 85.

33 The housing crisis was acute even before the war. The 1938 census reported over 200,000 people lived in crowded apartments all over Oslo with more than two people per room. Liv Schødt, "3 Typehus," *Bonytt* (July–August 1948): p. 126–131. Between 1947 and 1950, 72,000 new homes were built in Norway. Fallan, "Visionaries and Weathercocks," 106.

34 Helen Engelstad, *Norwegian Textiles* (Brighton: The Dolphin Press, 1952), 8. Poulsson was also involved in the decoration of "Lysebu," a residence constructed as a gift to Denmark from Norway for their help during World War II. Arne Remlov, "Lysebu", *Bonytt* (November–December, 1947): p. 200. Poulsson also created textiles for model rooms in "12 Right Ways", a 1950 exhibition on how to decorate new housing. Poulsson contributed to the decoration of the Norwegian Farmer Woman's association space. *Den Norske husflidforening gjennom 60 år.*, 93.

35 In 1948 she designed textiles and upholstery fabrics produced by the Association for the Grand Hotel, Oslo. Knut Greve and F.S. Platou, "Grand hotells vestibyle," *Bonytt* (Christmas 1948): p. 191–195. Two years later, in collaboration with the Association, she designed the interior textiles for the *Norsk Folke-Feries* resort, Dovrefjell Hotell, Dombas, a ski resort owned by the Norwegian Workers Union. *Den Norske Husflidforening gjennom 60 år.*, 98.

36 Lien, *Norwegian Organization for the Promotion of Home Arts and Crafts*, 89; "Norwegian Women Revive All Ancient Textile Arts," *Milwaukee Journal*, 1938; De nye norske båtene," *Urd*, 1938. Poulsson also designed the textiles for the ships "Black Prince" and "Black Watch", as well as the textiles for the King's waiting room at the Oslo Train Station (Østbanen). See Else Poulsson, Artist Statement, Else Poulsson Archives, Norske Folkemuseum.

37 The Oslo City Hall took nineteen years to compete and officially opened in conjunction with Oslo's ninth centenary. Per Rom, ed., trans. Christopher Norman, *The Decorations of the Oslo City Hall* (Oslo: Municipality of Oslo, 1952), 7. See also Johan Borgen, "The Decorations of the Oslo

City Hall," trans. Christopher Norman, *Kunsten i dag*, vol. 13–14, no. 1–2 (1950): 27–47; Arnstein Arneberg and Magnus Poulsson, "Oslo rådhus," *Byggekunst*, 9–10 (1950): 145–173. For the textiles see Elise Jakhelln, "Tekstilene," in *Rådhuset i Oslo: annen del beskrivelse*, ed. Carl Just (Oslo: H. Aschehoug & Co., 1952), 240–8. For a comprehensive overview of the City Hall see Ulf Grønvold, Nils Anker, and Gunnar Sørensen, trans. Ruth Waaler, *The City Hall in Oslo* (Oslo: Aschehoug, 2000).

38 Elise Jakhelln, "Tekstilene," 246. The linen tablecloths and napkins for the banquet hall and the wall covering of the library were mechanically woven by Joh. Petersen, the same company that wove the wall coverings for the United Nations Security Council Chamber. Poulsson also designed textiles for cushion covers and curtains for the Chairman Hall, wall textiles and furniture textiles for the Aldermen's Assembly Room, and the Executive Committee Library. Ulf Grønvold, et. al., *The City Hall in Oslo*, 189–192; 216 and 238. In 2000 Poulsson was consulted on the refurbishments of all of the City Hall textiles. Hollekim, "Dette er liksom 'mitt' rom."

39 Aage Schou, "Arkitekt Magnus Poulsson som jeg husker han," *Bonytt* (October 1958): p. 203–205; Hollekim, "Dette er liksom 'mitt' rom." The architects had commissioned Tora Quiller to design the Mayor's office and Ingeborg Arbo to make the textiles for the Executive Committee Hall. It was only Poulsson, however, with the Association, who completed their tasks. Jakhelln, "Tekstilene," 240.

40 Ulf Grønvold, et. al., *The City Hall in Oslo*, 231–2; Halling worked with four assistants for two years to execute Poulsson's design. Annemor Sundbø, *Spelsau og samspill: Glansfull ull og lodne skjebnetråder* (Tvedestrand: Bokbyen forlag, 2015), 359; Candida, "Vårt nyeste billedteppe skal utstilles," *Morgenbladet*, 10 March 1948.

41 Englestad, *Modern Norwegian Textile Art*, 25–26. During the early 1940s, the Association started a collaboration with the director of the Oslo Museum of Decorative Arts and Design, Thor Kielland, to develop hand spun spelsau yarn for the City Hall tapestries. The Association completed three monumental tapestries, one by Else Poulsson and two by Kåre Mikkelsen Jonsborg for the Ceremonial Hall. Such commissions fell out of the range of what the Association could deliver and in 1947, it started Norwegian Tapestry A/S (Norsk Billedvev A/S), a collaborative weaving studio with the Norwegian Home Craft Association, and the Museum for Decorative Arts and Design in Oslo. In 1951, Else Halling assumed the position as artistic director. It worked on both public and private commissions based on historical motifs as well as from historical carpets and tapestries from the museum's collection. Sundbø, *Spelsau og samspill*, 359; *Den Norske Husflidsforening gjennom 60 år.*, 99 and 101. In 1948, an exhibition was mounted as part of a campaign to rejuvenate the breed. "Spelsauen i festsalen," *Dagbladet*, 11 March 1948.

42 Arnstein Arneberg and Magnus Poulsson, "Oslo rådhus," *Byggekunst*, 9–10 (1950): 168; Tommie, "Veggstoffer, gardiner, møbelstoffer," *Kvinner og Klær*, 17 June 1950, 20; Candida, "Vårt nyeste billedteppe skal utstilles," quoted in Sundbø, 359.

43 Arnstein Arneberg, "Litt omkring FN-bygningen i New York," *Byggekunst* 10 (1952): 201. Poulsson outlined her proposals for alternative furniture fabrics to Arneberg. Letter from Else Poulsson to Arnstein Arneberg, 20 October 1949, Arnstein Arneberg Archive, National Museum – Architecture, Oslo. The rear wall of the chamber is covered with traditional straw Biri wallpaper. The Arneberg archives contain correspondence between the United Nations Planning Office and Kunstnerforbundet – the Artist's Union – about obtaining the covering for use in the Security Council Chamber. Arneberg also used Biri wallcoverings for the Oslo City Hall. 26 February 1951. National Museum, Architecture Collection, Arneberg archive. Also see correspondence between Arneberg and Klare Schee. Arneberg had initially considered using Poulsson's same design as the one for the wall coverings for the Oslo City Hall. Arnstein Arneberg, undated notes. Arnstein Arneberg Archive, National Museum – Architecture, Oslo.

44 Arneberg considered weaving the fabrics in silk by the Parisian firm of Tassani & Chatel. 21 December 1949; 29 December 1949; 5 January 1950; and 21 February 1950, Arnstein Arneberg Archive, National Museum – Architecture, Oslo. In correspondence with Arneberg, Joh. Petersen director Joh. Brunæs quotes a cost of 140 Norwegian Crowns per meter. He informs Arneberg that they will use yarn from a Norwegian producer of synthetic silk, Kunstsilkefabrikken, Notodden. See correspondence from 24 March 1950 and 11 January 1951. Arneberg confirms the curtain order from Joh. Petersen on January 13, 1951 and asks him to rush the order since he is concerned that the walls will be "naked until the fabric arrives". 13 January, 1951, Arnstein Arneberg Archive, National Museum – Architecture, Oslo. The textile company Joh. Petersen was founded in 1854 by Ole Johan Petersen (1828–1906) in Bergen, Norway. By 1854, he had established a mechanical cotton mill, the Bergens Dampveveri (Bergen Steam Mill) that could produce multicoloured damask as well as an array of household textiles. By 1880, Petersen relocated the company from Bergen to Bryn and continued to expand its activities. Joh. Petersen AS, *En norsk tekstilbedrift 100 år: Joh. Petersen aktieselskab, lin-og bommulsvarefabrikker* (Oslo: Joh. Petersen, 1954, 6–16).

45 Letter from Michael H. Harris to Arneberg, 15 January1951. Arnstein Arneberg Archive, National Museum – Architecture, Oslo. In a letter to Secretary General Trygve Lie, Arneberg sheepishly shared the news that fire had damaged the fabrics during a flame test and would need to be replaced. Arneberg to Trygve Lie, 5 January 1952. In addition to the fabrics needing to be altered, so too did the original idea of using Norwegian pine for the delegate's table because it did not meet fire codes. Ingeborg Glambek, "The Council Chambers in the UN Building in New York," *Scandinavian Journal of Design History* 15 (2005), 19. Also, see Winton, "A Striking Juxtaposition," 186. For more about the United Nations and its construction see Arnstein Arneberg, "Litt omkring FN-bygningen i New York," *Byggekunst* 10 (1952): 196–202; Victoria Newhouse, *Wallace K. Harrison: Architect* (New York: Rizzoli, 1989).

46 Henry Stern Churchill, writing in *Architectural Record*, described the room as, "curiously antique". Henry Stern Churchill, "United Nations Headquarters: A Description and Appraisal," *Architectural Record*, July 1952, 118. *Architectural Forum* found the chamber so lacking that it chose not to review it at all. *Architectural Forum*, April 1952, 109. Excerpts from *Architectural Forum* were reproduced in *Bonytt*. See "Skandinavia innreder i F.N. bygningen," *Bonytt* (May–June 1952): p. 112. Also see "An Unodious Comparison: The Three Council Chambers of the United Nations," *Interiors*, July, 1952, 49.

47 Helen Engelstad, "Norsk tekstilindustri 1952: en utstilling i brukskunst," *Bonytt* (February 1953): p. 30. It's possible that Arneberg found using real silk too expensive. His first proposal was over the budget allotted by the United Nations and he was asked to reduce costs. Glambek, "The Council Chambers in the UN Building in New York," 18.

48 Engelstad, *Norwegian Textile Art*, 85; Winton, "A Striking Juxtaposition," 181–193. Winton discusses the work of Marianne Richter and Paula Trock located in the Economic and Trustees Council Chambers. For a period analysis of hand woven textiles at the United Nations, see Lili Blumenau, "Textiles in the United Nations Building," *Handweaver & Craftsman*, Winter, 1952–53, 10–12.

49 In 1966 the National Museum of Decorative Arts and Design featured Poulsson's work in the exhibition "Wood and Textiles by 3", commemorating the 60th anniversary of the Association, and in 1971 her work appeared at the Kunstindustrimuseét, The National Museum of Decorative Arts and Design, Oslo, in "Norwegian Textiles Now," as well as various other exhibitions. Solo exhibitions included at the noted Kunstnerforbundet Artist's Union, Oslo, (1961); an exhibition of ryas designed in collaboration with yarn producer Rauma ullvarefabrikk (1961); and "The Set Table" (*Dekkede Bord*) with ceramic designer William Knutzen. Oscar Thue, "Utsillinger i Oslo høsten 1961," *Kunst og Kultur* 45, 1 (1962): 51. "Tre og tekstil ved 3: Tre husflidsdesignere: Else Poulsson, Agnes Sykkelstad, og Aage Schou," Kunstindustrimuseet i Oslo, 1966; Karen Sundbye, "Tre og tekstil ved 3," *Dagbladet*, September 3, 1966; "Husflidsjubileum med fin utstilling i Kunstindustrimuséet," *Verdens Gang*, nd. Else Poulsson Archive, Norsk Folkemuseum, Oslo; Norsk Tekstil *NÅ*, 1971. Sponsored by the Norwegian Applied Art and Textile working group, Norwegian Society for Arts and Crafts, Kunstindustrimuseet, Oslo. Later in her life when she was no longer able to weave, Poulsson painted watercolours. Shows include: "The Cube," Sandvika, Bærum (1979), the Galleri Chac Mool, Oslo (1982), "Akvareller: Else Poulsson". Rastad & Relling (1983) and the Bekkestua Bibliotek, Oslo (1984). See Else Poulsson, Artist Statement, Else Poulsson Archives, Norsk Folkemuseum.

50 Thank you to Elisabeth Hoff, Kari-Anne Pedersen, Tone Rasch, and Mats Linder for their help in preparing this article; and to Malin Graesse for her research and translation assistance.

Linda Veiby
Norway's Role in the Restoration of the Security Council Chamber

1 Letter from the Ministry of the Environment to the Ministry of Foreign Affairs. Case number: 201005211-/ETB. Also e-mail from the Ministry of the Environment to the Directorate for Cultural Heritage, dated 5 January 2011, case number: 09/571-7. The role of the Directorate for Cultural Heritage was thus purely advisory, and the directorate had no authority to impose any desired action.

2 Letter from Ministry of the Environment to Ministry of Foreign Affairs. Case number: 201005211-/ETB.

3 I have described the process as a restoration rather than a refurbishment. To be sure, during the process many new items were added, but this was done with full awareness that this is a historical space. To perform a restoration is to return and reconstruct a building or object entirely or partly to an earlier condition.

4 The large conservation project that went under the name "Statens kulturhistoriske eiendommer" (Cultural-Historical Government Properties) involved key architectural momuments of the postwar period, including Erling Viksjø's government buildings.

5 Modernism's cultural heritage distinguished itself from the architecture of earlier periods by the fact that, to a large degree, it consisted of serially produced parts, some of which are no longer in production. Many felt that It was In the nature of modernistic architecture that it should look new and modern, and that it did not age well or tolerate patina in the same way as traditional architecture.

6 Espen Johnsen, "Brytninger mot modernismen: 1945–55", i *Brytninger. Norsk arkitektur 1945–65*, ed. Espen Johnsen, (Oslo: National Museum of Art, Architecture and Design, 2010), p. 41.

7 Letter from Arnstein Arneberg to Sven Markelius 5 March 1951, National Museum, Architecture Collection, Arneberg archive.

8 Letter from Arnstein Arneberg to R.B. Skylstad 19 November 1949, National Museum, Architecture Collection, Arneberg archive.

9 Letter from Arnstein Arneberg to R.B. Skylstad 17 November 1949, National Museum, Architecture Collection, Arneberg archive.

10 Letter from Arnstein Arneberg to R.B. Skylstad 19 November 1949; Letter from Arnstein Arneberg to the Ministry of Foreign Affairs 13 September 1951, National Museum, Architecture Collection, Arneberg archive.

11 Letter from Arnstein Arneberg to Trygve Lie 12 June 1950, National Museum, Architecture Collection, Arneberg archive.

12 Business card from Klare Schee, dated 31 August, no year given. "Architect Arnstein Arneberg Oslo, I have taken the liberty of placing my new kind of straw wallpaper at your office in the hope that you will show it to Mr. Harrison. I hope you have 5 spare minutes for the Biri straw! Yours cordially, Klare Schee."

13 Letter from Arnstein Arneberg to Wallace K. Harrison 7 June 1950.

14 The Capital Master Plan (CMP) is the name of the project that was given the responsibility for the renovation of the United Nations Headquarters complex in New York. The costs for the CMP would be covered by and shared among the member nations.

15 See Michael Adlerstein's article.

16 The textile wallpaper was changed in 1997. In 1966 a more extensive restoration fo the space was undertaken. Its dimensons are unknown. EYP/Memo. To Kathrine Grenier from Anthony Cohn. 16 June 2009. UN archives.

17 E-mail from Jan Skrefsrud 7 February 2011. The Gudbrandsdal material that was delivered in 1997 was a wool-based variant *(85 % wool / 15 % polyamid)*. It is clear that it was a copy of a copy. The smoke-damaged and faded second version with a greyish blue colour had served as the foundation for a woollen wallcovering of the same drab blue colour.

18 EYP/Memo. To Kathrine Grenier from Anthony Cohn. 16 June 2009. UN archives.

19 Letter to Harrison from Arnstein Arneberg. Undated. Probably 6 June 1949. National Museum, Architecture Collection, Arneberg archive.

20 Letter from Arnstein Arneberg to Trygve Lie 11 January 1952. National Museum, Architecture Collection, Arneberg archive.

21 Letter to Harrison from Arnstein Arneberg. Undated. Probably 6 June 1949. National Museum, Architecture Collection, Arneberg archive.

22 *Fra tråd til tekstil: temporærutstilling i anledning 100-årsjubileet for organiseringen av norske bekledningsarbeidere: Norsk teknisk museum.* (Oslo: Fellesforbundet, 1990).

23 E-mail to Erlend Arneson Haugen 24 June 2011. The thread count was evaluated by the curator at the Norwegian Museum of Decorative Arts and Design (Kunstindustrimuseet).

24 E-mail from Linda Veiby 4 January 2012. Krivi says that in a potential production of this fabric, they will be able to enhance quality by working with the details in the pattern, the weave, thickness, and glossiness. The Directorate for Cultural Heritage estimates that Krivi can come reasonably close to the original material quality, but that they will be unable to reproduce a satisfactory copy, because the compactness of the warping cannot be replicated. This affects both the strength of colour and the precision in the textile's pattern. The Ministry of Foreign Affairs will have to assess whether they wish to issue a new call for tender for the project.

25 E-mail to Cecilie Ramse 14 November 2011. Order: a replica of the 1952 textile based on Else Poulsson's original design. The textile should be made of woven rayon textile and should visually and materially correspond to the original material. The textile should have a thread count that is equal to, or close to, that of the original.

26 E-mail from Martin Fossum 13 July 2012. "A misunderstanding is averted in regard to the straw wallpaper, where the formulation 'mounted horizontally' turns out to be ambigious. The UN has decided that the straw on the Biri wallpaper should be horizontal, but this means that the wallpaper must be mounted vertically, that is to say, not in the same way that the consulate, the Directorate, and Biri itself had been prepared for. This means that Biri must make an adjustment in production, but this change will probably not cause delays. The adjustment will mean a small price increase because the long sides of the wallpaper now require a more thorough treatment and use of sealant on the part of the manufacturer."

27 Ban Ki-moon, Remarks at the inauguration of the renovated Security Council Chamber. 16.4.2013. Security Council Chamber.

Loraine Sievers
The Security Council Chamber through the Eyes of Those Who Meet There

1 Article 28(3) of the UN Charter provides that "The Security Council may hold meetings at such places other than the seat of the Organization as in its judgment will best facilitate its work." In addition to the meetings of the Security Council in temporary locations prior to 1952, four sets of official Council meetings have been held away from UN Headquarters: (1) In 1972, Council meetings were convened in Addis Ababa to give special attention to African questions; (2) Meetings were held in Panama City in 1973 to consider peace and security in Latin America; (3) One meeting was held in Geneva in 1990 to discuss "the situation in the Occupied Arab Territories" after the United States, as the UN Headquarters Host Country, let it be known it would not grant a visa to Palestine Liberation Organization Chairman Yasser Arafat if such a meeting were convened in New York; and (4) Four meetings were held in Nairobi in 2004 to foster a peace agreement between the Sudan and South Sudan, and to consider other matters related to Africa.

2 S/PV.574 of 4 April 1952.

3 Chinmaya R. Gharekhan, *The Horseshoe Table: An Inside View of the UN Security Council.* (Delhi: Dorling Kindersley, 2006).

4 This is not the case in the chambers of the other major UN organs, and in most UN conference rooms, where delegates speaking from the floor usually have their backs to many members seated in the room.

5 S/PV.7811 of 16 November 2016.

6 S/PV.6341 of 16 June 2010.

7 The one visually noticeable modification related to the earlier practice of having a rectangular table within the horseshoe table for the UN staff who wrote press releases and verbatim records for Council meetings. With the older microphones, they needed to sit close by because if delegates turned their heads, their words could be lost. However, with modern technology by the time of the CMP, Council members felt that the writers' table could be moved to a side location where they would be less distracting.

Siri Wolland
The Security Council Chamber in the media

1 Linda Sue Phipps, "'Constructing' the United Nations headquarters: Modern Architecture as Public Diplomacy" (Ph. D. Harvard University, 1998), p. 312.

2 Lewis Mumford, *From the Ground and Up: Observations On Contemporary Architecture Housing Highway Building And Civic Design* (Harvest Books, Harcourt, Brace & World inc. 1953), p. 35.

3 Mumford, *From the Ground and Up*, p. 25.

4 Mumford, *From the Ground and Up*, p. 28.

5 Mumford, *From the Ground and Up*, p. 66.

6 Henry Stern Churchill, "United Nations, A Description and Appraisal", *Architectural Record* (1952).

7 Viollet-le-Duc (1824–1879) was a noted French architect who became famous for his restoration of medieval buildings in the 19th century.

8 Churchill. "United Nations, A Description and Appraisal", p. 119.

9 Read more about this in Linda Sue Phipps, "'Constructing' the United Nations headquarters: Modern Architecture as Public Diplomacy", pp. 301, 305, 312, 317.

10 I have found 306 hits for the searchword "UN building" (in Norwegian) and 36 for "Security Council Chamber" and 3 radio reports from 1952 in the archives of the Norwegian National Library.

11 After searching for the term "Security Council Chamber" (in Norwegian) for the period 1952–2017, I got 2293 hits; 1614 were from newspapers, 356 from books, and 318 from periodicals. The search was made in the archives of the Norwegian National Library.

12 Retriever, *Medieanalyse av Sikkerhetsrådets sal*, 2008–2015.

Literature

A Home for U.N.O.: Must We Repeat the Geneva Fiasco? Press release, Museum of Modern Art, New York, 1946.

"An Unodious Comparison: The Three Council Chambers of the United Nations". *Interiors*, (July 1952): 46-67.

Anker, Nils. "Else Poulsson Moe". *Aftenposten*, 18. mars 2002.

Arneberg, Arnstein and Magnus Poulsson. "Oslo rådhus". *Byggekunst* 9-10, (1950): 145-173.

Arneberg, Arnstein. "Lieset, Rugeldalen". *Byggekunst* (1952): 12-13.

——. "Litt omkring FN-bygningen i New York". *Byggekunst* 10, (1952): 196-202.

Ashby, Charlotte. *Modernism in Scandinavia: Art, Architecture and Design.* London: Bloomsbury, 2017.

Askeland, Jan. *Freskoepoken: Studier i profant norsk monumentalmaleri.* Oslo: Gyldendal Norsk Forlag, 1965.

Atmer, Ann Katrin Pihl. *Livet som leves där måste smaka vildmark. Sportstugor och friluftsliv 1900-1945.* Stockholm: Stockholmia förlag, 1998.

Aubert, Andreas. *Norsk kunst og kultur.* Kristiania, 1917.

Auther, Elissa. *String Felt, Thread: The Hierarchy of Art and Craft in American Art.* Minneapolis: University of Minnesota Press, 2009.

Baal-Teshuva, Jacob. *Art treasures of the United Nations.* New York: Yoseloff, 1964.

Blumenau, Lili. "Textiles in the United Nations Building". *Handweaver and Craftsman* 4, no. 1 (1952-53): 10-12.

Borgen, Johan. "Kunsten i Oslo Rådhus". *Kunsten i dag* 13-14, no. 1-2 (1950): 27-46.

Bøhn, Annichen Sibbern. *Norwegian Knitting Designs.* Oslo: Grøndahl & Søn, 1952.

Caro, Robert A. *The Power Broker: Robert Moses and the Fall of New York.* New York: New York Vintage, 1975.

Cordier, Andrew W. and Wilder Foote, *Public Papers of the Secretaries-General of the United Nations.* Volume 1. New York and London: Columbia University Press, 1969.

Churchill, Henry Stern. "United Nations Headquarters: A Description and Appraisal." *Architectural Record*, July (1952): 103-123.

Det norske husflidsbolag. *Den Norske Husflidsforening gjennom 60 år.* Oslo: Morten Johansens boktrykkeri, 1951.

Eden, Anthony. *The Reckoning. The Memoirs of Anthony Eden, Earl of Avon.* Boston: Houghton Mifflin Co., 1965.

Eldal, Jens Christian. *Norsk kunstnerleksikon*, "Arnstein Arneberg". 9.1.2018. URL: https://nkl.snl.no/Arnstein_Rynning_Arneberg

Elmlund, Peter and Johan Mårtelius (ed.), *Swedish Grace. The forgotten modern.* Axel and Margaret Ax:son Johnson Foundation: Stockholm, 2015.

Engelstad, Eyvind. "Husfliden jubilerer". *Bonytt* 26, no. 9 (1966): 254-56.

Engelstad, Helen. *Norwegian Textiles.* Brighton: Dolphin Press, 1952.

——. "Modern Norwegian Textile Art" *Norway Arts and Crafts*, ed. Conrad Hofgaard, 25-30. Oslo: Norges Eksportråd, 1950.

——. "Norwegian Textile Art". *Bonytt* 11, no. 4-5 (1951): 85.

——. "Norsk tekstilindustri 1952: En utstilling i brukskunst". *Bonytt* 2, no. 13 (1953): 28-30.

——. "Til Paris V: De håndvevde tekstiler". *Vi selv og våre hjem*, 5 (1937): 32- 34.

Fallan, Kjetil. *Designing Modern Norway: A History of Design Discourse.* London and New York: Routledge, 2017.

——. "Visionaries and Weathercocks: Norwegian Furniture Design c. 1920-1965." In *Scandinavian Journal of Design History* 13, (2003): 100-113.

——. "Love and Hate in Industrial Design: Europe's Design Professionals and America in the 1950s." In *The Making of European Consumption: Facing the American Challenge*, ed. Per Lundin and Thomas Kaiserfeld, 50-53. Basingstoke: Palgrave Macmillan, 2015.

Fra tråd til tekstil: temporærutstilling i anledning 100 års jubileet for organiseringen av norske bekledningsarbeidere. Exhibition catalogue, Norsk teknisk museum. Oslo: Fellesforbundet, 1990.

Gharekhan, Chinmaya R. *The Horseshoe Table: An Inside View of the UN Security Council.* Delhi: Dorling Kindersley, 2006.

Giedion, Siegfried. *Space, Time and Architecture. The Growth of a New Tradition*, 5. edition. Harvard University Press: Cambridge, Mass., 1966

Glambek, Ingeborg. "Norway." In *International Arts and Crafts.* Ed. Karen Livingstone and Linda Parry, 286-293. London: V&A Publications, 2005.

——. "The Council Chambers in the UN Building in New York". *Scandinavian Journal of Design History.* Volume 15 (2005): 8-39.

Grønvold, Ulf, Nils Anker and Gunnar Sørensen. *Det store løftet. Rådhuset i Oslo.* Oslo: Aschehoug, 2000.

Guldberg, Jørn. "'Scandinavian Design' as Discourse: The Exhibition Design in Scandinavia, 1954-57." *Design Issues* 27, (Spring 2011): 41-58.

Halèn, Vidar and Kerstin Wickman. *Scandinavian Design Beyond the Myth: Fifty Years of Design from the Nordic Countries.* Stockholm: Arvinius Förlag / Form Förlag, 2003.

Hjeltnes, Guri. "McCarthyismens inntog i FN" p. 32-53 in *Arbeiderhistorie 2004*, ed. Knut Einar Eriksen. Arbeiderbevegelsens arkiv og bibliotek, 2004.

Hjeltnes, Guri. "Tapte horisonter: Nordisk eller atlantisk: Striden om Atlanterhavspolitikken 1940-1945", in *Selvstendig og beskyttet: Det stormaktsgaranterte Norge fra Krimkrigen til NATO*, ed. Roald Berg. Bergen: Fagbokforlaget, 2008.

Hølaas, Odd. "Norsk brukskunst: en introduksjon". In *Norsk Brukskunst.* Gøteborg: Röhsska Konstslödjmuseet / København: Det Danske Kunstindustrimuseum, 1951.

Håberg, Kirsten Røvig. *Fra skyggetanter til yrkeskvinner: Livet, tiden og menneskene ved Den kvinnelige Industriskolen fra 1875 til 1950.* Oslo: ABM-media, 2012.

Ifversen, Karsten R.S. and Birgit Lyngbye Pedersen. *Finn Juhl i FN. Et dansk mesterværk i New York.* København: Strandberg Publishing, 2013.

I.S. "Våre kvinnelige tekstiltegnere: Else Poulsson i Den Norske Husflidsforening." *Urd* 41, (1937): 144-145.

Isitt, Mark and Åke E:son Lindman. *United Nations. The story behind the headquarters of the world.* Stockholm: Max Ström, 2016.

Jakhelln, Elise. "Tekstilene". In *Rådhuset i Oslo: annen del beskrivelse*, ed. Carl Just, 240-248. Oslo: H. Aschehoug & Co, 1952.

Johnsen, Espen. "Brytninger mot modernismen: 1945-55", in *Brytninger. Norsk arkitektur 1945-65*, ed. Espen Johnsen. Oslo: Nasjonalmuseet for kunst, arkitektur og design, 2010.

Johansson, Gottard. "Design in Scandinavia." In *Design in Scandinavia: An Exhibition for the Home from Denmark, Finland, Norway, Sweden*, Exhibition catalogue, Brooklyn Museum, ed. Arne Remlov, 11-28. Oslo: Kirstes boktrykkeri, 1954.

Kirkham, Pat and Lynne Walker. "Women Designers in the USA, 1900-2000: Diversity and Difference." In *Women Designers in the USA 1900-2000: Diversity and Difference*, ed. Pat Kirkham, 49-84. New York and New Haven: Bard Graduate Center and Yale University Press, 2000.

Krohg, Per. "Under Fugl Fønix' vinger". *Dagbladet* 7.6.1951

Krohg, Per. "FN-maleriet" *Kunsten i dag*, årg. 6, nr. 2, 1952.

Krohg, Per. *Per Krohgs memoarer.* Oslo: Gyldendal, 1966.

La Norvège à Paris: Catalogue du Pavillion de la Norvège à L'Exposition Internationale de Paris 1937. Exhibition catalogue. Oslo: Blix, 1937.

Lie, Trygve. *Syv år for freden.* Oslo: Tiden Norsk Forlag, 1954.

Lie, Trygve. *In the Cause of Peace: Seven Years with the United Nations.* New York: The Macmillan Company, 1954.

Lien, Marie. *Norwegian National Organization for the Promotion of Home Arts and Crafts.* Oslo: Fabritius & Sønner, 1946.

Lunde, Jo. "Den Norske Husflidsforening: 60 år i brukskunstens tjeneste". *Bonytt* 11, no. 9 (1951): 149-153.

Meisler, Stanley. *United Nations: The First Fifty Years.* New York: Atlantic Monthly Press: 1995.

Moe, Per R. "Den våpenløse kamp." Dagbok brev og erindringer fra læreraksjonen 1942. Ms.4° 4470: 2. Private archive of Per R. Moe, unpublished closed manuscript. Monte Sol. Villa Joyosa, February 6th, 1978.

Mumford, Lewis. *From the Ground and Up: Observations on Contemporary Architecture Housing Highway Building and Civic Design.* New York: Harvest Books, Harcourt, Brace & World inc. 1953.

Mørck, Ole Morten, Arnstein Arneberg. *Mennesket og arkitekten, byggverkene og byggherren.* Oslo: Bastion forlag, 2006.

Tre og tekstil ved 3: Tre husflidsdesignere: Else Poulsson, Agnes Sykkelstad, Aage Schou. Exhibition catalogue. Oslo: Kunstindustrimuseet, 1966.

Newhouse, Victoria. *Wallace K. Harrison, Architect.* New York: Rizzoli, 1989.

Nergaard, Trygve. *Bilder av Per Krohg.* Oslo: Aschehoug forlag, 2000.

Nisi, Aaste, Kjetil Tjønnås and O.A. Quamme. *Gransheradsoga.* Notodden: Notodden kommune, 1977.

"Norwegian Women Revive All Ancient Textile Arts." *Milwaukee Journal* (1938).

"Norsk Tekstil *NÅ*," 1971. Exhibition catalogue. Oslo: Kunstindustrimuseet, 1971.

"Norsk ånd i verdenskunsten", *Dagbladet* 12.8.1952.
"Oslos Michel Angelo skal dekorere i FN", *Morgenbladet* **12.**8.1952
Petersen, Joh. AS. *En norsk tekstilbedrift 100 år: Joh. Petersen aktieselskab, lin-og bommulsvarefabrikker.* Oslo: Joh. Petersen, 1954.
Phipps, Linda Sue. "Constructing" the United Nations headquarters: modern architecture as public diplomacy. Ph. D. Harvard University, 1998.
Poulsen, Sverre. "Genève-komedien", *Byggekunst* no. 4 (1928) s. 62–63.
Poulsson, Else. *Rutemønster for strikking og broderi*. Oslo: J.W. Cappelens Forlag, 1945.
Rasch, Tone. "Den kvinnelige industriskole sett innenfra." *FORMakademisk*, vol. 5, 2 (2012): 1–3.
Rasch, Tone and Kari-Anne Pedersen. "Interview with Else Poulsson, November 3, 1998." Audio file, archive reference: NFAV.016-001Alimit. Norsk folkemuseum.
Remlov, Arne. "Foran gjenreisningen: en utstilling i foreningen brukskunst." *Bonytt* 6, no. 9–10 (1946): 154–159.
——. "Merkbar framgang." *Bonytt* 9, no. 10 (1949): 175–179.
Ritter, John. *World Parliament.* "The League of Nations Competition, 1926", in *Architectural Review*, (July 1964).
Rom, Per. *Utsmykkingen av Oslo Rådhus*. Oslo: Oslo kommune, 1952.
Rovine, Arthur W. *The First Fifty Years. The secretary-general in World Politics 1920–1970.* Leyden: Sitjhoff, 1970.
Rudberg, Eva. *Sven Markelius, Architect*. Stockholm: Arkitektur Förlag, 1989.
Sandvik, Maria Veie. "Iconology of a New World Order: Per Krohg's Painting in the United Nations Security Council" i *Vereinte Nationen: German Review on The United Nations*, Vol. 62, nr. 4, (2014).
Schnitler, Carl W. "Arneberg og Poulssons raadhusplaner", *St. Hallvard* (1918).
Schøning, Trond L., *Det Norske Hus. Oslo Rådhus – en historisk sammenligning*, Master in Art History, Universitetet i Bergen: 2001.
Seip, Elisabeth. *Norsk biografisk leksikon*, "Arnstein Arneberg". 13.2.2009. URL: https://nbl.snl.no/Arnstein_Arneberg
Sievers, Loraine and Sam Daws. *The Procedure of the UN Security Council.* 4th edition. Oxford: Oxford University Press, 2014.
Sinding-Larsen, Henning. *Per Krohg.* Exhibition catalogue. Bergen and Trondheim: 1965.
Smith, T'ai. *Bauhaus Weaving Theory: From Feminine Craft to Mode of Design.* Minneapolis: University of Minnesota Press, 2014.
Stavenow-Hiedemark, Elisabet. "Scandinavia: 'Beauty for All'". In *The Arts and Crafts Movement in Europe & America*, ed. Wendy Kaplan, 179–217. London: Thames and Hudson med The Los Angeles County Museum of Art, 2004.
Sundbø, Annemor. *Spelsau og samspill: Glansfull ull og lodne skjebnetråder.* Tvedestrand: Bokbyen forlag, 2015.
Tannum, Per. "Norway Designs for Living." *Bonytt* 11, no. 4–5 (1951): 64.
Thue, Oscar. "Utstillinger i Oslo høsten 1961." *Kunst og Kultur* 45, no. 1 (1962): 47–60.
Urquhart, Brian. *A Life in Peace and War*. New York: W.W. Norton & Company, 1987.
Vogt, Carl Emil. *Fridtjof Nansen. Mannen og verden*. Oslo: Cappelen Damm, 2011.
Vreim, Halvor. *Norwegian Decorative Art Today*. Oslo: Fabritius & Sønner Forlag, 1937.
Winton, Alexa Griffith. "A Striking Juxtaposition: Hand-Woven Textiles in the United Nations Conference Building Interiors." In *The Journal of Modern Craft* 8, no. 2 (July 2015): 181–193.
Zeckendorf, William and McCreary, Edward. *Zeckendorf, The Autobiography of William Zeckendorf*. New York: Holt, Rinehart and Winston, 1970.
Zetterlund, Christina. "Just Decoration? Ideology and Discourse in Early-Twentieth-Century Sweden". In *Scandinavian Design: Alternative Histories*, ed. Kjetil Fallan, 103–116. London: Berg, 2010.

Archives

Arnstein Arneberg archives, Architecture Collection, National museum, Oslo.
Archives of The Ministry of Climate and Environment, Norway
Archives of National Association of Norwegian Architects, The National Archives of Norway
Archives of Sven Markelius, National Centre for Architecture and Design, Stockholm.
Electronic archives of the Ministry of Foreign Affairs, The National Archives of Norway
Else Poulsson archives, Norwegian Museum of Cultural History, Oslo.
UN Archives, New York.

Contributors

Michael Adlerstein (b. 1945) is adjunct professor at Colombia University, graduate school of Architecture Planning and Preservation. Previously, Mr. Adlerstein served as the Chief Historical Architect for the National Park Service, recognized as the national expert in the field of historic preservation. In 2007 United Nations Secretary-General Ban Ki-moon appointed Mr. Adlerstein as the Assistant Secretary-General of the UN for the Capital Master Plan.

Nina Berre (b.1964) received a degree in architecture from the Norwegian Institute of Technology in 1992, and earned a doctorate in modern architectural history from the same institution in 2002. She is a former director of Norsk Form, and has served as director of the architecture department at the National Museum since 2010. Berre curates, lectures, edits and publishes regularly on architecture and architectural history.

Ingeborg Glambek (b.1939) is a professor emeritus in art history (design and architecture) at the University of Oslo. Previously, she spent many years as an employee of the Statens lærerhøgskole i forming, Oslo. She has written several books on art and a wide range of articles, many of them about Nordic and German architecture and design.

Ulf Grønvold (b.1947) is an architect and architectural historian. He has served as editor of *Byggekunst* and director of the National Museum of Art, Architecture, and Design for 17 years. He received the King's Medal of Merit (Gold) and is an honorary member of the Academy of Art in Stockholm. He has published several books about architecture.

Vibeke Waallann Hansen (b. 1970) is an art historian and has been a curator at the National Museum since 2006. Waallann Hansen is a specialist in Nordic art of the 19th and early 20th centuries. At the National Museum, she has curated and written the catalogues for several exhibitions in recent years.

Guri Hjeltnes (b. 1953) is director of the Norwegian Center for Studies of the Holocaust and Religious Minorities (HL-senteret) in Oslo. Hjeltnes is a historian and author who earned her doctoral degree with a dissertation about the history of the Norwegian merchant fleet during the Second World War. Hjeltnes has published extensively on Norwegian war history, press history, and general social history. In 2015, her book *Hverdagsliv i krig* (Everyday Life in War) was named one of the ten most important books on WWII to be published in Norway. Hjeltnes is currently writing a biography of Trygve Lie.

Jørn Holme (b.1959) has been the Director of Cultural Heritage since 2009. A legal scholar with an expertise in legal history, he spent years in government administration, serving as a police official, judge, chief public prosecutor, parliamentary secretary to the Minister of Justice, and head of the Norwegian Police Security Service. Holme was also acting assistant Director of Cultural Heritage in 1997. He has written and edited books about cultural preservation and historic buildings.

Sarah A. Lichtman (b.1970) is an assistant professor of design history at Parsons School of Design, where she directs the MA program in the History of Design and Curatorial Studies, offered jointly by Parsons and Cooper Hewitt, Smithsonian Design Museum. She received her MA and PhD from the Bard Graduate Center and her work has appeared in the *Journal of Modern Craft*, *Design and Culture*, *West 86th* and the *Journal of Design History*, for which she serves on its editorial board.

Maria Csaszni Rygh (b.1984) received a master's degree in art history in 2009 and works at the Directorate for Cultural History. She has done further study in Norwegian architectural history and has contributed to a book about postwar Norwegian architecture.

Loraine Sievers worked at the UN for over 30 years, concluding her career as Chief of the Security Council Secretariat Branch, in which capacity she worked with Council members on a daily basis. She also served with the Afghanistan and Sierra Leone Sanctions Committees. She has co-authored The Procedure of the UN Security Council and maintains a website on Council procedure at www.scprocedure.org.

Linda Lovise Veiby (b.1978) is an art historian who serves as section chief at the Directorate for Cultural Heritage. She is a former member of the boards of ICOMOS Norge and DOCOMOMO Norge. Her work is focused especially on 20th-century architecture, a subject about which she has written several articles. Veiby represented the Directorate of Cultural Heritage at the restoration of the Security Council Chamber up through the completion of the process in 2013.

Siri Wolland (b.1962) is director of communications for the Directorate of Cultural Heritage, where she has worked since 2009. She has many years of experience in the media, both in Norway and abroad. She studied photography and journalism and received a Masters degree in art history from the University of Oslo. Wolland published a book about communications in the public sector in 2017.

Photo credits

Cover: Ivan Brodey
pp. 1–8, 49–64, 145–160, 217–224: Ivan Brodey

All pictures including Per Krohg's mural: Per Krohg: *Maleri i sikkerhetsrådets sal i FN-bygningen, New York.* © Per Krohg / BONO 2018

pp. 16–17: UN Photo
pp. 18–19: AP Photo / NTB scanpix
pp. 20, 22–23, 24: Ezra Stoller / Esto
p. 27: Albert Fox / UN Photo
p. 29 (both pictures): UN Photo
p. 30: MB / UN Photo
p. 31: CV / UN Photo
p. 34: ES / UN Photo
pp. 36–37: MB / UN Photo
pp. 38–39, p. 40: Albert Fox / UN Photo
p. 42 top: MB / UN Photo
p. 42 bottom: Albert Fox / UN photo
p. 43: NAMT.aar621.019 / National Museum, Architecture collections. Photo: Annar Bjørgli / National Museum
p. 44: Arnstein Rynning Arneberg / NAMT.aar621 / National Museum, Architecture collections Photo: Annar Bjørgli / National Museum
p. 46: Bildesamlingen / Nasjonalbiblioteket
p. 66: DEXTRA Photo / NAMF.00160.001 / National Museum, Architecture collections. Photo: Dag Andre Ivarsøy / National Museum
p. 67: Arnstein Rynning Arneberg / NAMT.aar756.001 / National Museum, Architecture collections
p. 68: Arnstein Rynning Arneberg / NAMT.aar436.001 / National Museum, Architecture collections
p. 69: NAMF.00182.002 / National Museum, Architecture collections
p. 70: Axel Revold: *Jordbruk og fiske*. Freske i Oslo Rådhus © Axel Revold / BONO 2018 Photo: Jiri Havran
p. 72 top: Arnstein Rynning Arneberg / NAMT.aar621.005 / National Museum, Architecture collections Photo: Annar Bjørgli / National Museum
p. 72 bottom: Arnstein Rynning Arneberg / NAMT.aar621.004 / National Museum, Architecture collections Photo: Andreas Haarvik / National Museum
pp. 74–75: Arnstein Rynning Arneberg / NAMT.aar621.002 / National Museum, Architecture collections
pp. 76–77: Arnstein Rynning Arneberg / NAMT.aar621.018 / National Museum, Architecture collections
pp. 78–79: Arnstein Rynning Arneberg / NAMT.aar621.003 / National Museum, Architecture collections Photo: Andreas Haarvik / National Museum
p. 80: Aktuell / NTB scanpix
p. 83: Arnstein Rynning Arneberg / NAMT.aar326.003 / National Museum, Architecture collections Photo: Dag Andre Ivarsøy / National Museum
p. 85: Arnstein Rynning Arneberg / NAMT.aar436.002 / National Museum, Architecture collections Photo: Annar Bjørgli / National Museum
p. 86 top: Arnstein Rynning Arneberg / NAMT.aar621.00025 / National Museum, Architecture collections Photo: Børre Høstland / National Museum
p. 86 bottom: Arnstein Rynning Arneberg / NAMT.aar621.013 / National Museum, Architecture collections Photo: Andreas Harvik / National Museum
p. 87 top: Arnstein Rynning Arneberg / NAMT.aar621.008 / National Museum, Architecture collections
p. 87 bottom: Arnstein Rynning Arneberg / NAMT.aar621.009 / National Museum, Architecture collections
p. 89: MB / UN Photo
pp. 90, 92–93, p. 94–95: UN Photo
p. 96: Picture collection / National Library
p. 99: AP Photo / NTB scanpix
p. 100: Sverre A. Børretzen / Aktuell / NTB scanpix
p. 105: AP Photo / NTB scanpix
p. 107: UN Archive
p. 108: UN Photo
p. 110: Keystone Pictures USA / ZUMAPRESp.com / NTB scanpix
pp. 112–113: Per Krohg: Mural in Security Council Chamber, New York (detail) © Per Krohg / BONO 2018. Photo: Ivan Brodey
p. 114: Arnstein Rynning Arneberg / NAMT.aar621 / National Museum, Architecture collections. Photo: Annar Bjørgli / National Museum
p. 117: Aktuell / NTB scanpix
p. 118: Per Krohg: Fresco in East Gallery in Oslo City Hall. © Per Krohg / BONO 2018 Photo: Jiri Havran
p. 122 Aktuell / NTB scanpix
p. 124 top: Candido Portinari: *War*. Mural in UN building, New York. © Candido Portinari / BONO 2018 Photo: Lois Conner / UN Photo
p. 124 bottom: Candido Portinari: *Peace*. Mural in UN building, New York. © Cândido Portinari / BONO 2018 Photo: Lois Conner / UN Photo
p. 125: José Vela Zanetti, *Mankind's struggle for lasting peace* (detail). UN complex, New York. © José Vela Zanetti / BONO 2018. Photo: John Isaac / UN Photo
p. 126, pp. 128–131: National Museum, Architecture collections Photo: Annar Bjørgli / National Museum
p. 132: Arnstein Rynning Arneberg / NAMT.aar621 / National Museum, Architecture collections. Photo: Annar Bjørgli / National Museum
pp. 134–135: Matt Flynn / Smithsonian Institution
p. 136: Aftenposten / NTB scanpix
p. 139: Haakon Harris / Norwegian Folk Museum
p. 142 top: Mats Linder / matslinder.no
p. 142 bottom, p. 143: Jiri Havran
p. 163: Paulo Filgueira / UN Photo
p. 165: Michos Tzovaras / UN Photo
p. 166: Martin Lerberg Fossum / The Royal Norwegian Consulate General, New York
pp. 168, 170–171, 172: Mark Mahaney
p. 175: Arnstein Rynning Arneberg / NAMT.aar621 / National Museum, Architecture collections. Photo: Annar Bjørgli / National Museum
p. 177 top: JC Mcllwaine / UN Photo
p. 177 bottom: The Royal Norwegian Consulate General, New York
p. 178: Linda Veiby / Directorate of Cultural Heritage
p. 179: Capital Master Plan (CMP)
p. 180 top: Lasse Moe / The Royal Norwegian Consulate General, New York
p. 182: Harry Harris / AP Photo / NTB scanpix
pp. 184–185: MH / UN Photo
p. 186: Richard Drew / AP Photo / NTB scanpix
p. 188: MB / UN Photo
p. 191: Manuel Elias / UN Photo
p. 192: JC Mcllwaine / UN Photo
p. 193: Paulo Filgueiras / UN Photo
p. 194: UN Photo
pp. 196–197: Paulo Filgueiras / UN Photo
p. 198: Arnstein Rynning Arneberg / NAMT.aar621 / National Museum, Architecture collections. Photo: Annar Bjørgli / National Museum
p. 200: UN Photo
p. 203: Mary Altaffer / UN Photo
p. 204: Manuel Elias / UN Photo

NORWAY
NIGERIA

POLAND
PERU

ENGLISH
FRENCH
RUSSIAN
EXIT
KUWAIT
DIRECTOR
PRESIDENT
CHINA

ENGLISH
EXIT
UNITED STATES